Communication and Social Change

Global Media and Communication

Communication and Social Change

A Citizen Perspective

THOMAS TUFTE

polity

First published in 2017 by Polity Press

Polity Press
65 Bridge Street
Cambridge CB2 1UR, UK

Polity Press
350 Main Street
Malden, MA 02148, USA

ISBN-13: 978-0-7456-7037-9
ISBN-13: 978-0-7456-7038-6 (pb)

A catalogue record for this book is available from the British Library.

Typeset in 11 on 13pt Adobe Garamond Pro by Servis Filmsetting Ltd, Stockport, Cheshire
Printed and bound in the UK by CPI Group (UK) Ltd, Croydon, CR0 4YY

The publisher has used its best endeavours to ensure that the URLs for external websites referred to in this book are correct and active at the time of going to press. However, the publisher has no responsibility for the websites and can make no guarantee that a site will remain live or that the content is or will remain appropriate.

Every effort has been made to trace all copyright holders, but if any have been inadvertently overlooked the publisher will be pleased to include any necessary credits in any subsequent reprint or edition.

For further information on Polity, visit our website: politybooks.com

Library of Congress Cataloging-in-Publication Data

Names: Tufte, Thomas, author.
Title: Communication and social change : a citizen perspective / Thomas Tufte.
Description: Malden, MA : Polity, 2017. | Series: Global media and
    communication | Includes bibliographical references and index. |
    Identifiers: LCCN 2016050714 (print) | LCCN 2017013008 (ebook) | ISBN
    9781509517800 (Mobi) | ISBN 9781509517817 (Epub) | ISBN 9780745670379
    (hardback) | ISBN 9780745670386 (paperback)
Subjects: LCSH: Social change. | Communication--Social aspects. | Mass
    media--Social aspects. | BISAC: SOCIAL SCIENCE / Media Studies.
Classification: LCC HM831 (ebook) | LCC HM831 .T84 2017 (print) | DDC
    303.4--dc23
LC record available at https://lccn.loc.gov/2016050714

Contents

Foreword

By Silvio Waisbord

Everything we knew about the nexus between communication and social change is up for grabs. Technological and social innovations constantly bring up new themes and questions and nudge us to rethink arguments about how and why communication matters for social change.

Even as more than half of the world does not use the Internet, digital technologies have upended traditional media industries and ushered in revolutionary forms of communication. The traditional divisions between interpersonal and mass, private and public, hierarchical and horizontal, one-way and multiple-way communication are no longer tenable. Digitalization has reshaped social interactions and deepened the mediatization of society. From reasonable debate to emotional discourse, the politics of voice are common despite concentrated economic power and elite politics. Just as digital technologies are used by power to enhance profit-making and surveillance, they are also utilized to monitor power and hold it accountable. The proliferation of communication platforms has spawned the disaggregation of the public spheres in multiple, parallel and scattered spaces.

Just like communicative transformations, social change is everywhere. Noisy, messy offline and digital activism attests to the vitality and unpredictability of politics. Organized publics mobilize to express demands and redress inequalities. Participation is not confined to specific, time-bound moments such as elections and referenda, but is a fixture of everyday life. Citizen participation and social mobilization facilitated by digital networks have shaken up the institutional architecture of liberal democracy and authoritarian regimes. The gradual incorporation of consultative mechanisms and citizens into public debates and policy-making in several countries attests to democratic governance in flux.

Significant advances in human rights in the past decades, too, reflect positive social changes. Even in a deeply unequal world, social movements have succeeded in several areas, such as women's and children's rights, political representation, cultural pluralism, sexual diversity and communication rights. In past decades, progress in girls' education, global public health and poverty reduction offer glimmers of hopes about social justice.

Amid progress, reactionary backlash often rears its ugly head. Recurrent episodes of xenophobia, racism, sexism and political persecution are symptomatic of deep-seated forms of hatred. Intolerance is not exclusive to one corner of the world. The politics of hate and bigotry have no borders. Globally, large segments of the public stubbornly refuse to recognize diversity and human rights and cling to old orders. Governments of various ideological stripes resort to assorted tactics to curb or eliminate dissent. Opportunist demagogues whip up intolerance by appealing to the worst angels of our nature.

Against this backdrop, it is clear that no gain on the side of social justice is ever secured. Blowback is always a possibility. Excessive optimism is unwarranted.

This mixed picture of social change comes as no surprise. As a long line of progressive activists has contended, the betterment of the human condition is not a straightforward, sure-footed process. It is dotted with ups and downs, steps forward and backwards. Actions in support of emancipation are bound to run up against established powers and nostalgia for a world of social hierarchies and privileges of class, race, ethnicity, gender, nationalism, sexuality and religion. Sepia-tinted sentiments dangerously infuse resentment and reactionary politics in a world of rapid, constant changes.

Understanding the multiple dimensions of fast-moving social and communication transformations is challenging. The complexity and chaos of contemporary global societies make it difficult to produce neat and comprehensive accounts. Making sense of academic dispersion and turbocharged changes demands a panoramic view and considerable intellectual heft.

This book gets us closer to a better comprehension of scholarly debates about communication, collective action and social change. Thomas Tufte offers a valuable roadmap, packed with insightful, sophisticated and provocative ideas. He is a voracious reader and a thoughtful interpreter of debates and developments. The book deftly walks the reader through a dense theoretical maze – from modernization to post-colonialism. It exhibits a cosmopolitan sensibility that nimbly swings from Europe to Latin America to Africa, and taps into Tufte's vast research experience that blends academic analysis and ethnographic work in the global South.

The book connects scattered literatures in order to build a fresh argument. Doing this is not easy considering that 'communication and social change' includes myriad lines of research – from digital insurgency to community dialogue, from aid/development programmes to information campaigns, from social movements to media criticism. Making sense of this intellectual smorgasbord demands familiarity with different bodies of research. Tufte takes a bird's-eye perspective to make sense of a fuzzy field that overlaps intellectual and disciplinary traditions. He is not interested in repeating complacent, dogmatic approaches or rehashing tired debates about theoretical models and research paradigms. Instead, he brings together studies around the notion of citizen-driven changes, and shows that, time and time again, citizens are the protagonists of communication actions responsible for progressive change.

Tufte makes a call to put communicative citizenship at the centre of the analysis. Communication is another word for debate and collective action; it is not synonymous with information, public relations, branding, and the kind of 'magic thinking' common in the aid industry. The book provides plenty of examples showing that mobilized citizens and critical communication drive changes. It reminds us to be sceptical of 'silver bullets' that capture the ever-fleeting attention of aid agencies, corporate philanthropy and non-governmental organizations. Citizens are the true agents of change as they express demands, outline actions, criticize power, pressure governments and international agencies, draft proposals and so on. Yet the analysis does not offer a sentimental view of citizenship. Rather, it proposes a sober, clear-eyed view of when and why citizen participation makes a positive difference. Espousing an agency-centred view of communication and social change is essential, but we should not *ex ante* praise collective action. Not every form of participation necessarily contributes to progressive changes. Citizens can come together to achieve virtuous changes or push progress back. However, as Tufte shows, long-lasting, progressive social transformation necessarily demands citizenship.

In sum, the book makes a persuasive, evidence-based call to scholars, students, agencies and practitioners to focus on how communication processes articulate citizenship and positive social change. Tufte challenges us to think critically and to find analytical bridges between various streams of communication research. This is necessary to comprehend multiple dimensions of social change and inform practice.

Acknowledgements

Writing a book about communication and social change today is like running a marathon where the 'finish line' keeps moving and you can never really reach the end. We are living at a time of continuous and profound change in society. Technological, political and social transformations constantly influence citizens' everyday lives and in particular their opportunities to engage in social change processes. Understanding these processes, and the role of communication herein, was at the core of this book project.

I have often felt that, and experienced how, governments and the organizations involved in international development cooperation contain a degree of inertia at their core, in the way they communicate to and with their constituencies. This has often limited and constrained the opportunities and abilities of citizens to participate in social processes influencing their own lives. At the same time, non-governmental organizations and social movements in particular have seemed to offer a more dynamic space for citizens to claim voice and visibility and engage in social change processes. However, as this book shows, the equation is not that simple.

This has in many ways felt like a seminal book for me to write. I have long experience of work as a researcher, consultant and co-director of the Ørecomm Centre for Communication and Glocal Change, as well as in teaching and lecturing in many countries and contexts. With this book, I have tried to pull together my research interests and lines of experience to offer my take on how to understand the current challenges facing, and opportunities for, successful citizen-led processes of social change. The world has changed a great deal since Andrea Drugan at Polity first contacted me back in 2011, and many people have helped me understand these changes and translate them into the analytical debates and insights offered in this book.

I would like to thank my co-director at Ørecomm, Oscar Hemer, for having read and commented on the full manuscript, but also for our many valuable debates about communication and social change over the years. Likewise Colin Chasi, with whom I have kept up an ongoing and inspiring dialogue throughout these years. Teke Ngomba, Morten Giersing and Leo Custodio have all read sections of the manuscript. All their comments were thoughtful and constructive, challenged me on my analysis and perspectives, and helped me improve the manuscript. In the process I have also had valuable student assistance from Sara Gevnoe Rasmussen, Charlotte Marie Hermann and Carlos Manuel Moraleda Melero.

Many other students and colleagues have been both helpful and inspirational. Numerous lectures given, doctoral courses taught and conference presentations offered across Latin America, Africa and Europe have offered me opportunities to broaden my perspective and enrich my analysis. This process has in particular involved students and colleagues at the University of Tirana, Albania; Universitat Autònoma de Barcelona; the University of Johannesburg; Moi University, Kenya; Universidad del Este, Paraguay; Universidade Metodista and ESPM, both in São Paulo, Brazil; Universidad del Norte, Colombia; and Universidad de Aguascalientes, Mexico. The entire argument about contesting ethnocentrism and criticizing the Western concept of development, which I make in this book, has grown out of my constant exposure to many different realities and ways of thinking. My thanks to all of you who were part of this ongoing dialogue.

In the world of organizations carrying out practical work on communication and social change, I found a lot of expertise on, and many insights into, how to translate concepts and approaches into practice and how practice can and must influence research. My year-long collaborations with Femina HIP in Tanzania, ADRA Denmark and ADRA Malawi, Soul City in South Africa and UNICEF, with Rafael Obregon in particular, were all extremely important parts of the process of writing this book. Numerous conversations, interviews and focus group discussions with citizens throughout the countries I have worked with helped to remind me of the need to ground the debates about communication and social change in the everyday lives of people, in the realities of people living and organizations working at community level.

Writing this manuscript also required silence and space for reflection. A month-long stay with Víctor Marí Sáez at the University of Cadiz in 2012 produced excellent discussions and time for immersion. The latter was also possible during a similar stay at the Danish Institute in Rome in 2014. Two shorter stays at Klitgården in Skagen in 2014 and 2016 offered similar opportunities for immersion, as have numerous stays in Birte's safe havens in Sejrobugten and Portugal. My thanks to all who helped carve out these quiet spaces for me to reflect and write.

In pulling this all together as a book manuscript, thanks are also due to the anonymous peer reviewers, for their comments, and not least to the great and patient team at Polity – from the initial collaboration with Andrea Drugan to the further work with Elen Griffiths, Ellen MacDonald-Kramer and their colleagues in the production team. A special thanks goes to

Andrew Mash, who read and reread all the drafts of the manuscript prior to its final submission to Polity, showing me the hard way just how difficult it is to write perfect English.

A special mention must go to Roskilde University and Malmö University, the two universities that constitute the institutional base for Ørecomm, which Oscar and I have co-directed since its inception in 2008. For many years Ørecomm constituted my home base for engagement and reflection in the field of communication and social change. I wish to thank the core Ørecomm team in recent years: Marie, Norbert, Jonas, Nina, Yuliya, Anders, Micke, Hugo, Ronald, Kathrine and Tobias, who all contributed to the realization of the Ørecomm Festivals and Symposia held in 2011–16. The Centre has been a base for international debate with researchers, practitioners, artists, students and consultants interested in understanding and engaging with communication and social change from a citizen perspective. This interest and commitment I have also found at my base at the University of Leicester. Thanks to all of you who have taken part.

Finally, I wish to dedicate this book to Laura, Anna and Pernille. Without your patience, support and smiles, this book would never have been written.

Leicester
6 December 2016

1   Towards a New Social Thought in Communication and Social Change

A Call for a New Social Thought

The French sociologist and theorist of new social movements Alain Touraine makes a powerful call for 'a new social thought' in his book *Thinking Differently* (Touraine 2009). Touraine abandons the 'exhausted evolutionism' of the dominant discourse and seeks to recognize that the subject should be based on the right of all individuals and groups to be recognized and respected:

> The most profound thing about the social thought we inherited was the positivistic conviction that modernity meant the elimination of . . . any kind of reference to the consciousness of actors. We were taught to content ourselves with two principles when it came to analyzing behaviours: the rational pursuit of self-interest or pleasure, and the fulfilment of the functions required by the perpetuation and evolution of social life. (Touraine 2009, 5)

Touraine's call for a new social thought is a timely commentary on the dominant neoliberal development discourse, which increasingly seems to be incapable of respecting the rights and needs of every individual and group to be recognized and respected, but instead allows market logic to determine who is heard, who can voice their concerns and who is empowered to act.

There is a growing questioning of the dominant Western model of economic growth. A highly detailed example of this critique comes from the French economist Thomas Piketty. His book *Capital in the Twenty-First Century* (Piketty 2014) questions the ability of a capitalist economy to prevent inequality. The critique of the neoliberal economic model is much broader, however, as reflected in the post-colonial critiques of Western development paradigms (Escobar 1995; Bhabha 2004; Fanon and Markmann 1952; Mbembe 2001) and seen in the emergence of new ways of conceiving development, such as the 'Gross National Happiness Index' in Bhutan (Ura, Kinga and Centre for Bhutan Studies 2004) or the notion of 'Buen Vivir' in Latin America, which emphasizes sustainability and ecology as elements of a good life (Silva 2011).

The idea of this book is to approach contemporary studies of communication and social change within this wider call for a new social thought (Touraine 2009, 92) that is embedded in a sociology of the subject and agency. This is a sociology that recognizes at the outset the potential power of active sense-making and the action of the individual. Furthermore, it places this sense-making and action within the domain of the collective. What is proposed in this book is a notion of the subject that is radically different from the dominant paradigms within communication for development.

I propose a 'citizen perspective' on communication for social change that is embedded in this broader sociological call for a new social thought. This opens up opportunities to revisit the concepts of modernity and development, and the ideas of individual action and of social movements. It will require a deeper analysis of the underlying cultural models that influence local processes of deliberation and activism. However, a citizen perspective is first and foremost a proposition for a notion of the subject that opposes functionalist approaches to processes of change, and consequently to communication for development and social change. As Touraine argues, we 'have to get away from anything that defines sociology as the study of social systems and their functions . . . the most important thing is that the behavioural conformity is no longer imposed by particularity of a culture of society, but by the way everyone is constructed as a subject who has universal rights as well as an individual being' (Touraine 2009, 8).

This approach enables communication for development scholars to take an often neglected step back from analysing the particular strategies for communication implemented by specific organizations and social actors, and instead embed and review the communication practices and relations between subjects and institutions from a much broader social and cultural perspective. Only then can we start to construct a deeper and less instrumental understanding of the relation between communicative practice and social change. For many within the field of communication for development, this is more about 'unlearning' established perspectives on strategies of communication, loosening up and becoming more open to seeing communication as a fundamentally social, relational and dynamic process.

Emerging questions

In reviewing the changing character of communication practices between citizens and institutions, a number of concrete questions emerge:

- How do scholars and practitioners understand and conceptualize development, agency, participation, media use and communication practices?
- How are today's young citizens making use of the digital media? What synergies are sparked between old and new media and communication practices?
- How do institutions communicate with their constituencies? To the degree that they are pursuing social change objectives, what notion of social change informs their communicative practice?
- What outcomes are the social movements achieving? Can they sustain their mobilizations beyond the short term?
- How, if at all, are social movements and their communicative practices influencing the ways in which United Nations agencies, governments, non-governmental organizations (NGOs) and other stakeholders communicate with citizens?
- Have the massive civic engagements and their multiplicity of demands influenced the global development debate? If so, what novel notions of development are we seeing?

This first chapter offers a critical review of the main lines of research on social change- and social justice-oriented media and communication practices. This book has grown out of an interest in the interdisciplinary field that deals with the role of communication in processes of development and social change, but is written at a time when this discipline is almost drowning in its own success. A prolific research interest has emerged around the dynamics between media, communication, civic engagement and social change. It is being approached from a variety of perspectives, many of which have evolved in parallel with each other – but with only limited cross-fertilization.

With the objective of challenging the impermeability of this 'silo thinking', this book identifies and discusses how each of these fields contributes to a deeper academic insight into the relations between media, communication, civic engagement and social change. First, however, this chapter retrieves key developments in the field of communication and social change from the silos with which it has traditionally been associated. As a first step, let us visit two locations where citizens engage in communicative practices that offer examples of the different dynamic relations that exist between practices of communication and processes of social change.

Liberating Pedagogy in Rural Malawi

On a hot afternoon in the south-eastern corner of Mulanje, Malawi, a group of farmers, mostly women, has come by bicycle or on foot to a 'difficult-to-access' deep rural site, a wall-less school building on the outskirts of a village some 50 kilometres by dirt road from the nearest town. The meeting has been arranged by ADRA Malawi, an NGO that works with dialogic communication, using face-to-face communication to enhance processes of empowerment that enable local communities to advocate for their rights, hold their local governments accountable and improve their livelihoods. ADRA Malawi is a national NGO but part of the larger Adventist Development and Relief Agency (ADRA), which has national organizations across the globe. One of the development programmes run by ADRA Malawi is 'Action for Social Change' (ASC). It receives the bulk of its support from the governmental bilateral Danish International Development Agency (DANIDA), which supports ASC through ADRA Denmark.

Assisted by the training facilitated by ADRA, community-based groups gain insights into their potential role as civil society actors and are enabled to hold dialogues with the relevant authorities and advocate on issues that affect them. ADRA complements this community-based work with the radio dramas it produces for a national audience, which are broadcast in the early morning before the farmers go off to their fields. The television drama ADRA produces is not relevant in this area, where nobody has a television, but is instead directed at the more urban populations it also works with.

Characteristic of ADRA's work in East and Southern Africa, and in Malawi in particular as the pioneering country in this respect, is the strong strategic use of media and communication as a way to inform, engage and mobilize, as well as raise awareness of and advocate on citizen-driven issues pertaining to the development themes of HIV/AIDS and livelihood/food security. ADRA Malawi has made an explicit and strategic effort to work with both mass media, in the form of radio and television programming, and interpersonal communication, in the form of community dialogue sessions, in its efforts to deal with these development challenges.

The farmers I meet are organized in a so-called REFLECT group, which stands for 'Regenerated Freirean Literacy through Empowering Community Techniques'. The communication principles practised in these groups originate from the Brazilian adult educator Paulo Freire, whose ideas of a liberating pedagogy have been widely used and incorporated into education policies around the world, and become a strong strand of thinking in the field of communication and social change. Freire's ideas have travelled far, from his work on literacy and a bottom-up liberating pedagogy in Brazil in the 1950s and early 1960s, to work focused on participatory communication led by the Institute for Development Studies in Sussex in the 1980s. The REFLECT methodology was later spread further by Action Aid, and is now widely used by many development NGOs.

Since 2011, ADRA Malawi has incorporated the creation of REFLECT groups into its community-based work with rural communities, building on its work since the early 1990s, but now with an explicit long-term development goal of strengthening 'a vibrant, locally rooted civil society in Malawi which can be a dynamic actor in social, political and economical development processes in areas of livelihood/food security and health' (Action for Social Change: ADRA Malawi Programme 2010). Thus, although communication practices and the strategic use of media platforms are central to its work, the overarching agenda is advocacy and social change in the areas of health, food security and livelihoods more generally.

What I witness on an afternoon in August 2012 is a group of local villagers meeting at one of its regular assemblies to discuss the challenges faced by group members, taking turns to draw problem trees, identify possible solutions and, facilitated by an ADRA 'community facilitator', formulate strategies to deal with these challenges (see figure 1). The group members

Figure 1. REFLECT group at work in a village in southern Malawi
Source: Thomas Tufte

5

seem very confident with each other, and also with the ADRA community facilitator, who is from the region and regularly rides his motorbike out to the village to participate in the meetings.

Central to pursuing the group's programme goals is a training methodology built around the REFLECT pedagogical and operational methodology. This helps ADRA enhance the capacity of local communities to organize themselves, and communicate and advocate on core issues relevant to stakeholders in order to achieve improved services, better prices and – at the end of the process – improved livelihoods.

The inbuilt logic of ADRA's work with REFLECT is the assumption that synergies can be created between development challenges such as HIV/AIDS prevention, food security and improved livelihoods. ADRA's work with REFLECT also contains a component focused on building ADRA's capacity to become part of and further support the development of a vibrant civil society in Malawi. Finally, the work on REFLECT and community orientation is linked to ADRA's development of dynamic national and local media platforms that can enhance the social processes articulated at the community level.

The important question is therefore: is ADRA succeeding in communicating for social change? What I observed on that afternoon, and what I have seen repeatedly in ADRA's work over a decade, is the unfolding of a gradual and expanding awareness-raising process that is enabling communities to articulate demands and engage in collective action. Numerous results have been achieved, such as successfully holding the local government accountable for rebuilding a broken bridge, negotiating better subsidies on fertilizers, and achieving better facilities for voluntary counselling and testing for HIV and AIDS. Less visible, but fundamental, is what Paulo Freire called the process of 'conscientization' or, for want of a better phrase, the awareness-raising process that led to processes of collective action, mostly at the community level.

ADRA has replicated this type of work in several hundred similar communities across the region. These efforts have been linked closely to processes of organizational development, from the formation of community-based groups to registering as formal associations and establishing networks at the local, regional, national and even international levels. All this has been complemented by ADRA's strategic use of the mass media to engage all relevant stakeholders in 'national conversations' around the topics that emerge from community dialogue sessions in the villages.

Although it is not possible to deconstruct fully the processes of change, or the institutional objectives guiding these processes, one key lesson to learn from this example is that at a time heavily influenced by social uprisings and social movements, and their ability to articulate social change, and at a time when new technologies are attributed significant roles in some of these social change processes, we must remind ourselves of community-based efforts to communicate for social change. These are efforts that do not make headlines in the media, and are often considered 'silent' vis-à-vis the criteria for visibility in the public sphere. They are therefore less visible, less 'noisy' and not as articulate as some of the more recent social uprisings. However, they are possibly achieving more concrete development results, and thus social change outcomes that equal or surpass some of the many social movements across the globe that are mobilizing and communicating their way to achieving social change.

Having flagged the merits of this community-oriented practice of communicating for social change, let us contrast this with an illustration of how media activists in Brazil work to enhance processes of change through mediated citizen responses to current development challenges.

Mídia NINJA: Media Activists in Brazil

It is a warm day on the *sertão*, the dry, rural outback of north-east Brazil, in October 2013. In the city of Juazeiro, the local university is organizing a panel on 'New Media and Social Movements', and that same evening a new journal on communication and social change in rural settings is to be launched. I have been invited to sit on the panel and to join the editorial board of the new journal. Yet another bottom-up communication initiative is emerging in Brazil, a country known for its 10,000-plus community radio stations and vibrant civil society; but also for being the sixth-largest economy in the world and for some of the most powerful media institutions, such as Rede Globo, the world's largest producer of television fiction, and *Veja*, a weekly magazine with one of the world's largest print runs. Furthermore, Brazil is a country with more than 100 postgraduate degree courses in communication, more than 15 doctoral programmes in communication and 4,000–5,000 participants in the annual national assemblies for researchers and students of communication. In many ways, Brazil is a world leader in community media presence, print media volume, fiction media output, and media and communication research. However, because it is all produced in Portuguese, it achieves limited distribution in the Anglo-Saxon world.

The small city of Juazeiro lies in the region where, some fifty-five years earlier, Paulo Freire used his liberating pedagogy and participatory communication to teach literacy and raise critical awareness among landless peasants. That time marked a moment of change in the history of Brazil, when conflicting visions of development in the country led to clashes between power holders and the people, which ultimately resulted in a military coup and more than two decades of military dictatorship (1964–85).

This colossal nation is once again experiencing conflicting visions of development. In June 2013 protests were sparked by increases in bus prices in São Paulo, but soon spread to more than 400 cities across Brazil to articulate a nationwide rebellion and give voice to a set of complaints that fundamentally questioned the ability of power holders to provide social justice, health and education for all. The rebellions emerged in the period preceding and during the mega-event of the FIFA World Cup, which was held in twelve cities across Brazil in June-July 2014, but also contained references to and critiques of the Rio Olympics, held in 2016. Massive demonstrations were organized to protest against corruption and the mismanagement of public funds, the eviction of citizens and violations of human rights.

One of the activists, Thiago Dezan, was also on the panel in Juazeiro. Thiago is a tall, pale young man, then aged 23. He is from the provincial city of Cuiabá but lives in Rio. He seemed more focused on his iPhone than on the several hundred students in the audience. Demonstrations in Rio and São Paulo the night before had resulted in mass arrests, and he had been awake most of the night, communicating with fellow activists.

Thiago is a key member of Mídia NINJA, a network of media activists and citizen journalists committed to giving voice to and a fairer representation of ordinary citizens in the mediated public sphere. They are present at protests and demonstrations with their cameras and smartphones, and they film and then post and disseminate their images and messages online. They also actively seek to prevent Globo from filming and transmitting, out of a conviction that it is misrepresenting events. Fundamentally, Mídia NINJA represents an alternative vision of how to represent ordinary citizens in the media and voice their struggles.

Mídia NINJA has been highly successful at making many of the street demonstrations and grassroots activities visible through active and efficient online networking and dissemination. These were fully integrated into the vast and diverse network of social movements that erupted into the massive demonstrations of June 2013, and gradually developed and continued to demonstrate their discontent during preparations for and the progress of the World Cup. Mídia NINJA's role was strategic in the sense that it worked consistently to gain maximum coverage for trusted activists in the network in order to secure visibility for the demonstrations and other street events. The growing national network also ensured that the nationwide dimensions of the uprisings were communicated and disseminated online. Thus, when Thiago Dezan attended the seminar in Juazeiro, his participation ensured visibility for Mídia NINJA's role in the social movements, and provided an opportunity to network and show solidarity with local social movements mobilizing around the same set of causes.

'Noisy' Activism and 'Silent' Community Work?

Taken together, the NGO-facilitated liberating pedagogy in rural Malawi and the media activism by discontented urban youth in Brazil represent the variety in citizen responses to contemporary development challenges – responses that have media and communication practices at the heart of their strategies.

Mídia NINJA, which arose from within the Brazilian social movements, is just one example of the newer forms of social movement media experience. It converges with the more classic, community-based, communication for social change type of work carried out by ADRA in rural Malawi, work I consider to be equally innovative and just as able to articulate collective action and social change.

ADRA is an example of an NGO-driven process articulating community mobilization and collective action. Mídia NINJA, on the other hand, is a more multipolar and even fragmented process of social groups and movements connecting in networks and organizing through communication. Their dynamics, orchestration and organization of mobilization and social movements, as well as their use of social media and their overall communicative approaches, highlight a whole new way of both organizing and communicating for social change. Both are examples of the communication practices for social change that this book analyses in detail, bringing empirical insights into dialogue with new and relevant theory on communication for social change. Many questions guide this dialogue between theory and practice. Most notably: how can communication researchers, planners and practitioners conceptualize, strategize and act out their ways to social justice and social change? To answer such questions, I draw on and seek to connect the many parallel debates found in the social movement-based activism, on the one had, and the more institutionalized experiences led by NGOs, CBOs and even by governments, on the other.

Although different in many ways, a common denominator can be found in their explicit critique of policies and of negative social impact on ordinary people. The groups' demands have also been quite similar, as seen in the struggles for social justice, human rights and inclusion in governance processes. A multitude of citizens, many young, but not all, took to the streets in numerous countries across the globe to contest political dictatorships, financial crises and mass unemployment, producing a global wake-up call around the societal costs that many decades of autocratic leadership and neoliberal development have produced.

This plethora of agency has in many cases been 'noisy' in the sense of attracting attention, and although often slow at the beginning, ended up being highly visible in the public sphere. It has been focused on activism outside of established institutions and achieved what can be seen as spectacular results, not least the overthrow of presidents in Tunisia and Egypt. This 'noisiness' has also been seen in the expressions of mass popular outcry – of which the examples are many beyond Tunisia and Egypt, and include Iran, Greece, Spain, Thailand, Chile and Brazil, as well as Hong Kong and South Africa, to mention just a few. Less noisy in this sense, however, and more embedded in existing civil society organizations and structures, are the far greater number of examples of agency that can be found in ongoing 'development work' on the ground, of which the Malawi case is one example.

One of the key challenges of communication for social change today, as a field of both theory and practice, lies in recognizing and exploring the common challenges of the 'noisy' activist social movements often seen in cities, and the more 'silent' community work of civil society organizations, often seen in rural areas. The latter are well known for their long-standing work on communication for development and social change. This arena has been instrumental in the development of key concepts and theories dealing with communication and social change, and is today centrally placed in the field of communication for development. The concepts and theories in this field, however, are being challenged by the creativity, performance and media dynamics seen, for example, in the social movements in Brazil.

It is my belief that as the situation unfolds following the apparently 'noisy' peaks of the current waves of protest, the underlying social movements from which these often spring are increasingly being faced with classic challenges well known from the long-term and more silent development work of civil society – the challenges of organization, sustainability, legitimacy, strategic thinking and funding. This situation invites comparative analysis and the posing of similar questions to both processes of social change, including an inquiry into how each conceptualizes social change, and the role of media and communication practices in their social change processes.

The vast social uprisings as well as the long struggle for development even in remote rural Malawi are affected by a profound globalization of economies, politics and social relations. We are witnessing a gradual unfolding of cosmopolitan values and realities, and the transnationalization of social networks and civic engagement. All this is combined with a deepening process of mediatization that is influencing the logics of communication in the everyday lives of both systems and subjects. This is a general trend, but its processes vary significantly from the high end, in the connected countries of Europe, to places such as the villages in Mulanje or many other similar regions found across not only Africa, but also Latin America, where access remains a huge challenge. In this context, how can the 'new social thought' that Touraine calls for emerge and place ordinary people at the centre of contemporary visions and practices of development? The fact is that the examples from Malawi and Brazil both work to achieve exactly that.

The global wave of activism which the world has experienced, combined with developments in new digital media, have brought powerful dynamics into the equation of relations between citizens, the state, government, the media and the private sector. They have sparked a long list of questions that many, especially younger, scholars are grappling with today. It seems to be the technological innovations and the condensed moments of insurgency involving visible and immediate transformations that are catching the eye of the social scientists.

As my example from Malawi indicates, a lot of work on the ground – community work, social work and work in rural areas on health, agriculture, environmental issues, peace and education – is where much of the development and social change takes place. These processes, however, appear currently to be at the margins of the fashionable focus on social movements and citizen engagement. To reiterate my metaphor: the noisy, mainly urban process of transformation is gaining a lot of attention, while the quieter process of transformation, less visible and often in rural settings, captures far less attention but is definitely making noise in its own way. While research into social movements tends to concentrate on the peaks of mobilization and contestation, development research and communication for development research have traditionally been far more oriented towards the slow, less noisy and difficult-to-see-or-grasp processes of change.

Many current citizen-driven practices of media and communication are embedded in this dilemma between wishful optimism and a belief in fundamental changes happening in the immediacy of contemporary collective action, on the one hand, and recognition that fundamental social change requires long struggles in order to challenge power structures, cultural practices and the socio-economic realities of everyday life, on the other. This has been seen in many social uprisings of recent years, such as in Egypt in 2011, Brazil and Turkey in 2013, but also in the student uprisings in South Africa in 2015. Nick Couldry was therefore expressing timely scepticism in mid-2011, a time of intense upheaval across the world, when he wrote: 'Much is made of the use of social media in, say, times of political protest, but political upheavals are poor guides to wider change, since they are precisely exceptional. Entertainment and the basic necessities of holding things together may be a much more useful guide' (Couldry 2012, 19).

What cuts across from the farmer in the REFLECT group in rural Malawi to Mídia NINJA's media activism in Brazilian street demonstrations is their concern to position ordinary citizens in processes of social change, and claim their role as actors in social change processes. This book shares this concern and is particularly focused on exploring the role of the media and communication practices used during the positioning of ordinary citizens in contemporary social change processes. A notion of the subject that opens up space and generates attention for the ordinary citizen to be recognized as a fundamental social actor in processes of change became highly visible in the social uprisings that swept the world, but is also notable in the less spectacular community work for social change. Exploring some of the spaces that were opened up and how communication played a role is at the heart of this book. First, however, let us take a step back to explore some of the roots and past trajectories of communication for development, which will help us to understand the current challenges for the field.

The History of Communication for Development and Social Change

The well-known story of the history of communication for development and social change is the story of two competing paradigms – the paradigm of 'diffusion of innovations' (Rogers 1995) and the participatory paradigm (Freire 2001). In the multiplicity of communication approaches that have been applied to development over the years, these two main schools have dominated and still coexist as the main conceptual orientations in the practice of communication for development. On the one hand, the diffusion model is based on Everett Rogers' diffusion theory of the early 1960s, but encompasses a broad range of strategies all of which aim to resolve the problem of a 'lack of knowledge and information' (Rogers 1995). These strategies are primarily expert-driven. They have external change agents as their drivers and little or no room for participatory processes. The essence of these approaches is linear, monologue-like communication in top-down processes.

On the other hand, there is the participatory model based on Paulo Freire's liberating pedagogy from the 1960s, but renewed in the context of the post-development development paradigm (Escobar 1995). This school of thought brings the issues of globalization, transnational networking, new media and governance into the thinking on strategic communication, and these issues help to determine the objective of strategic communication. Rather than being about communicating the correct or relevant information to specific target groups, this becomes about articulating specific processes of collective action and reflection. The communication for social change approach takes many of these issues into account. The central focus is on the empowerment of citizens through their active involvement in the identification of problems, the development of solution strategies and their implementation. This is a dialogic, bottom-up approach to communication and development.

If we review the discursive histories and unpack these two main lines of thought, many competing discourses are revealed – each centred on its own concept, and each informed by different epistemological approaches. Of these many discourses, four dominate: development communication (DevCom), communication for development (ComDev), Latin American alternative communication, and communication for social change (CFSC). This overview excludes the whole separate field centred on more activist approaches and on social movements and their communication practices and media uses. I return to those specifically in chapter 4, as a separate set of discourses that is producing significant effects on the overall thinking on agency, communication and social change.

DevCom

Development communication originated in Los Baños in the Philippines in the early 1970s with the scholar Nora Quebral, but has strong conceptual ties to the United States. For many scholars and practitioners, DevCom is considered the dominant discourse within this field of research and practice. It emerged from the functionalist tradition within media and communication studies, but has since has broadened its scope. The US Agency for International Development (USAID) has been a strong institutional driver over the years, as have some of the key UN agencies, especially in large-scale agricultural and health communication interventions with a strong behaviour change focus.

ComDev

Communication for development originated from the critical thinking pervasive in European institutions, but also had clear parallels in some Latin American thinking in institutions in Colombia, Paraguay and Bolivia, among others. ComDev has links with the critical perspective of 1980s European cultural studies, with its rehabilitation of popular culture and recognition of the importance of audience sense-making processes which grew out of reception studies in the 1980s. It is also tied to critical studies of globalization, which question the notion of development and argue for stronger post-colonial notions of development. Although these perspectives do not characterize all ComDev research and practice, it is this interdisciplinary blend of perspectives that has informed the thinking and academic activities carried out at the Ørecomm Centre for Communication and Glocal Change, which I have co-directed with Oscar Hemer since its inception in 2008, and the Masters in Communication for Development at Malmö University which preceded it in 2000.

Alternative Communication

While the notions of DevCom and ComDev emerged in the 1970s and 1980s, Latin America was, in parallel with these discourses, using its own very different language to speak rather of *alternative communication* (Grinberg 1981) and *horizontal communication* (Beltrán 2006 [first published 1979]; Gerace 1973). Latin American scholars and practitioners carefully avoided the concept of 'development', which for decades was so closely associated with the autocratic and top-down development plans of the military dictatorships. In spite of this legacy, however, this view on 'development' is now changing (Tufte 2011; Peruzzo 2014). In Peru, Ecuador, Colombia, Paraguay, Bolivia and Uruguay universities have started to use 'communication for development' as well as 'communication for social change' when naming degrees and as frames of reference. These efforts are often developed in close collaboration with civil society and governmental efforts to enhance development through communication. A fairly recent and influential concept growing out of Latin American and Ibero-American experience is that of 'citizen media', substantiated by Clemencia Rodriguez in her 2001 book *Fissures in the Mediascape*, which connects to the broader international discourse on alternative media, ranging from 'radical media' to tactical media, social movement media and emancipatory media activism. I return to this in chapter 4.

CFSC

Finally, a discourse that has gained significant momentum since the turn of the millennium, in part due to the articulation of the concept and approach by the US-based Communication for Social Change Consortium, is communication for social change (CFSC). CFSC emphasizes using communication strategically to address and often challenge the structural conditions that inform social change processes. This could, for example, be the power dynamics in society that generate wider social injustice, the gender inequalities informing unequal access to education or the influence of the lack of health infrastructure in a community on the HIV/AIDS situation in that community. The lack of adequate health infrastructure, gender inequality and general levels of social injustice, and the alarming poverty levels in many societies were central topics in the debates about how to fight HIV/AIDS using CFSC strategies. CFSC as a strategy has placed strong and insistent emphasis on bottom-up perspectives such as participatory communication as an empowering and process-focused approach.

Overall, a deconstruction of these differences in discourse and approach within communication and development necessarily leads on to the need to analyse the political economy of this field. As this brief overview implicitly suggests, it is a field packed with power struggles, hierarchies and conflicts of interest. The actors in the field range from social movements to governments and businesses to a multiplicity of organizations, communities and groups in civil society and different regions and countries, each with its own set of historical, socio-cultural and political-economic contexts – and the list continues to grow. I analyse the political economy of the field of communication and development in chapter 7.

Communication and Development and Social Change: Past Models

Following an initial mapping of the prevalent discourses and concepts in the debates about communication, development and social change, let us take a closer look at three models developed to operationalize this field. These are far from the first to set out their take on this field of communicative action. What they have in common, however, is that they use communication strategically for pro-social purposes. They are also generic, and seek in systematic ways to offer and outline the key organizational traits and the prevailing strategies of the dominant paradigms in this arena of thinking.

It is important to note that a highly significant real-life experience lay between the models developed in the late 1980s and early 1990s and the three models presented here, all of which date from the mid-2000s: the rise of HIV/AIDS and the massive mobilization to fight this pandemic. This was a catastrophic experience that led to millions of deaths, and most actors – governments, civil society, and communication scholars and practitioners included – failed to find appropriate and efficient responses. Thus,

15

the struggle against HIV/AIDS was one of the most significant development challenges and led to heated debates about how to communicate for development and social change, and these experiences and debates very much informed the CFSC models of the mid-2000s.

Similarly, we may possibly in the future argue that the 'Arab Spring' and the new media developments of recent years together provided a real-life experience that created a similar epistemological rupture, shifting our perspectives on and understandings of how media, communication and social change interrelate. There will be more about that as this book unfolds. At this point, the three models I present here are my own model of three generations of communication for development; Colombian scholars Rafael Obregon and Mario Mosquera's 'convergence model' in communication for development; and Malawian media and communication scholar and practitioner Linje Manyozo's six schools of thought in communication for development.

Three generations of communication for development

My three-generation model, conceived in 2004, was heavily inspired by my own practical experience in the field of HIV/AIDS prevention. Since the late 1990s I had been carrying out both research and consultancy work in the field of HIV/AIDS communication and prevention, mainly working in sub-Saharan Africa where the pandemic struck the hardest. The three-generation model serves as a heuristic framework with which to analyse communication for development practice (see table 1).

The model contains three conceptual approaches, each represented by a 'generation' of experiences. The first generation of communication for development is that of diffusion of innovations (Rogers 1995), focused on dissemination of information and tied closely to the experience over decades with individual behaviour change communication. The second generation is a life-skills approach to communication, promoting the development of core life skills or competencies as the basis for people's ability to handle their own life's challenges. This competency-based approach has traditionally been closely tied to educational communication but has become an increasingly mainstream approach in the work of NGOs and UN agencies.

The third generation is the communication for social change approach, which emerges from Freire (2001). Each generation defines the development problem in its own way. These distinct problem definitions become the key distinctive features between the three generations. Rather than emphasizing chronology, the key distinction lies in how they define development problems. It is the way the problem is defined that determines

Table 1. Three generations of communication for development

Communication for Development	1st Generation	2nd Generation	3rd Generation
Definition of the problem	Lack of information	Lack of information and skills	Structural inequality Power relations Social conflict
Notion of culture	Culture as obstacle	Culture as ally	Culture as "way of life"
Notion of catalyst	External change agent	External catalyst in partnership with the community	Internal community member
Notion of education	Banking pedagogy	Life skills Didactics	Liberating pedagogy
Notion of audience	Segments Target groups Passive	Participatory Target groups Active	Citizens Active
What you are communicating	Messages	Messages and situations	Social issues and problems
Notion of change	Individual behaviour Social norms	Individual behaviour Social norms Structural conditions	Individual behaviour Social norms Structural conditions Power relations
Expected outcome	Change of norms and individual behaviour Numerical results	Change of norms and individual behaviour Public and private debate	Articulation of political and social processes Structural change Collective action
Duration of activity	Short-term	Short- and middle-term	Mid- and long-term

Source: Tufte (2004)

the nature of and need for the communication response. If the problem is defined as an information problem, the response will obviously be information dissemination. However, if the problem is of a more complex nature, referring to the underlying causes that influence behaviour, norms and values, then a whole different set of communication strategies evolves. It is thus the nature of the development problem to which they seek to respond that defines the core difference between the generations.

In addition to defining three different types of problems, the heuristic framework offers nine core concepts to help flesh out the conceptual and strategic differences between the three generations. It thereby becomes a useful tool for conceptually positioning any communication for development experience.

The Convergence Model

The Convergence Model (Obregon and Mosquera 2005) emerged out of an in-depth analysis of approaches within health communication, but has since been developed into a more clear-cut typology of interventions (see figure 2). This typology distinguishes between five categories of communicative intervention. These are placed in a continuum between the two dominant paradigms: diffusion of innovation and participatory/structural. Obregon and Mosquera make the point that most communication for development practice draws on a mix of these typologies. It speaks to pragmatism and the field's embeddedness in practice, making it less ideological and theory-driven than Manyozo's in the next outline, but giving it a more dynamic understanding of the interrelations between the approaches than my three-generation model implies. There is no magic formula and each communication intervention is unique.

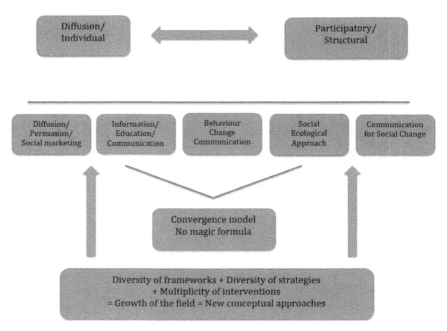

Figure 2. The convergence model in communication for development

Source: Obregon and Mosquera (2005)

Six schools of thought

In 2004, Linje Manyozo suggested bringing together the many conceptual approaches and real-time stakeholders involved around three nodes: geographical setting, institutional affiliation and ideological stand. He outlined six schools of thought in communication for development: the Latin America school; the Bretton Woods school; the Los Baños school; the African school; the Indian school; and the Post-Freire school, emphasizing participatory development communication (Manyozo 2004; 2006). Manyozo brings together an at times confusing mix of individual scholars, media, strategies, geographies and institutions, but the outline correctly communicates a crucial point. Communication for development and social change is a broad field, with institutions, scholars and communication experiences spread all over the globe and a breadth of conceptual approaches. Ironically, however, there is no mention of the Arab world, from where some of the most prominent recent communication for social change processes have emerged. Manyozo developed these thoughts further in 2012, and I return to this in chapter 2.

Common traits

When comparing the three models outlined here, a number of common traits emerge. These can help us to define communication for development as *a specific object of study* around which we can analyse and theorize. First, they all emerge from the *institutionalized* practice of communication, tied up with the logic of thinking of an organization or a system. This will be crucial to understand when later in this book I compare these communication practices with those of the social movements that typically stand outside of institutionalized settings and organizational practices. The inertia and logic of thinking in an organization tend to narrow its focus down to exploration of its own singular impact, leaving aside broader, deeper and more complex questions of development and social change. The dynamics and synergies of what really articulates social change are often ignored or underestimated.

This last point speaks to a second common trait: they all tend to contain *an implicit imperative of having predefined goals*, that is, they have established a set of tangible targets, often quantifiable outcomes related to ambitions of information transfer. What are left aside are the more open-ended processes of social change that are implicit in notions of empowerment, citizen engagement and not least 'social change'. A lot of institutionalized communication for development practice is so focused on predefined goals that at best it operates within the category of 'unintended outcomes', as the parking lot for the change processes that were not made explicit in the design and in the established indicators of the planned evaluation. Predefined goals make many things easier in terms of being precise, focused and to the point in assessing outcomes, but there are serious limitations and downsides regarding all the facets of social change that are not captured.

A third common trait lies in *the common concern for strategic communication* as a means to reach these predefined goals. This entails a systematic approach to the whole communication process. Again, the obvious advantage of this is the ability to track a particular type of observable outcome, often with a short time line, demonstrating impact in the immediate aftermath of the intervention. However, this advantage contains its own disadvantage: not being attentive to synergies, to intangible change processes and to the longer-term outcomes that could well be sparked or reinforced by the particular strategic communication intervention.

Finally and most importantly, all three models, including my own, contain *a normative framing of development.* It is clear in their discourses that they are committed to common concerns of social justice, equity and human rights, although how explicit this normative grounding is does vary. Their characteristic framing reflects different degrees of commitment to what Touraine has termed 'the return of the political' (Touraine 2009), articulating a pro-poor, pro-social approach in the communicative intent, and recognizing the need to question the implicit model of development – the neoliberal discourse. However, as is examined in the course of this book, there seems to be a range of contradictions and discrepancies between overarching ambitions for social change and some of the actual approaches of institutionalized communication for social change. It is in facing this dilemma that new contexts, stakeholders and dynamics emerge and contribute to the formulation of a new generation of communication for social change research and practice, driven from below.

Revisiting the Epistemology of Communication for Social Change

The main lesson to take away from this brief review is the variation in the epistemological and ontological approaches to communication and social change, along with, quite frankly, the confusing range of terminology scattered across the field. In such a context, this book settles on using the concept of *communication for social change* to outline an epistemology that emerges from the critical tradition within the field of communication for development and social change. In further developing a critical theoretical grounding for communication for social change, this book takes as its starting point opposition to and a critique of the instrumentality and narrow behavioural focus so prevalent especially in the history of the 'DevCom' tradition. In repeating the initial call I made for a new social thought where agency, processes of empowerment and collective action are guiding principles, this book suggests a theory-building of communication for social change that is centred on four key components. These components relate to specific understandings of communication, media development, social change, and governance and agency.

- First, communication is understood in a holistic and 'ecological' manner – emphasizing a practice approach that focuses on uses and appropriations, but does this within a broader framework which factors in the political economy of the media.
- Second, media are viewed as deeply embedded in and contributing to the configuration of social and political spaces. Media cannot be dissociated from these contexts. As Couldry argues: 'a media phenomenology not grounded in political economy is blind, but a political economy of media that ignores the phenomenology of media use is radically incomplete' (Couldry 2012, 30).
- Third, we must clarify how to understand social change. A critical stance towards the ethnocentrism implicit in a lot of social change thinking is crucial, and the vibrant debates on development and social change emanating from post-colonial and post-development debates are at the core of the approach advocated here. This entails a clear analysis of power relations, and is guided by normative stands on social justice, equity and thus positive social change. Social change is a non-linear, complex and often contested process. The complex relation between media use and social change processes is implicit in this approach.
- The fourth perspective on communication for social change is about notions of agency and governance. Media uses and appropriations are viewed as active sense-making processes, which, however, is not the same as saying that all sense-making activity is about citizen engagement. With a particular interest in citizen engagement, this book draws on the Mexican scholar Jorge González (2014) and others in suggesting a notion of sustainable and bottom-up governance. Such governance processes are based on the citizen-driven social change processes that emerge from the development of localized knowledge bases, information systems and communication practices (see chapter 5).

2   Changing Contexts and Conceptual Stepping Stones

Societal Processes Influencing Communication for Social Change

The prospects for citizen engagement in social change processes have radically changed in recent years. When examining contemporary challenges for communication for social change, a myriad of new contexts, stakeholders and societal dynamics can be identified. These are observable and concrete societal processes that can be broadly structured around four meta-processes in society: the emergence of a new generation of social movements; the substantial growth and expansion of civil society organizations across the globe; the increasing critique of Western development paradigms and the substantiation and circulation of significant alternatives; and, finally, new media developments, especially in digital media. This section discusses the way in which these societal processes constitute 'game-changers' for research in and the practice of communication for social change.

Informed and affected by these meta-processes, but also influenced by the significant limitations of previous communication for social change outcomes, a growing critique and self-critique have emerged within research in and the practice of communication for social change. The following section outlines this growing awareness of the complexities tied to the practice of communicating for social change. This awareness has gathered around three challenges that it is important to make explicit in our pursuit of conceptual ground on which to position citizens' needs, rights and responsibilities at the heart of communication for social change. These challenges are linked to reclaiming the political, cultural and 'mediatic' in communication for social change.

The third section provides a deeper analysis of the theoretical perspectives and challenges associated with a so-called pro-poor approach to communication for social change. This discussion is informed by Colin Sparks' proposal for a pro-poor and social-justice-focused communication based on 'radical participation'. The fourth section goes a step further by providing a similar analysis and discussion of what a post-colonial and culture-centred approach to development implies for communication for social change. A relevant framework to spark this debate is Mohan Dutta's culture-centred post-colonial development discourse. His points and argument are put in perspective by ideas on the same issue from several other post-colonial and post-development scholars. They confirm that Dutta's refreshing analysis echoes long-standing insights that local knowledge and popular culture are cornerstones of any sustainable social change process.

The fifth section explores the notion of media, which is conceived differently in the different schools of thought within communication for social change. Using Martin Scott's and Linje Manyozo's critical analyses of media development, as well as Manyozo's distinction between media as content, as structure and as process, proves extremely useful. Both these scholars help us to navigate conceptually within the different communication for social change debates, while also connecting communication for social change to some of the contemporary debates about the role of digital media and social movements in processes of social change. As we shall see, we cannot discuss the role of media development in communication for social change processes without also discussing issues of power, policy and participation. The concluding section outlines the preliminary contours of a conceptual framework for a citizens' perspective on communication for social change, a framework that is further elaborated in chapters 3, 4 and 5. First, however, I turn to the societal processes that configure the new contexts, stakeholders and dynamics which currently challenge communication for development.

The emergence of a new generation of social movements

The social movements that have emerged in recent years have sent shock waves through many societies across the globe. Many examples illustrate this, from the popular participation in writing a new constitution in Iceland in 2009, to the overthrow of presidents in Tunisia and Egypt in 2011, massive student protests in Chile in 2012, popular revolts in Brazil, Spain and Thailand over several years and the protests by South African students in 2015. Today's social movements share some traits with the identity-based *post-material* social movements that emerged in the 1960s and 1970s (Inglehart 1977; Melucci 1985; Touraine, Duff and Sennett 1981). However, the current wave is also articulating highly material demands for jobs, an income, housing, food and education. The students in South Africa took to the streets due to increases in tuition fees at their universities, while Brazilian protests were sparked by rising bus fares and the Spanish population came on to the streets with a polyphony of demands, most notably on jobs and affordable housing. In this way, the social and economic demands of the new generation of social movements resonate more with the social movements of the industrial era. It is perhaps fair to say that the new generation of social movements is characterized by its multi-vocal narrative.

Some of these narratives are unpacked in what follows, where I echo Kevin McDonald (2006) by claiming that they are 'experience movements' that have moved beyond traditional political claims of representation and instead touch on a fundamental emotional need to feel included in processes of change, especially processes that affect people's own lives. First, however, it is useful to look back at previous social movements.

The post-material social movements of the 1960s and 1970s put a heavy emphasis on specific social groups with specific social and cultural claims, often tied up with questions of identity and universal human rights. They thereby distinguished themselves from the first generation of social movements, which emphasized more material demands and rights. In the 1990s a wave of insurgency across the globe saw the emergence of the Zapatistas, the global social justice movement, the anti-globalization movement, and other similar uprisings with strong transnational networking features.

Transcending the old boundaries of 'North' and 'South' in the Western development paradigm, the most recent wave of social movements is less specific in its demands than the classic industrial movements, more material than the post-material movements, and, despite the intense transnational networking of some, possibly more national than the global movements of the 1990s and 2000s. This local orientation is manifest, for example, in the way each country named its social uprising in a way relevant to the local or national context, such as Occupy Wall Street in New York in 2011, the Gezi Park uprising in Istanbul in 2013 or the Umbrella revolution in Hong Kong in 2014. Their national features and characteristics notwithstanding, however, today's social movements have come together as a wave of worldwide social mobilizations. Despite their many variations, they resonate with each other in their fundamental critique of the marginalization of large sectors of society and in arguing for the right to be included in defining the direction of and participating in their nation's and region's, but also global, development processes.

The Italian theorist of social movements Mario Diani maintains that social movements are distinct social processes that are characterized by conflictual relations with clearly identified opponents, are linked by dense informal networks and share a distinct collective identity (Della Porta and Diani 2006, 20ff). Diani's characteristics cut across the generations of social movements outlined here, and also resonate with the current wave of insurgency. However, Lisa Thompson and Chris Tapscott rightly remind us to be cautious about our understanding of social movements being too caught up in Western paradigms, as their 'genesis, form and orientation are likely in many, but not all, instances to be significantly different' (Thompson and Tapscott 2010, 2). There may be some generalizable traits in the mechanisms through which social actors engage in collective action, but it is essential to localize these dynamics and understand the concrete departure point that gives rise to collective action and social movements.

As my generational approach to social movements suggests, each time and age has its own features, challenges and opportunities, but underlying these generational generalizations and global trends is a world of variations. With regard to the most recent wave of social movements, several studies have shown the many differing features of their objectives, participants and forms of mobilization, as well as the specific local historical trajectories that led to insurgency in each case (Galindo Cáceres and González-Acosta 2013; Gerbaudo 2012; Juris 2008; 2012; Kavada 2014; Treré 2011; Wildermuth 2013; 2014). This is analysed in more detail in chapters 6 and 7.

The growth and expansion of civil society

The period since the early 1990s has seen a significant development of civil society locally, nationally and transnationally (Gaventa and Tandon 2010; Jordan and van Tuijl 2006. Drawing on Scholte (2001), Lisa Jordan and Peter van Tuijl define civil society as 'the realm (that is, the public sphere) where citizens associate voluntarily, outside families or businesses, to advance their interests, ideas or ideologies' (2006, 9). It includes NGOs, civil society organizations (CSOs) and social movements, but not profit-making or governmental activity. Jordan and van Tuijl do not distinguish between NGOs/CSOs and social movements, a point I make elsewhere in this book to underscore the significance of different starting points, that is, being embedded in an institutional setting or not.

NGOs in particular have carved out a central role in development processes as key agents of advocacy and change, with all the rights, risks and responsibilities that this entails, and equally with the resources, strengths but also inertia that the institutional setting provides. This stands in contrast to many social movements that often lack some of the resources NGOs have to offer, such as organizational capacity, access to funding and professional experience. It is beyond the scope of this chapter to delve into the details of the differing roles of NGOs in development, but two different discourses exist regarding their virtues. On the one hand, there is the optimism expressed around the potential for increased citizen engagement in social change which the rise of civil society has enabled, and where media and communication play key roles. On the other hand, there are critical voices arguing that NGOs have come to dominate the development discourse and sometimes have difficulty remaining accountable downstream to their constituencies. Some speak of 'NGOization' within communication for development, and not necessarily in a positive way.

From service delivery to advocacy and human rights

Seeking to identify patterns and trends in civil society development, Lisa Jordan and Peter van Tuijl identify five dominant syllogisms in NGO activity since the early 1980s:

1. the classic role of complementing government, particularly with delivering services to the citizen that otherwise should be the responsibility of the state, but which the state for a variety of reasons does not fulfil, 1980–89;
2. the strong emphasis on civil society development now closely associated with democracy and governance, 1989–95;
3. the emphasis on the importance of good governance, legitimacy and establishing self-regulation mechanisms, 1995–2002;
4. the return of the supremacy of the state, since 2002; and
5. the main syllogism today – a human-rights-based approach which focuses on balancing multiple responsibilities to different stakeholders, using a variety of mechanisms (Jordan and van Tuijl 2006, 9–13).

Jordan and Van Tuijl focus their book on the fifth syllogism, which, I would argue, is that of exactly the period when we begin more profoundly to see a shift from service delivery to advocacy agendas in the work of NGOs.

Social accountability

With the emergence of a new generation of participatory communication embedded in civil society, where media and communication play central roles, the debate about accountability has sparked heated discussions about the correspondence between actions and objectives. As Jordan and van Tuijl explain, changes in development paradigms have produced changes in emphasis on NGO accountability. It is within the human-rights-based approach that we see NGOs using digital media as social accountability mechanisms. The case of Kenya is relevant here. After the crowd-sourcing mechanisms developed by Kenyan software experts were used during the post-election violence of early 2008 to monitor crackdowns by the conflicting parties, the use of such mechanisms took off, mainly for the purpose of holding governments accountable for the policies they implemented. A multiplicity of social accountability mechanisms have been developed, with Ushahidi, Uchaguzi and Huduma some of the most widely used (Wildermuth 2013; 2014).

Changing development paradigms

Reinforced by the global financial crisis of 2008, which was largely associated with the Western model of economic growth inherent in neoliberal economic thinking, changing concepts of development are increasingly nuancing what development means. Long before the financial crisis, long-standing debates questioned the Western development discourse that had dominated since 1945, but which is now losing its global ascendancy. The fundamental critique of Western development discourse is based on its narrow focus on economic growth and the centrality of market logic, its lack of concern for social consequences and its lack of long-term considerations of sustainability.

These critiques have over the years been accompanied by the emergence of new paradigms. These paradigms range from China's technocratic growth model, centred on national economic growth mixed with Confucianism, to Latin American claims of a sustainable development process informed by notions of 'good living' (*buen vivir*) (Silva 2011). In parallel with this questioning of the economic growth model spearheaded by the West, competing economies from the Global South and beyond have become strong 'economic game-changers', or at least competitors within a neoliberal economic development paradigm. This can be seen, for example, in the BRICS group encompassing Brazil, Russia, India, China and South Africa, building its own economic and commercial alliances. China has taken a number of its own powerful initiatives, investing heavily in African development under numerous bilateral agreements with African countries, boosting many of these fairly small economies, but in the process securing natural resources for China's continued economic growth. China is also spearheading the newest development bank, the Asian Infrastructure Investment Bank (AIIB), which was founded in 2014.

Among the general questioning, one of the paradigms that fundamentally challenges the growth-oriented focus of Western notions of development is the 'capabilities approach'. The Indian economist and philosopher Amartya Sen developed this concept in the 1980s and 1990s, defining development as 'a process of expanding the real freedoms that people enjoy' (Sen 1999,

293). His approach is characterized by four elements: first, development is understood as a process, not an outcome; second, it focuses on freedom of choice in all spheres – the personal, social, economic and political; third, it puts people at the centre of development; and, fourth, people themselves define what they value. Sen's capabilities approach connects well with Touraine's call for a new social thought, placing the capacity and aspirations of the individual at the centre of development.

Despite its influence on the development of the United Nations Development Programme Human Development Index in the early 1990s, Sen's approach remains surprisingly marginalized vis-à-vis the mainstream development organizations, mainly due to the difficulty of translating his ideas and philosophy into concrete policy and operationalizable frameworks. The German geographer Dorothea Kleine has developed an interesting analytical framework inspired by Sen within the subfield of information and communication technologies for development (ICT4D). In her book *Technologies of Choice? ICTs, Development and the Capabilities Approach*, Kleine (2013) explores how Sen's approach can be used to empower people to make choices in their lives. I return to this in chapter 4.

Surprisingly, the Bhutanese Gross National Happiness index has gained international attention and been developed into a system of thematic pillars with no fewer than thirty-two indicators with which to operationalize and assess how happy the Bhutanese people are (Ura, Kinga and Centre for Bhutan Studies 2004). It is an operational way of emphasizing some of the qualities of life that might otherwise be seen as rather intangible ways of measuring progress. The Latin American concept of *buen vivir* resonates with some of these concepts of good living, happiness and a sustainable way of life. In the United Kingdom, the then prime minister, David Cameron, launched a happiness index in 2010, involving annual measurements of well-being. In my own country, Denmark, a new political party emerged in 2014, 'The Alternative', which questioned economic growth as a natural given in the Danish development paradigm. In their way, each of these initiatives speaks to a fundamental questioning of how to measure development, and seeks ways to move beyond the historical focus on economic growth as the main indicator of development. The recent social uprisings and social movements already mentioned also constitute a fundamental questioning of the neoliberal development paradigm that lies at the heart of the dominant Western model of development (Couldry 2010).

New media developments

Complementary to and deeply embedded in these three meta-processes is a fourth, connected to the massive global diffusion of mobile telephony and the Internet. These technological advances have in many cases developed in dynamic synergy with the new social and political dynamics. Initial discussions on the causal relations between the use of new social media and citizen insurgencies and political change were marked by a polarizing debate between techno-optimists and techno-pessimists. On one side, Shirky unfolded his techno-optimistic approach with an emphasis on the 'almighty power of social media as a means of collective action' (Shirky 2011, 7). By way of contrast, there is Morozov's pessimism about online activism as 'a feel good activism that has zero political and social impact' (Morozov 2011). He further elaborates this techno-pessimism in *The Net Delusion*, in which he warns against the risks of 'slacktivism'.

Many research projects have recently explored or are currently exploring the emerging relations between decision-makers and citizens, media and activists, and offline and online spaces of deliberation. This serves to ground and nuance the previously polarized debate. Examples of such studies include: Jeffrey Juris' study of the Catalan anti-globalization movements of the 1990s (Juris 2008); Mirjam de Bruijn et al.'s study of mobility and mobile telephone use in West Africa (De Bruijn, Nyamnjoh and Brinkman 2009); Castells' studies of the revolutions and movements in Tunisia and Egypt, the Indignados in Spain, Occupy Wall Street in the USA and the Kitchenware revolution in Iceland (Castells 2012); Kavada's studies of transnational social movements (Kavada 2011; 2014); Marí Sáez' studies of associations, NGOs, social movements and ICT4D in Spain (Marí Sáez 2011); Wildermuth's studies of crowd-sourced social accountability mechanisms in Kenya (Wildermuth 2013; 2014); and Tufte's studies of civil-society-driven media platforms and social change in Tanzania (Tufte 2011; 2014a).

These studies reveal some of the complexities in the social and cultural dynamics emerging from the increased incorporation of new media into everyday life. Thus, in addition to offering new media and communication infrastructures, with access to an infinite world of cultural imaginings, it is on the actual uses of these new media that fascinating new research is happening – studies of how social relations, cultural identities and citizen engagement are mediated by these new media developments.

Beyond the new media developments and their mediations in everyday life, a third and more fundamental analytical entry point for understanding the new media developments lies in the overall process of mediatization. This process, which is intrinsically entangled with processes of globalization, is seen by some scholars as one of the determining features of contemporary development. As the German media researchers Friedrich Krotz and Andreas Hepp write in the description of their research project, 'Mediatized Worlds', mediatization is 'a comprehensive development process similar to globalization and individualization' (Stark and Lunt 2010). This speaks to the increasing pervasiveness of the media not only in the cultural practices of ordinary people, but also in the logics and practices of organizations and institutions in society. This all-encompassing presence of the media in society has led to a proliferation of studies on mediatization (Hjarvard 2008; 2013; Couldry and Hepp 2013; Hepp and Tribe 2013; Lundby 2009; Esser and Strömbäck 2014). However, it has also led to an increasing critique of the concept and its media-centrism for attributing to the media an overly large role in processes of change (see Deacon and Stanyer 2014).

While recognizing the limitations of the mediatization concept and its explanatory value when analysing media and social change, private sector media companies have emerged as strong drivers of change in a variety of roles. Mobile banking is a good example of an interesting innovation driven forward by private companies in Kenya many years before it reached Europe or other places in the Global North. These companies operate within and often reinforce a highly specific development process that is not only a market-driven economic growth model, but also closely affiliated to the Western development discourse, and connected to the values of the modernization paradigm and consumerism.

Another dimension linked to the emergence and growth of a whole new generation of media companies is the controversies around surveillance, which technologically presents unprecedented possibilities. Many of the largest companies, such as Facebook, Google, Microsoft, Yahoo, Apple and AOL, base their business models on new modes of organization and communication in which they have millions, and in some cases billions, of users across the globe. They own valuable information about the digital footprints of the ordinary citizens and their tastes and preferences in a broad spectrum of areas – knowledge that in some cases has been made available to government institutions for surveillance and security purposes.

Edward Snowden's publication in 2013 of huge numbers of confidential government files revealed close monitoring not only of key leaders and decision-makers but also of ordinary citizens. This was often information obtained by governments, in one way or another. Snowden's action and the WikiLeaks affair in 2010, when Julian Assange published massive amounts of confidential government material online, are iconic, albeit contested, examples of how new media developments challenge relations between citizen and state, with private companies playing at times controversial roles. In academia, the critical neo-Marxist field of Internet studies (Fuchs 2008; 2014b) has become a strong research trend, as has surveillance studies (Jansson and Christensen 2014). This serves to illustrate that new media developments contain a range of opportunities for pro-social, civic engagement to unfold, but also for governments and companies to exercise unprecedented forms of surveillance over their citizens.

Overall, these four societal processes – a new generation of social movements, the growth and expansion of civil society, a strengthening of post-development discourses and the proliferation of new digital media – are defining new contexts, bringing in new stakeholders and sparking many new social, cultural, economic and political dynamics, within which we must redefine the discipline and practice of communication for development and social change. This is the starting point for our revision and redefinition of communication for social change.

A game-changer for communication for social change?

In the light of the societal processes already outlined, what exactly is being challenged in the thinking and practice of communication for social change? What specifically are the game-changing factors? Have the high social costs of neoliberal development, the re-emergence of non-formal activism outside of institutions, the multidirectional, open-ended use of communication through digital media and the all-round pervasiveness of media in society made communication for social change as we know it obsolete?

Has the field of theorizing on practice in communication for social change been overrun by the communication for social change occurring in real-time, informal, activist-oriented settings? Or do our all-encompassing digital footprint, the surveillance of it and the fear generated result in either self-censorship among the silent majorities or stark rebellion, demonstrations and activism by angry citizens?

Rather than its being made obsolete, we are experiencing a proliferation of communication with a social change agenda, but this proliferation is appearing in new contexts. We will indeed continue to see the institutionalized practice of health communication, knowledge-sharing systems in the rural sector, environmental education campaigns, peace communication and community-based communication – but we will also see a lot more. The many opportunities provided by the new contexts, stakeholders and dynamics are offering innovative and cutting-edge pathways.

The practice of communication for social change is both expanding and changing character. Despite the development of civil society, and the heated debates about development paradigms, technological innovations and the mass use of digital media, it is what we might term *the global citizen insurgency* that is de facto contributing to the largest wake-up call for communication for social change. I refer to the vast growth in social uprisings – insurgencies – but more importantly to the deeper social movements they are part of. These insurgencies and movements with their often globally networked practices of communication have gained significant momentum in recent years. They are achieving the type of results that more traditional communication for social change initiatives strive for in public debate/ deliberation, civic engagement, community development and even sectoral outcomes around specific development topics.

However, the global citizen insurgencies are also vulnerable. They contain organizational weaknesses linked to funding and their ability to sustain their demands, among other things. In some cases they have failed or pro-voked political responses. In Egypt, for example, the mass social uprising in 2011 and the overthrow of President Mubarak was followed by politi-cal turmoil when the Muslim Brotherhood's candidate, Mohamed Morsi, won the presidential election only to be overthrown by the military. A new election brought the former defence minister and long-serving member of the Supreme Council of the Armed Forces, Abdul Fattah al-Sisi, to power in June 2014. This 'taking turns' by the established sectors of the political elite was far from the visions and aspirations of the activists in the Egyptian revolution.

We need to understand the global citizen insurgencies and the communi-cative practices linked to them. Only then can we better grasp what lessons can be learned, and which practices of both the individual social uprisings and the longer-term underlying social movements can inspire and challenge the institutionalized communication of the development industry. The rhetoric of the activists in many social movements and that of the institu-tionalized civil-society-driven media and communication initiatives is often the same – they are pursuing similar goals but with different approaches. There is a specific analysis of social movements and their communicative practices in chapter 4. Before that, let us dig deeper into previous experi-ences with communication for development and social change and the lessons that can be learned from them.

Reclaiming the Political, Cultural and Mediatic

The massive challenge of fighting HIV/AIDS with communication is the single most significant development challenge that scholars and practitioners of DevCom, ComDev and CFSC have faced. This long-standing struggle therefore illustrates well a number of the recurrent debates, and reveals the key challenges and limitations of communication for social change. The Ebola crisis, mainly in West Africa but with global spill-overs, echoed some of the challenges that emerged over decades around that fight.

When the Joint United Nations Programme on HIV and AIDS (UNAIDS) initiated a global consultation on experiences in HIV/AIDS communication in 1997, it received a mass of feedback highlighting the lack of consideration of context in HIV/AIDS communication. One critique was that HIV/AIDS communication had simply taken over the methods and approaches that had proved successful in the area of family planning since the 1970s, based on a narrow focus on behaviour change. The strong message from the field was that HIV/AIDS communication had to move from an exclusive focus on individual behaviour change to address the many contexts that influence the social behaviour of individuals. The UNAIDS Communication Framework, first published in 1999, made a convincing argument for the need to consider five key contexts in HIV/AIDS communication: gender relations, policy environments, socio-economic conditions, spirituality and culture (Airhihenbuwa et al. 1999).

The UNAIDS Communication Framework became highly influential and was widely disseminated. Its shortcoming was that while it was policy-oriented and clear about the key shortcomings in HIV/AIDS communication, it was difficult to operationalize, something that has required time and experimentation ever since. In the years that followed, there was a broadening of the overall agenda in the fight against HIV/AIDS. Many cases from sub-Saharan Africa through the 2000s and up until today bear witness to the effort of more context-sensitive approaches. The fight against HIV/AIDS developed from being defined as a health problem with behavioural roots and embedded in ministries of health, to be defined as a broad inter-sectoral problem of a socio-economic, cultural and spiritual nature which required inter-ministerial collaboration. National responsibility for the fight moved from single ministries to the offices of vice-presidents or presidents. Nonetheless, despite climbing the political agenda, the strategic communication approaches within communication for social change remained rather narrow in their focus.

Many of the scholars participating in or analysing these processes expressed fatigue and frustration with the dominant discourse within 'first-generation communication for development' and its inability to deliver communication interventions that could provide new knowledge, or change attitudes let alone practice. An often-heard problem was what came to be known as 'the KAP gap'. KAP was a popular acronym in behaviour change communication that emphasized that changes in knowledge, attitudes and practice were linear and sequential targets. The gap in the equation, which kept emerging, signified the alarming gap between what ordinary citizens knew about a particular topic, in perhaps health or farming – their knowledge levels; and their actual practice and behaviour. It became iconic and exemplary of what a lot of first-generation communication for development grappled with: the assumption of a causal relationship between the dissemination of information and a change in the individual behaviour of citizens. The problem was that this illustrated a false chain of events, where acquiring knowledge was assumed to lead to changes in behaviour. A lot of research has since documented that there is often no causality in that relationship unless the communication interventions are deeply embedded in contextual factors, partnerships are established with key stakeholders, and long-term, sustained action is ensured.

The poor explanatory power found in how researchers and practitioners were conceiving social change and the role of communication in articulating change processes led to a growing critique and self-critique. The 'distinct lack of progress led to a movement to replace rather than replicate the mistakes, theories and practices of the past'. There was now 'a broad-based movement challenging academic-, political-based leadership, NGOs, development theory, practices, motives, roles, paradigms as well as agendas and methodologies' (McPhail 2009, 2). The call grew for innovation in theory, concept and practice.

Reclaiming the political dimension

Consequently, a critique of the practice of communication for social change unfolded, resulting in a proliferation of new publications exploring a variety of critical issues. Three debates dominate this new wave of communication for social change research. The first is on *the different underlying assumptions of social change*: how it is defined and consequently what aims can be pursued by working strategically with communication. Moving beyond the false chain of events of the KAP gap, we find recurrent calls for deeper analysis and clarification of how social change is conceived (Obregon and Tufte 2014; Tufte 2012). The focus has been on the pursuit of narrowly defined objectives, however, and the wider challenges of development, that is, the visions and directions of development and social change, have remained unclear.

In the example of HIV/AIDS the objectives of the communication interventions translated for many years into a more limited but arguably also a more manageable focus on marketing the messages of abstinence, being faithful or using a condom – the famous ABC of HIV/AIDS prevention – rather than challenging the underlying causes of gender inequality, unemployment, poverty or lack of health services. Communication interventions were reduced to addressing behaviours rather than profound social change. This was a prescriptive strategy of communication, or 'directed social change' as it were. Some of the critical reflexivity around these traditional approaches is captured in, for example, Srinivas Melkote's edited volume, which contains self-critical reflections on experiences with directed social change (Melkote 2012; Tufte 2012). Similarly, Wendy Quarry and Ricardo Ramírez' book *Communication for Another Development: Listening before Telling* speaks to the prescriptive intention of a lot of communication for development, arguing that a lot can be learned from studying the failures in the field. Quarry and Ramírez (2009) highlights that one of the largest failures in the communication for development business has been the lack of ability to listen to the ordinary citizen. This critique is in line with the prescriptive communication already being criticized by Paulo Freire in his book *Extensión o comunicación?* (Freire 1998).

It is significant that a lot of the instrumental, functionalist and prescriptive approaches to what communication was expected to achieve survived the first, but also permeated the second and even the third, generation of communication for development. Such communication strategies took a techno-centric approach to the immediate objectives of many projects and programmes, failing to tackle in any depth the deeper structural causes underlying many project issues. This resulted in communication for development remaining for decades presumably neutral as a discipline, value-free and intentionally framed as non-political. Meanwhile, in order to speak of social change in any depth, or tackle structural constraints, socio-economic conditions or human rights, will necessarily require a stronger political perspective. Making the underlying social change assumptions explicit is about reclaiming the political dimension of communication for social change.

Culture-centred development

A second debate emerged strongly over the role of culture in development and the relation between culture, agency and social change. Who are the catalysts of change? What role do local knowledge and popular culture play vis-à-vis, for example, expert knowledge? How do these differing perceptions play out in communication strategies? What content is produced? Does it resonate with local popular culture, such as traditions of storytelling or of communication? The issue of being culture-centred is closely tied up with issues of power relations, social hierarchies and opportunities for participation, and is furthermore associated with exploring the deeper understanding of agency inherent in communication for social change initiatives. This speaks to power issues as well as to the need to define where change comes from, and who defines the aims and the pathway to achieving change. Consequently, the political economy of the field of communication for social change cannot be dissociated from the rest of this complicated equation of defining a communication for social change strategy.

Youth, for example, are often put forward as significant agents of change: but how does each culture define youth and what power do they have to influence development and social change in their societies? Florencia Enghel and I edited a book in 2009 on the role of youth in communication for social change, exploring the multiplicity of roles, functions and institutional set-ups, and even the mere ages of people – all culture-specific issues to be clarified when associating youth engagement with communication for social change initiatives (Tufte and Enghel 2009). Being culture-centred is about clarifying the role of local communities, their ways of life, their experiences and their knowledge, information and communication systems in proposed communication strategies for change. It is also about voice and the ability to listen. Whose voice is heard in a communication for development intervention – that of a community, a group, an NGO, a government or a donor? Power, policy and participation go hand in hand in culture-centred approaches.

If the many questions raised here on the relation between culture, agency and social change are taken on board, a far more complex monitoring and evaluation scheme will be required than can be found in the vast majority of cases. The science and methodology of evaluating communication for social change are increasingly made more mysterious. June Lennie and Jo Tacchi provide a good example of capturing the complex relations between communication interventions and social change processes (Lennie and Tacchi 2013). This is expanded further in Tacchi's piece from 2016 where she challenges our ways of interpreting voice in the field, arguing that what we see cannot be taken for granted without in-depth understanding of the context. She gives a wonderful example of how a situation of voice is completely misunderstood in an Indian slum (Tacchi 2016).

At the other end of the equation we find 'theory of change', which has become the new generation of logical framework analysis. It has emerged as a somewhat value-free technical instrument with only limited social change theory and little or no development theory underlying its claims. It speaks to what Pradip Thomas polemically calls an obsession with results: 'The obsession with results-oriented projects, outcomes, and numbers had led to a skewed understanding of what communication in social change is all about' (Thomas 2014, 17). We dig deeper into this discussion in chapter 8.

Defining the role of media in the communication for social change agenda

A third debate refers to the role and definition of the various media in communication for development and social change. There has long been a subtle distinction between two quite different fields of research and practice. These sometimes converge but at other times run on parallel tracks with different agendas. On the one side, we find those scholars and media practitioners most interested in exploring media developments, questions of journalistic practice, citizen journalism, freedom of expression, media infrastructure, media law, capacity-building of journalists and now, with the Internet, issues of Internet governance, content regulation, and so on. For these practitioners and scholars, the common denominator is the media sector, be it new or old media, but the issue is developing and understanding the practice of this sector in society.

On the other hand, there are those who instead identify with a communication for development and social change agenda, where the emphasis is on the development challenges in which the media serve as tools for enhancing development and social change agendas. Media tools are strategically chosen to pursue these agendas. For this purpose, media are identified either as the relevant channel of communication, the relevant choice of genre, or the most efficient means of distribution or dissemination of content, and so on. For these practitioners and researchers, the focus is on communication rather than media, where communication is seen as the social processes which media in all its varieties can serve.

It is when focusing on agency – the actions of specific individuals or groups – that the two agendas can converge. It may be an interest in citizen journalism that sparks a relevant debate or makes an event visible, and thus articulates social and political processes. Identifying what makes media activism and communication for social change converge is an important strategic question, and a highly relevant research one to inquire further into.

Theoretical stepping stones in communication for social change

All three of the meta-debates outlined – politics, culture and media in communication for social change – involve substantial critiques and self-critiques of the theoretical framing and the practical design of the field. At the conceptual level, they open up three theoretical perspectives that must be addressed in order to deepen the theoretical basis of communication for social change.

First, there is the need to theorize the notions of development and social change within communication for social change. While the 'modernization' and 'participatory' paradigms of development have often been seen as the key conceptualizations of development within communication for development, a deeper understanding of development and social change and the implications for communication for social change strategies and interventions remain clearly under-researched. The British scholar Colin Sparks critically assessed four key development paradigms with the intention of exploring which communication for development approaches can best serve poverty alleviation. He argued ultimately for 'radical participation as the one which complies best with a rights-based and social justice oriented approach' (Sparks 2007, 225). We take a closer look at Sparks' analysis later.

Second, there is a need to explore the close association between culture and social change theoretically. The central role of local culture and knowledge in communication for development and social change strategies is not well theorized. There are, however, notable exceptions. Mohan Dutta (2011) provides a useful introduction to and argument for a post-colonial perspective on development, using it as his entry point to position culture centrally within communication for social change. As a post-colonial Indian scholar, Dutta delivers a harsh critique of the dominant Western discourses on development and argues for a culture-centred approach that is very much in line with Sparks' principles of radical participation. Furthermore, only with a culture-centred approach can we avoid ethnocentric bias in communication for social change models. In the anthology *Voice & Matter*, Oscar Hemer and I assembled a wide range of anthropologists and other culture-oriented scholars working in and around social change processes. We identify and argue for an emerging 'ethnographic turn' within communication for social change, a turn which manages to distance itself from the functionalist and interventionist impositions of traditional 'DevCom' strategies (Hemer and Tufte 2016).

Third and finally, there is a strong need for theoretical clarity about whether 'media' is to be understood according to the 'media sector approach', where it has a life and purpose of its own, or within the 'communication for social change' approach, as a set of tools useful in pursuit of a range of social and political agendas. In *Media, Communication and Development*, Linje Manyozo (2012) makes useful distinctions between media as content, media as structure and media as process, which help to clarify the many points of convergence between the two parallel approaches to the media outlined here. Furthermore, Manyozo makes a useful connection between media development and issues of power, policy and participation, underscoring some of the convergence points. These theoretical perspectives are explored in the next three sections.

Development Paradigms and the Challenge of Pro-Poor Communication

Throughout the history of communication for development and social change, it has been argued that there has been a close and dynamic relationship between the main discourses of development and the main approaches in communication for development and social change. I would contest that argument. The sequential and linear story often told with regard to the evolution of development theory speaks in broad terms of a move away from modernization theory to critical perspectives stretching from dependency theory to participation and post-colonialism, in parallel in recent decades with globalization and the neoliberal approach to development. Within communication for social change, scholars argue that the evolution has been from modernization (linked to the diffusion of innovations) to imperialism (the New World Information and Communication Order, NWICO, debate), participation (participatory communication) and globalization (ICT4D in its uncritical, techno-optimistic variant). This generalized intellectual history of development theory, and especially how it connects to the history of communication for development and communication for social change, is erroneous mainly for two reasons: the intellectual history of development theory is far from linear, and nor is that of communication for development and communication for social change. Both have been far more complex and entangled, with parallel tracks between coexisting approaches.

Consider the example of the history of participatory communication. It did *not* emerge with Paulo Freire in the 1950s or 1960s, with the civil rights movements in the USA in the 1960s or with the early experiences of the United Nations Food and Agriculture Organization (FAO) in the 1970s. Rather, it has been an experience and concern throughout the history of modern forms of communication, as reflected in Bertolt Brecht's 1927 vision of the participatory and dialogic potential of radio:

> The radio would be the finest possible communication apparatus in public life . . . if it knew how to receive as well as to transmit, how to let the listener speak as well as hear, how to bring him into relationship instead of isolating him. On this principle the radio should step out of the supply business and organize its listeners as suppliers. (Brecht 2006, 2)

It also precedes the history of mass media in so many examples of interpersonal communication, such as the 'community dialogue sessions' run by social movements like the cooperative movement across Europe in the nineteenth century, raising the awareness of peasants and industrial workers (see, for example, Reich 2002).

In addition, the history of development theory and of using communication to articulate social change far precedes the commonly acknowledged starting point of development and communication for development – the post-Second World War era. Many scholars speak of President Truman's inaugural address in 1949, where he conceptualized the notion of the 'third world' and the idea of development, as the beginning. Like ComDev, the DevCom paradigm sees the establishment of USAID in the early 1950s as the starting point, where communication was strategically linked to the articulation of social change processes. Latin American scholars disagree with this narrative, as do Indian scholars. Both refer to innovative community media experiences in their regions in the 1940s and 1950s as seminal moments in the early days of ComDev (Manyozo 2012, 37; Melkote and Steeves 2015).

Furthermore, referring to the early experiences with communication to articulate change, John Downing outlines – albeit only briefly – an interesting list of far earlier examples, ranging from the distribution of flyers during the Protestant Reformation in Germany and the revolutionary pamphlets of the English Civil War in the mid-1600s to the anarchist, socialist and Marxist posters in Spain and Catalonia in the 1930s (Downing 2014).

Conclusively, the history of development theory and of how it informs communication for development over time needs to be rewritten, looking beyond the Western development industry post-1945 to recognize cultural, regional, ideological and other differences. Manyozo's 'six schools of thought' (see p. 19) is a useful starting point in recognizing the complexity and diversity of communication for development.

Four development paradigms

The work of Colin Sparks is useful in pursuit of a citizen perspective on communication for development. Sparks (2007, 1) addresses the role media and other forms of communication can play in improving the conditions of life of the world's poorest and provides a critical assessment of four of the most important paradigms influencing media, communication and social change in the quest to address questions of poverty, inequity and injustice. He argues that the four most important paradigms are the dominant, the participatory, the imperialism and the globalization. The dominant paradigm is, as I explain in the preceding section, tied to the 'first generation' of communication for development – aligned with the modernization paradigm and a highly instrumental way of understanding what communication is able to achieve. It is also the paradigm that defines change most narrowly as individual behaviour change.

Both the imperialism paradigm and the participatory paradigm were formulated in opposition to the dominant paradigm. Each emphasizes its own level of change. The imperialism paradigm focuses on the meta-level of change, with particular emphasis on media developments in terms of ownership, infrastructure and content flow (Nordenstreng and Varis 1974), issues that were ever present in the NWICO debate of the 1970s and 1980s (Sparks 2007, 84). In contrast to these meta-analyses, the participatory paradigm emphasizes community-level change – bottom-up initiatives based on a variety of participatory approaches ranging from 'non-participation' to 'power-participation'. Sparks draws on a typology from the Brazilian communication scholar Cicilia Peruzzo (Sparks 2007, 70), which is elaborated further in chapter 4. His own final proposal, 'radical participation', is closely aligned with Peruzzo's notion of 'power-participation'. Finally, the globalization paradigm, Sparks argues, is equivalent to the neoliberal development project where social change dynamics are regulated by the market.

While all four paradigms have been significant and brought insights to the field, Sparks argues that in order to develop an emergent paradigm that builds on radical participation and social change driven from the bottom up, the participatory paradigm and a revised, updated version of the imperialism paradigm are the most important.

Pro-poor communication

In reviewing the past conceptualization of the role of media and communication in articulating social change for the poor, Sparks provides a traditional historical account that brings us back to the origins of the dominant paradigm and its emergence in the USA after the Second World War. In discussing the clear state-driven interest in using media and communication strategically, Sparks criticizes this top-down approach as ultimately disempowering for local populations. However, he argues that there are sections of the dominant paradigm that we can take with us in outlining what he calls 'a pro-poor communication paradigm for the future'. These sections he calls *the continuity variant* (Sparks 2007, 50).

The continuity variant grows out of decades of health communication that has promoted behaviour change for the improvement of public health, without ever really challenging the power structures in society. Sparks acknowledges that from the mass of experiences framed in this paradigm, the communication of what he terms 'technical modernity' remains valuable, although he also recognizes the limits of the work, such as overoptimistic expectations of what communication can achieve, and failure to recognize the difficulty of altering deep-rooted patterns of human behaviour or the interdependency of behaviours and other substantial social change (Sparks 2007, 195). Nonetheless, innovations and knowledge related to improving public health have been communicated to large constituencies with significant success. While the continuity variant of the dominant paradigm talks about participation, however, it remains a discourse in which the participation of audiences is controlled, never seriously allowing participation to challenge the pre-established aim set out by the organization responsible for the project.

Instead, it is within the participatory communication paradigm that a vision of real structural and social change for the benefit of the poor is articulated. While acknowledging this vision, Sparks criticizes the lip service paid to participatory communication and to genuine social change-generating practices (Sparks 2007, 195). Sparks highlights the paradox he found in his review of the literature: 'the dominant paradigm passed in theory, but retained a very extensive appeal in practice: the participatory paradigm, on the other hand, triumphed in development theory, but has failed to command any substantial support in practice' (Sparks 2007, 59). That participation became a buzzword in reports and project documents, as well as in science and research, is well documented (Brock and Pettit 2007; Cooke and Kothari 2001). According to Fair and Shah (1997, 10), participatory communication became the most frequently used theoretical framework within communication for development in the late 1980s and 1990s, but in practice its use remained very rare.

Contours of a new paradigm in communication and social change

In an attempt to argue his preference for the participatory paradigm and delineate some contours for a new paradigm of communication for social change, Sparks' concluding chapter fleshes out five challenges. The first is the need to be aware of the nature of the change agents in communication processes. This resonates with one of the nine conceptual concerns I outline in my heuristic framework of three generations of communication for development (see table 1 in chapter 1). Sparks emphasizes that change agents are necessarily political activists (Sparks 2007, 225). Radical participation is about reclaiming the political dimension of communication for development and social change, and moving beyond the instrumentality that proliferated in the first generation of communication for development.

Second, Sparks highlights the need to be democratic in essence, leaving no conceptual space for top-down approaches that oblige people to take a set course of action. This leaves little room for persuasive communication. Third, he argues for communication for development to be based on majority views, achieved through debate and discussion – what I would call the dialogic nature of communication for development. Fourth, he argues for a proper understanding of what imperialism means, moving beyond the old theories of centre and periphery, and instead considering a 'people's perspective' as a guiding principle in pro-poor initiatives: 'The poor of the world . . . are both oppressed and exploited. Their natural allies in the world are not governments or businesses but other people who have the same experiences' (Sparks 2007, 225). Only by recognizing interdependency across borders and pursuing the bigger connections in world development, as Pieterse (2010) would argue, can a communication for social change process have a more positive outcome. Finally, and most importantly, there is a need to decide on the nature of social change:

> On its own, the best communication cannot succeed in changing the situation. Only when the poor are organized and confident can the problems that face them be addressed, and it is social action that gives people confidence and organization. The media have a central role in this process because finding a public voice is one of the ways in which both confidence and organization can be built. (Sparks 2007, 226)

Post-Colonialism and a Culture-Centred Approach

A paradigm which was not given much attention by Sparks, but which I find crucial to understanding today's debates about development, is post-colonialism. There have been key contributions from India (Bhabha, Appadurai, Gupta, Spivak), Palestine/USA (Said), Algeria (Fanon), Cameroon (Mbembe), Uganda (Mamdani) and several Latin American countries (Argentina, Ford;

Peru, Alfaro Moreno; Mexico, Reguillo and González; and Colombia, Martín-Barbero and Escobar). While the Latin Americans in particular do not traditionally identify themselves as post-colonialists, they do have a common strand with the others in critiquing the long-standing dominance of the Western discourse in development studies, cultural studies and science in general. They are also critical of the lack of non-Western voices in development. Similarly, they all make a strong argument for the role of culture in social change processes.

The Indian media scholar Mohan Dutta has written an inspiring and refreshing book in which he proposes and advocates for a culture-centred approach to communication and social change. Referring primarily to the Indian scholar Gayatri Spivak, Dutta positions himself within the post-colonial discourse. Also using Spivak, Dutta locates communication theory within a post-colonial framework and argues for the mobilization of knowledge 'for the purposes of servicing the material inequities of neocolonialism' (Dutta 2011, 6). Using subaltern studies theory as a perspective to 'write history from below' (2011, 7), Dutta argues for a rewriting of the narratives that constitute the discursive space of history. His aim is deliberately to seek out and listen to the voices of marginalized populations, 'voices that have been systematically erased' (2011, 7).

Dutta's arguments connect well with those of the British media scholar Nick Couldry, whose book *Why Voice Matters: Culture and Politics after Neoliberalism* (2010) provides an elaborate critique of the neoliberal development model. Couldry's fundamental critique of this paradigm has influenced large development organizations across the globe. His main criticism is that our ways of thinking development have historically not been very inclusive. There have not been proper ways and means of securing citizens a solid voice in the processes of development. He concludes his book by outlining the challenges of a post-neoliberal politics, and some of the important new resources such a politics can draw on.

Couldry speaks of the 'new technologies of voice' (Couldry 2010, 139), outlining five new possibilities which media and technology are enabling. First, *the new technologies are allowing voice in public for a vastly increased range of people*. This is already apparent, although issues of lack of access, resources and competencies still produce significant digital divides. Second, *a greatly increased mutual awareness of these new voices has emerged*. We can circulate more stories, more quickly to more and more peers. In other words, the imagined communities Benedict Anderson wrote about in the era of the mass media a few decades ago (Anderson 1991) have materialized as real-time networked communities for a growing proportion of the world population. Third, we are seeing *new scales of organization thanks to the*

Internet. Events during the Arab Spring are a case in point. Many demonstrations are being organized through web-based communications. This ties in well with Kavada's emphasis on 'organizational self-structuring', a topic I return to in chapter 4 (Kavada 2011). Fourth, *our understanding of the spaces that are needed for political organization has now changed.* As the US political scientist Lance Bennett has argued (2008), the dynamic network becomes the unit of analysis in which all other levels – organizational, individual and political – can be analysed more coherently. However, this is the case in some societies but not in others. Finally, and very importantly, all these changes are generating the potential for *new forms of listening.* This resonates with Wendy Quarry and Ricardo Ramírez' call for greater attention to 'listening before telling' in communication for development practice (Quarry and Ramírez 2009). Governments are no longer able to say that they cannot hear the voices of the people, as new relations become possible between citizens and politicians.

While Couldry delivers a critique of the neoliberal development process from a British perspective, using many British examples, Dutta is embedded very much in an Indian post-colonial discourse which has traditionally aimed to interrogate many of the assumptions taken for granted in the West-centric production of knowledge. Without delving into that discussion vis-à-vis Couldry, Dutta's work constitutes an interesting parallel to both African and Latin American post-colonial discourses. Like Dutta, they also seek to position themselves critically vis-à-vis the dominant discourses of development and communication for development, and they also argue for voice, visibility and the inclusion of the marginalized. In Africa, the early post-colonial or anti-colonial scholar Franz Fanon (1952; Fanon and Farrington 1968) was particularly concerned with racial discrimination and exclusion. The post-colonial African discourse is further developed in the works of the Cameroonian scholar Achille Mbembe, especially in his seminal work *On the Postcolony* (2001), where he provides compelling analyses of our understanding of power and subjectivity in Africa.

In Latin America, several lines of thought raise similar questions to Dutta's. First, there is the groundbreaking work of the late 1980s on rehabilitating popular culture and reassessing the political potential of everyday social and cultural practices, not least communicative practices. The seminal book in this area is *Communication, Culture and Hegemony: From the Media to Mediations*, by the Spanish-Colombian scholar Jesús Martín-Barbero (1987; 1993) Alongside him, Néstor García Canclini, Gustavo Jiménez, Rosa María Alfaro Moreno, Renato Ortiz, Milton Santos, Muniz Sodré, Rossana Reguillo, Aníbal Ford and Valerio Fuenzalida, among others, produced a strong conceptual proposal for a culture-centred approach to development in Latin America. It is notable that this literature is not mentioned in Dutta's work, given that he argues so strongly for a culture-sensitive approach, and given that some of their key contributions began to appear in English in the early 1990s.

A more explicitly post-colonial Latin American scholar, published by Princeton University Press and known to Dutta, is the Colombian Arturo Escobar, who introduced the concept of post-development (Escobar 1995; 1998). He argues that we are living in a 'moment of possible (truly) post-modern and posthumanist landscapes' (Escobar 1995, 224) where the voices of the Third World are beginning to be heard, and can make unique contributions to a project where the agency of Third World people is recognized: 'If one were to look for an image that describes the production of development knowledge today, one would use not epistemological centers and peripheries but a decentralized network of nodes in and through which theorists, theories, and multiple users move and meet, sharing and contesting the socioepistemological space' (Escobar 1995, 225). It is in this space that post-development in the form of other discourses and other politics of representation can emerge. Again, despite the lack of references to each other's work, Escobar's and Jorge González' thoughts resonate well.

The work of Jorge González emerges from his decades of grounded cultural research, and from the Culture Program at the University of Colima, which he directed for many years together with Jesús Galindo Cáceres. His work around 'cultural fronts' and 'cyberculture' is an important contribution to Latin American research on culture, communication and social change. His main argument is that a culture of governance in any society requires the development of systems of information, of communication and of knowledge, and that these must be developed from within that society as bottom-up processes. In chapter 5, I propose a culture-centred approach to governance, communication and citizen engagement based on González' notion of a 'culture of governance', which González calls 'cibercultur@'.

Communication and social change: models and approaches

Returning to Dutta and his review of the communication for development literature, he, like Sparks, works around four approaches to communication and social change. He develops these approaches as entry points for understanding the breadth of the field (figure 3). On the vertical axis, Dutta places the aim of social change communication, with individually oriented behaviour change but no societal change, and therefore the 'status quo', at

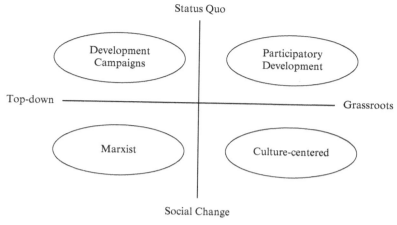

Figure 3. Theoretical framework for social change communication

Source: Copyright 2011 from *Communicating Social Change: Structure, Culture, and Agency* by Mohan J. Dutta. Reproduced by permission of Taylor and Francis Group LLC, a division of Informa plc.

the top. At the other end of the axis he places 'social change' understood as structural change. On the horizontal axis he places top-down approaches to the left and bottom-up, grassroots approaches as their opposite.

This results in four areas of praxis: at the top end, closest to 'status quo', he places 'development campaigns' as the top-down model and 'participatory development' as a more grassroots-oriented approach. Closest to a structural change orientation he places a 'Marxist' praxis as a top-down model along with his own proposal, the 'culture-centred' approach, as the more grassroots-oriented (Dutta 2011, 33). The 'development campaign' section resonates quite well with the dominant paradigm (Sparks) or first-generation communication for development (Tufte), while Dutta's 'Marxist' section fits well with the imperialist paradigm (Sparks). While this is in part a good starting point for a discussion on communication for social change, Dutta's model differs significantly from many others with regard to how he perceives participatory development. In direct opposition, for example, to Freire's argument, Dutta places participatory development as a status-quo-oriented category. Even the 'negotiated variant' of the participatory paradigm that Sparks outlines is more social-change-oriented than Dutta's interpretation of participatory development. Similarly, the Latin American scholarship on participatory development, well represented in the anthology Gumucio-Dagron and I edited (Gumucio-Dagron and Tufte 2006), argues strongly from a structural change perspective – it is its entire premise.

This illustrates only too well that the same concepts have very different connotations in the hands of different scholars. This confuses the reader and calls for more transparency and clarity on how concepts are defined and used. The Brazilian sociologist Evelina Dagnino has raised some of these dilemmas, referring to the lack of consensus on the definition of citizenship and similar concepts; and how this results in different takes on what participatory forms of media use and communicative practice entail and what they should aim to achieve. The debate is locked in what Dagnino has called a perverse confluence of two different political projects: 'The perverse nature of the confluence between the participatory and the neoliberal projects lies in the fact that both not only require a vibrant and proactive civil society, but also share core notions, such as citizenship, participation and civil society, albeit used with very different meanings' (Dagnino 2011, 419).

As I read it, Dutta's placement of participatory development as a status-quo-oriented approach runs the risk of undermining what participation is really about – it is a project of social change. Many scholars define participatory communication more or less as a contextualized, social-change-oriented communicative effort to articulate the voices and empower the actions of the most marginalized groups in society. Using such a definition of participation, there is no major difference between Dutta's culture-centred approach and the notion of 'participatory development'. Furthermore, this combined 'participatory-cum-culture-centred-development' approach is well aligned with Sparks' 'radical participation' approach. Consequently, my proposed revision of Dutta's conceptualization leads me to suggest the model in figure 4.

An issue not reflected in Dutta's model is the societal levels at which social change occurs – ranging from the local, community-oriented, to the national and regional, or the global. The interdependency of the different levels of change is present in Pieterse's notion of world development, and may well be implicit in others as well, but it is not reflected in Dutta's model.

With regard to the more explicit political positioning, Dutta's critique of the neocolonial agenda resonates well with contemporary critiques. In line with González' arguments (see chapter 5), Dutta highlights the problem of knowledge structures that remain situated in 'the realm of the materiality of colonialism and neocolonialism' (Dutta 2011, 45) and closely linked to 'mercenary interests'. Consequently, 'power differentials are continuously maintained in the realm of who comes to know the world, and who gets to be scripted as the subject of studies, as an artifact to be captured in mainstream narratives as constructed by the dominant knowledge structures' (Dutta 2011, 45). It is faced with this situation that he formulates

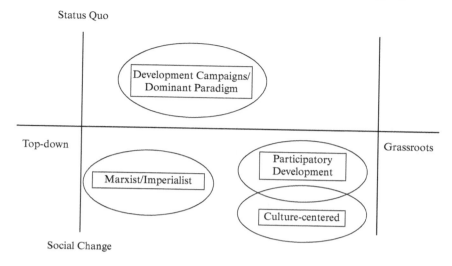

Figure 4. Positioning a 'participatory-cum-culture-centred development' approach

Source: Thomas Tufte

a 'resistive politics', spelling out the more activist elements of his culture-centred approach. He draws on Spivak and subaltern studies in his plea to document the agency and politics of the people (Dutta 2011, 54). His discussion of the important role of the subaltern agency in transformative politics has a clear parallel with the emphasis of Sparks, Thomas and others on political agendas and underlying structural inequalities as defining conditions in the practice and aim of communication for social change (Sparks 2007; Thomas 2014)

In conclusion, despite the limited framework of references to the rich work of many others on culture-centred approaches, Dutta's proposed pathway for rethinking communication for social change 'from below', emphasizing the subaltern, opposing the structural violence in society and articulating strategies of resistive politics, provides us with useful stepping stones towards a rethinking of communication for development in times of revamped social and political activism.

Dutta concludes his book by discussing the issues of praxis in communication for social change. In any further elaboration of a genuine pro-poor, bottom-up social change communication agenda it will be central for Dutta to deconstruct the culture of neoliberalism. As Dutta states: 'The culture of neoliberalism as embodied in the "Science" of communication interventions needs to be fundamentally deconstructed through sophisticated theoretical engagement that interrogates the ways in which specific legitimized knowledge configurations and relationships of power are embodied in these interventions' (Dutta 2011, 299). These issues are in line with the overall call for 'a new social thought', which I make in chapter 1. They also fit well with Jorge González' concept of 'cibercultur@', which constitutes a key frontier in developing a citizen perspective on communication for development and social change.

Media, Communication and Development

In chapter 1, I outline four common traits that characterize the current field of communication for development: the institutionalized practice of communication; the implicit imperative to have predefined goals; the common concern for strategic communication; and the normative framing of development. A noteworthy absentee from this outline was a role for the media to play in communication for development. Where do the media fit in to the equation? What role will they play in pursuing a communication for development agenda? These questions are difficult to answer because the media can mean so many different things, let alone the concepts of media development or media for development. Defining media development is like nailing jelly to a wall, as the British media scholar Martin Scott put it (Scott 2014, 75ff).

Departing from a media-centric nomenclature, both Scott and Manyozo have sought to map out the field of media, communication and development. Both use more or less the same three-pronged approach to media and development: *media for development, participatory communication* and *media development*. Scott furthermore discusses media relations to overall development processes, which I also discuss.

Within the nomenclature of communication for development, is it significant how the media is perceived? Are we dealing with media as institutions, discourses or uses? Or are we dealing with communication practices as agency and actions by groups and individuals? These are very different analytical approaches to defining and understanding communication for development. Manyozo attempts to build a bridge between media-centric and communication-centric focuses by expanding the naming of the field from 'communication for development' to 'media, communication and development', thereby carving out a more explicit role and higher visibility for media at a level equal to the practice of communication. Furthermore, this renaming of the field bypasses the 'causal or imperative' discourse that many raise and criticize when the field is named 'communication *for* development' (Wilkins 2014).

Manyozo formulates clear characteristics for each approach. Media for development has its focus on *media as content*, media development on *media as structure* and participatory communication on *the communication process*. To overcome further the implicit dichotomy between media-centrism and communication-centrism, which Manyozo refers to (Manyozo 2012, 13f), he brings in a political economy perspective by arguing that no matter which of these three approaches is taken, all must tackle the political economy of the field, and the powers of institutions and stakeholders over the practice of media and citizens. It is the same political economy perspective I argue for in chapters 1 and 7.

Taking a closer look at the different approaches, Manyozo analyses them according to their key concepts, origins/history, major theories, key theorists, functional objectives, levels of participation and key policy-makers (Manyozo 2012, 18–19). Media for development is seen as the instrumental use of media as tools to pursue the dissemination of information and achieve individual behaviour change. This resonates with my first generation of communication for development, and concurs that it has no social change agenda. The media-centrism of this approach remains clear: 'the media and communication experts are at the centre of the whole process' (Manyozo 2012, 17).

Second, there is 'participatory communication,' which emphasizes the processes inherent in participatory communication and highlights its key role in social change processes. However, Scott problematizes the many different approaches to participation, criticizing the widespread pragmatism and instrumentality inherent in the perceptions of participatory communication, and calling for a more clearly ideological stand (Scott 2014, 60). To this, we may say that Sparks' 'radical participation' approach contains a clear normative stand that argues for a bottom-up perspective in pursuit of social justice and human rights in pro-poor communication. This aligns well with Manyozo's understanding of a genuinely participatory approach as one where the different development stakeholders employ participatory communication in order to author development from below.

Third, the 'media development' approach treats the media sector as an independent entity. It is a sector per se which needs to be strengthened and supported to maximize the role of media in society. The agenda here is not about development or social change but about media freedom, press plurality, professionalism, capacity and an enabling environment, and the economic sustainability of the media organization. Scott and Manyozo coincide in their perceptions of media development, although Scott expands his notion to include media literacy. Media literacy is a concept which in recent years has evolved from the mere ability of citizens to protect themselves from possible harm by the media to include developing the skills necessary to create media or use them to communicate (Scott 2014, 87). It can be defined as 'the ability of citizens to access, understand and create communications and to understand the functions of the media and their rights in relation to it' (Scott 2014, 89). This definition opens the door to connecting communication for development debates and current studies of social movements with the outspoken media activism seen in many of these movements. The people's media literacy is a precondition for this media activism to take place, and media activism is often a strategic endeavour to pursue social change. I return to this in chapters 4 and 6.

Finally, Scott's fourth approach to media and development is about the question of how the media connects with the big challenge of 'development'. How can the media sector per se influence development? This discussion is tied in with the debate about democracy and good governance. Scott identifies three key roles for the media to play in underscoring this agenda: the watchdog function, the agenda-setting role, and the media as a civic forum in a more or less Habermasian understanding of the public sphere as rational deliberation and public debate in a public space. Scott's approach highlights the key roles the media can play in social change processes, while at the same time illustrating the limitations of a media-centric approach. It does not capture the everyday practices of communication that are mediated by the content and structures of the media.

The role of media in processes of communication for development and social change can be seen from a variety of perspectives. In figure 5 I have outlined some of the key relations, processes and dynamics, factoring in media-centrism and socio-centrism, and provided some characteristics of each of these perspectives as they pertain to media as structure, discourse and process.

Towards a Critical Perspective on Communication for Development

The current transitional period and all the movements we are experiencing in our time and age require a rethink of both research in and the practice of communication for social change. We are experiencing a process of social change that is resulting in many new contexts, new stakeholders and new dynamics, all of which influence the role of and possibilities for communication in sparking social change. This is resulting in the emergence of a whole new research agenda for communication for social change scholars. It is an agenda where we seek to redefine our understanding of media, communication and social change, and whose contours are informed by the issues dealt with in this chapter: *radical participation*, which emphasizes social change as

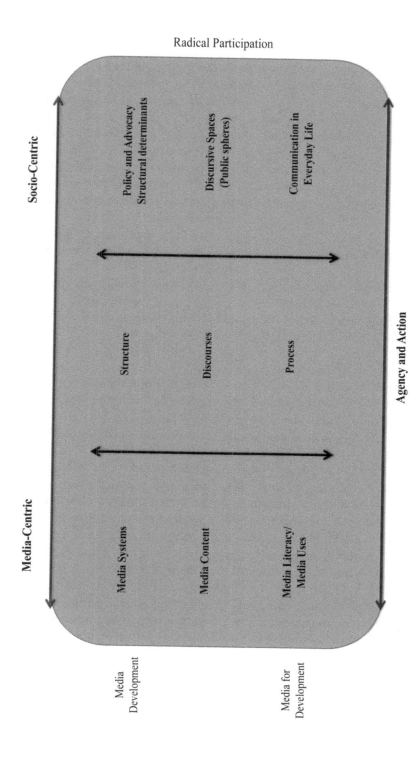

Figure 5. Communication for social change between media-centrism and socio-centrism

Source: Thomas Tufte

structural change, with conscious efforts to sustain such change; *a critique of the neoliberal agenda*, which questions Western development discourses, their emphasis on economic growth and their marginalization of non-Western development paradigms; *a proposed post-colonial perspective*, which opens up space for multiple approaches to social change from the perspective of the subaltern; *a culture-centred approach to development*, which enhances the voice of the marginalized and multiplicity as a principle; *socio-centrism*, which views any approach to the media, including new social media, digital communication and social networking opportunities, through this lens; *being political*, insisting on the fact that maintaining a subaltern perspective and an explicitly pro-poor communication agenda will require being political; and, finally, *recognizing mediatization in some parts of the world as an influential social force*. Together, these building blocks lead to the conclusion that communication for social change must call for a stronger embeddedness of this field in social theory – a social theory of the media and of communication.

Some of the new frontiers in research on and the practice of communication for social change will require further theorization, mainly in the areas dealing with the dynamic relations between media and communication, and agency and social change. The new frontiers include the wave of social and political dynamics that has emerged around media activism, empowerment and social change, and more specifically around organizing activism, using digital media and enhancing social movements. This calls for a more explicit, critical and political theorization of communication and change.

When critically assessing the institutionalized practice of communication for social change as we know it within the communication practice of UN agencies, governments and NGOs, we need to be clear about the fact that visions and ideals alone will not lead to sustained structural change. Nor will the optimism and opportunities offered by new generations of scholars and practitioners. Our current times, with a resurgence of activism, mainly in the form of social movements, call for further investigation into how we can navigate the tension between citizens wanting to remain 'free birds', autonomous, not organized and outside of the system, and the pressing needs in many of these bottom-up processes for organization and professional capacity and the resources to pursue their visions for a better world.

Moving into these research challenges calls for a conceptual framework that is embedded in a new social thought. This calls for further theorization, which will unfold in the next three chapters of this book, where a number of issues are explored: participation as an explicit project of transformation;

the relations between movements and media as well as communication and social change in times of activism and digital media; and the theoretical underpinnings behind the concept of 'cultures of governance'.

3   Participation: A Project of Transformation

The history of participation dates back to the writings of the utopian socialists, and the communitarian ideals and civil society activism of earlier times (Stiefel and Wolfe 2011, 19). A focus on participation as a transformative project was a common root of participatory thinking. Historically, therefore, participation has been tied not to the specificities of development cooperation, but to more fundamental visions of citizens engaging in articulating social and structural change.

Consequently, the concept has been closely associated with popular participation in social movements, from struggles of resistance and rebellion, to citizen engagement in processes of deliberation and the enhancement of voice and visibility in the public sphere. Discussing participation in social change processes is thus discussing questions of voice and agency, and activism and empowerment.

This chapter assesses the key debates linked to the concept of participation. The first section outlines the key frameworks and definitions, illustrating how the issue of participation has been linked not only to the larger processes of societal change but also to community development, governance processes at all levels and specific development projects – a variety of perspectives, each of which defines participation in its respective way. Based on Arnstein's classic *ladder of participation* and complemented by Cicilia Peruzzo's typology of participation, the next section discusses how different approaches to participation signify different degrees of commitment to and pursuit of citizen power in social change processes. It is in no way a given that a discourse about participation has anything to do with citizen power in social change processes. Arnstein's and Peruzzo's approaches are contextualized within Paulo Freire's liberating pedagogy, a founding paradigm in participatory communication.

The level of operation where participation has been most enhanced over the years is the community level, in processes and projects of community development. This experience is critically assessed in the third section. Most of the participatory methodologies developed in the 1980s and 1990s were specifically tied to this local level of development. There are, however, some risks in localism linked to maintaining a community focus (Mohan and Stokke 2000). There are also difficulties in moving beyond the local to participation in national or transnational processes of change, especially if you wish to ensure that the power of citizens is decisive in these change processes.

Participation in national and global processes of advocacy and change was a significant new development in the late 1990s. The 1990s also saw increased civic engagement in governance processes. Participatory governance is therefore the focus of the fourth section, in particular the different ways in which accountability can be enhanced, as a process articulated by government and as a bottom-up and citizen-driven process. The fifth section illustrates this with reference to the iconic Brazilian experience of participatory budgeting in the 1990s.

The role of communication in enhancing participation is central to practically all types of participatory efforts. What does this entail? How can we systematically conceptualize the communicative aspects of such societal processes? What does the umbrella concept of 'participatory communication' cover? The sixth section cuts across the different approaches to participation and focuses on the variety of takes on participatory communication and the lessons to be learned from them for a transformative agenda on participation. The chapter concludes by briefly revisiting the notions of *'invited' and 'claimed' spaces of participation* vis-à-vis our aim of conceptualizing participation as a transformative project.

History of Participation: Discourses and Practices

Participation in processes of change has been approached from a variety of perspectives over the years. A confluence of discourses and practices has characterized the field, which calls for clarity and systematic assessments of who participates, at what level in society and in which processes. Early discourses on participation appeared in the final years of colonialism – the 1950s and 1960s. These were paternalistic approaches, often framed as offering opportunities for people to mobilize and engage in order to access public goods such as health and education. In no way did they challenge power relations between colonizers and the colonized.

Some of the rhetoric of colonial times was taken on by the leaders of the newly independent states, who often established one-party rule. Their ideals were often formulated as free competition of ideas, involving criticism and two-way communication between citizens and their elected leaders as the frame of reference (Stiefel and Wolfe 2011, 20). However, the discursive practices of the leaderships were most often top-down calls for people's participation in development processes. This approach was also seen in the media systems developed by these newly independent nations, which were state-owned national media organizations.

In the 1970s, the notion of 'another development' (Dag Hammarskjöld Foundation 2014) inspired many young nations, mostly in Africa, to orchestrate 'people's participation' through mass organizations, using a wide range of mass organizations to legitimize power for often one-party systems. Pluralism was not an issue. Authoritarian regimes, some of which were revolutionary and/or socialist one-party systems, had people's participation institutionalized in organizations for 'the masses'. Key representatives of this ideal were communist China and President Nyerere's socialist government in Tanzania. 'People's participation' was important, but remained in social processes controlled from above.

In parallel with these often revolutionary, sometimes progressive but top-down calls for people's participation were the new social movements that emerged, largely in Western Europe and Latin America, which viewed participation as a bottom-up process that could eventually lead to a broad social movement and challenge the power structures in a country. The Latin American social movements fighting repressive military regimes in the 1960s and 1970s were a revolutionary symbol and reference point for the European social movements, although their 1970s vision of overthrowing authoritarian regimes was not accompanied by any aspirations for a stronger participatory system of governance. When, for example, the Sandinista revolution overthrew the Somoza dictatorship in Nicaragua in 1979, Daniel Ortega's Sandinista rule remained a one-party system, similar in many ways to Castro's Cuba, but also to Nyerere's African equivalent in Tanzania. At the time, people's participation was organized around popular movements, mass organizations and national development schemes, but not reflected in the visions or practices of a pluralist democracy.

In the 1970s and 1980s new discourses and practices of participation developed around the growing orientation towards community development. Community development initiatives focused on bottom-up processes of self-determination. In the 1980s a new language of participation emerged that echoed the rise of neoliberal development discourse and emphasized 'localized self-help' in a time of shrinking states. Participation in this scheme was reoriented towards 'technical fixes' that aimed to make development projects – often community-based – work better. However, neither the design nor the direction of the development process was to be questioned, reducing any aspiration for structural change to issues of technicalities. 'Good' participation, the dominant discourse prescribed, was about adding 'the missing ingredient' (Stiefel and Wolfe 2011, 23) and making community-based projects more efficient and effective. It was not about contesting 'structural violence' or pursuing social transformation, but focused on service delivery in the most efficient manner.

Discourses on participation evolved further in the 1990s. Most notable was the emergence of the rights-based approach to participation, in which the political perspective and attention to power relations resurfaced. This discursive frame, I would argue, remains the dominant discourse on participation today. This *re-politicization* of the field was connected to the emerging critique of Western development paradigms and the articulation of post-development, post-colonial, cosmopolitan and other discourses on development (Dutta 2011; Gupta 2012; Escobar 1998). The 1990s, and particularly the new millennium, saw a strong focus on participation in governance, including participation in policy processes and especially as a means to enhance public sector accountability.

Recent developments in new media have led to a proliferation of new policy-oriented processes of participation as well as a strengthening of transnational but still participatory advocacy initiatives, many tied to social movements and agendas driven by civil society and media activism. Demands for transparency and accountability have been at the heart of these initiatives, while the new ICTs have enabled a proliferation of experiences with crowd-sourcing, auditing and participatory mapping mechanisms. Thus, technological solutions have opened up a pathway for participatory governance and improved service delivery, for example in health and education, on the one hand, while many participatory initiatives have been driven by a generalized sense of indignation and feelings of exclusion, on the other. Examples can be found in the mass participation in the anti-globalization movements of the 1990s and early 2000s, from the Treatment Action Campaign in South Africa in the late 1990s for reduced prices for AIDS medication to more recent campaigns for housing in Spain, education in Chile and South Africa or health services in Brazil. Thus, the discourses on and the practice of participation have evolved substantially over the years. Participatory strategies have been a constant negotiation between a neutral and technical concern with efficiency in, for example, service delivery, on the one side, and versions of participatory democracy and participatory governance as more transformative and political projects, on the other.

Towards Citizen Power

One of the classic texts in research on participation is 'A Ladder of Citizen Participation' by Sherry Arnstein (Arnstein 2011, first published 1969). Arnstein's work on citizen power and her concept of the 'ladder of

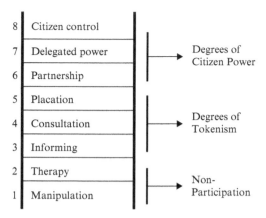

Figure 6. Sherry Arnstein's 'ladder of participation'

Source: Arnstein (2011, 5)

participation' have their roots in the civil rights movement and local governance processes in the United States in the late 1960s. Her thoughts were developed through her study of experiences with citizen involvement in planning processes in the USA, but were also heavily inspired by the student mobilization in France in 1968. After the emergence of social movements in the 1960s, models and typologies were developed as a means of conceptualizing and systematizing thinking around processes of participation. Many of these were tied to engaging citizens in community development schemes. Arnstein's model (see figure 6) remains a key reference.

For Arnstein, 'citizen participation is a categorical term for citizen power which allows citizens otherwise excluded from political and economic processes to be included: It is the strategy by which the have-nots join in determining how information is shared, goals and policies are set, tax resources are allocated, programmes are operated, and benefits like contracts and patronage are parceled out' (2011, 3). Arnstein's aspirations for citizen power defined what later became known as participatory governance, in this case processes that could enhance social reform and enable citizen access to decision-making on public policy and the control of public resources.

Arnstein's higher levels of citizen power resonate with Saxena's definition of *people's participation*. Rather than just being about participating in consultations and information sharing, Saxena emphasizes that it is 'a process by which the people are able to organize themselves, and through their own organization are able to identify their own needs, and share in the design, implementation and evaluation of the participation action . . . decision-making and initiating action are important and essential components of participation' (Saxena 2011, 31). High levels of citizen power are closely connected to the ability to control decision-making and initiate action.

There is thus a clear *power dimension of participation*, implicit in the notion of empowerment that follows from it. Despite this power dimension, a lot of participatory development initiatives in the 1970s and 1980s focused on community-level projects facilitated by either development agencies or the state, and channelled into organizational forms and levels where they may have been about empowerment but were tied to highly local processes, disconnected from the societal ambitions of changing power relations by addressing the structures or political-economic determinants of wider society. This was particularly evident in the rapidly growing business of development cooperation, where large multilateral organizations such as the United Nations FAO and bilateral organizations such as the UK Department for International Development (DFID) coincided in their strong focus on participatory development. The FAO had been a pioneer in the use of participatory methods in development since the late 1960s (Fraser and Restrepo-Estrada 1998). However, the consequence of a strong institutional and technical framing of participation was often a disconnection from policy change and structural change, and as such a depoliticization of the field.

A far more articulate claim for power was found in the new social movements of Europe and the USA in the 1960s and 1970s or the new social movements in Latin America, especially in the 1980s. Cicilia Peruzzo has produced an interesting although brief historiography of the different phases of Brazilian social movements as they developed throughout the 1970s and 1980s, which makes the important point that social movements converge in their trajectories and adaptation to political realities. In the progress from protest against the authoritarian regime of Brazil's former military dictatorship towards opportunities for freedom of speech, the history of Brazilian social movements shows that they managed to breed new social structures and values (Peruzzo 1996, 164). One of the key values that the population cherished enormously was that of direct participation. Another was that of collective and public rights – to a home, to health care and to education. A third was the value of autonomy, in the sense of being free from the supervision of public institutions, political parties and so on (Peruzzo 1996, 165). Peruzzo emphasizes that these values are *cultural values* that change with the civil society of a country. Her point underscores the process dimension of change: it comes gradually and is tied to cultural values, sensibilities and types of action (Peruzzo 1996, 165).

The lack of uniformity and the process orientation which Peruzzo underscores result in popular participation meaning different things. This is comparable with Arnstein's ladder of participation, although Peruzzo simplifies the process by distinguishing between three key perceptions of participation: non-participation, controlled participation and power-participation. Peruzzo argues that *non-participation* is also a form of participation – passive participation. This is seen when citizens choose not to engage, for instance, in the mobilization around the democratic management of a local school or with policies established by public entities. *Controlled participation* occurs when, for example, a local municipality organizes participatory budgeting (PB) events in Brazil, and limited participation is put into the system. Similarly, and more recently, the Kenyan government asked for input into the budget through social media. Finally, *power-participation* is based on 'democratic, authentic, autonomous participation that best facilitates people's growth as individuals'. The exercise of power is a shared process, and the power-participation can take the form of co-management processes or a more advanced form of 'self-management', which would be the form most closely affiliated with Arnstein's citizen control (Peruzzo 1996, 169ff). However, while Peruzzo's power-participation seems to emphasize individual participation, it is in practice often tied to community-driven processes, where it emphasizes the growth of community-based collectives more than individuals. This issue draws attention to the role of culture in development. To identify the form of power-participation, it must be assessed vis-à-vis collectivist cultures and/or individualist cultures, especially when it refers to democratic participation as Peruzzo does.

The Brazilian adult educator, lawyer and philosopher Paulo Freire was a fundamental source of inspiration to the Latin American social movements of the 1970s and 1980s. His ideas on a liberating pedagogy that was dialogic, reflexive, critical and action-oriented fitted well with the social movements. It was beyond question that Freire's aspirations were political. Participation was about a political project where unjust power relations were challenged, and where the 'Freirean method' became not only participatory but also liberating in the sense of tackling social injustice. Freire's ideas contributed in important ways to the 'democratic awakening' throughout Brazilian society, as was seen in the course of the 1980s, culminating in the overthrow of the military dictatorship in 1985, the adoption of a new Constitution in 1988 and the election of the first democratically elected president since 1960 in 1989.

While Arnstein's ideas grew out of the civil rights movement in the USA and were inspired by the student uprisings in France, Peruzzo's and Freire's ideas grew out of the dramatic social injustice in Latin America. Although they are difficult to compare, because Arnstein's major lasting contribution was the ladder of participation, while Freire contributed a whole philosophy of education and transformation, Arnstein and Freire converged in their efforts to promote citizen power through participation. Despite the very different realities they grew out of, both inspired the work of participatory development over several decades.

Participatory Methodologies

Participatory development has been a core but also contested strand in debates about social change. Many visions of transformation have been articulated around the prospects for participatory development, but there have also been many processes of co-optation where organizations have reduced participation to techniques for the efficient delivery of service-oriented development projects, far from the 'radical participation' that Colin Sparks pursued in his vision of participation (Junge 2012, 411).

The growing international attention paid to the virtues of participatory development led to a proliferation of approaches. Many methodologies were developed in the 1970s and 1980s, and a number of Latin American scholars were instrumental in developing the wide range of participatory methodologies in development. The notion of 'participatory action research,' developed by the Colombian Orlando Fals-Borda, became one of the most widely used techniques for participation. It in turn inspired the Institute of Development Studies (IDS) to develop participatory rural appraisal (PRA) (Fals-Borda 2006). Paraguayan Juan Diaz Bordenave's concept of participatory communication, and specifically his operationalization of participatory strategies in agricultural extension work in Latin America, successfully influenced the work of many international organizations, especially the Inter-American Institute for Cooperation on Agriculture (Bordenave 2006). Bolivian Luis Ramiro Beltrán's most notable contribution was at a more conceptual level, represented best by his article 'A Farewell to Aristotle', where he aligned himself with Freire in reinforcing the notion of 'horizontal communication' as a guideline for any participatory development process (Beltrán 2006).

From a performance perspective, one of the most notable contributors to participatory development was the Brazilian Augusto Boal, and his work with the theatre of the oppressed (Boal 2006). One of his many participatory techniques, Forum Theater, has allowed generations of practitioners to work with social change processes at the local level, in communities but also in more recent times in institutions, where people have enacted situations, produced dilemmas on stage and invited audience members not only to suggest solutions, but also to act out how they can be resolved, resulting in a highly empowering process for those involved.

The Latin American contribution was significant but, particularly in the 1970s, there was a parallel track in the UK centred on the work of Robert Chambers at the IDS (Chambers 1985; 1981) PRA was a technique where external development experts would visit an area to generate experience and local knowledge from citizens by inviting them to participate in a number of processes in which they visualized and in other ways articulated what they knew about a particular topic. It is a highly emic approach to knowledge production, and many techniques and manuals have been developed on this approach.

The conceptual framework of PRA drew on, among other things, Orlando Fals-Borda's participatory action research and Paulo Freire's concept of *conscientização* (awareness-raising). The REFLECT method, mentioned in chapter 1, also drew on Freire, illustrating the convergence between Freirean thinking and the British-/IDS-driven operationalization of these approaches. Later, PRA gained prominence, and was incorporated into development cooperation at all levels. Participatory Poverty Assessments and Community Action Plans are two examples of where PRA became central. However, the British development researcher Andrea Cornwall, a prominent scholar and articulator of PRA, is well aware of the pitfalls of the approach: 'without a more careful process in which interests are differentiated and negotiated, the Community Action Plans emerging from brief exercises can mask inequity and dissent' (Cornwall 2000, 71).

The risk of 'localism'

One of the problems associated with the strong strand of locally oriented participatory development is its tendency to celebrate the local without a clear consciousness of the politics of the local. British development scholar Giles Mohan and Norwegian human geographer Kristian Stokke delivered a thorough and well-argued critique, showing through a series of compelling examples that discourses on 'the local' can have conflicting connotations (Mohan and Stokke 2000). In other words, the 'perverse confluence of discourse', which Dagnino famously drew international attention to in her critical reflections around discourses of citizenship (Dagnino 2011), is equally in existence in discourses about 'the local'. Core concepts in the development discourse, such as citizenship, participation, empowerment and the local, come to mean very different things, creating a lack of clarity and ultimately a counterproductive situation in which some of these concepts become abused buzzwords with little meaning. This critique of participation was clearly visible in *Participation: The New Tyranny?* (Cooke and

Kothari 2001) and has remained an issue to be aware of when discussing its possibilities and limitations.

In the case of participation and its close association with local development processes, Mohan and Stokke critique the tendency to essentialize the local over the general. They argue that both post-Marxists and neoliberals have this tendency (Mohan and Stokke 2000, 248), resulting in convergences in the way both the new left (inspired by Laclau and Mouffe) and the new right (inspired by rational choice) articulate the local. Mohan and Stokke argue that the focus on the local contains a number of dangers. One obvious problem is the tendency to romanticize it, which means that local social inequalities and power relations are downplayed. Another problem is the tendency to view the local in isolation from broader economic and political structures.

Participation beyond the local: the rise of the network society

The local and community-focused approach to participation was challenged in the late 1990s and the 2000s. The rise of the network society in the form of technological developments facilitated participation at the national and global levels – the Zapatista revolution in 1994 became a significant early symbol of emerging forms of transnational networking and political participation, with a high degree of international commitment and involvement in a process that was well rooted in local realities of marginalization in southern Mexico, but also became an iconic act of transnational advocacy and solidarity where social media played a crucial role. (See the analyses of, for example, Juris 2008; Kavada 2014; Milan 2013; Olesen 2005.)

As the proliferation of social media enabled an unfolding of networked relations across time and space, citizen participation in national and transnational processes experienced a revival and a new dynamic. Bottom-up processes that addressed the national and the global became more feasible and realistic. There have been numerous examples, from the bottom-up campaigns by NGOs such as the Treatment Action Campaign in the mid-1990s to the anti-globalization campaigns and the many transnational campaigns by Avaaz.org (Kavada 2014, 362). All these combined local cases with national and transnational advocacy and mobilization.

In these articulations of social change dynamics since the late 1990s, the move often came from below in the form of community-driven processes that then networked and created participation beyond the local, and were often incorporated into transnational advocacy networks (TANs) by platforms such as Avaaz.org. This was the beginning of a new time of advocacy, driven forward by social movements and community-based organizations (CBOs), or often driven by transnational civil society initiatives. This opened up new forms of being political at the levels of everyday citizen engagement, but where a lot of the participatory development connected with transnational levels of action and advocacy. Mass self-communication (Castells 2009) was a key feature of these processes.

However, while many of these initiatives were driven by bottom-up processes of citizens claiming influence, it was the more system-driven initiatives that came to be termed 'participatory governance' that increasingly displayed a new dynamic with potentially transformative prospects for citizen participation. Within the politics of participation, the pendulum had once again swung towards participation as a transformative project, this time developed within social movements and community-based initiatives, as already outlined, but also within a more systemic framework where participatory governance took hold first as a top-down process, but increasingly in reverse order, as bottom-up processes.

Participatory Governance

> From the perspective of poor people worldwide, there is a crisis in governance.
> Narayan et al., *Voices of the Poor*

Just as Cicilia Peruzzo captured social movements in Brazil developing new structures and new values in their rebellion against the system's inability to meet social, cultural and economic demands, so a lot of the social unrest experienced across the globe in recent years speaks to the intriguing gap between the needs of the people and the services provided by the systems. As the epigraph shows, the discrepancies between the needs and aspirations of citizens and the ability of governments and systems to govern in sync with these demands form one of the most severe development challenges of our times. It is not that we cannot afford to provide services for the people: it is our lack of ability or commitment to do so. The Canadian political sociologist John Gaventa flagged this challenge and the need to review *relations between ordinary people and the institutions in society*, particularly the state which is supposed to service them. Gaventa argues that there seems to be a growing gap in these relations (2011, 253). These calls by scholars had an almost prophetic ring to them, given what later happened in the Arab Spring and its aftermath.

It is in this tension and the gap between government services and citizens' demands that participatory governance emerges. Bridging this gap was approached from the bottom up, with citizens protesting, rebelling, mobilizing and demanding to be heard, but it was also approached from the system's side, through efforts to offer space for participation and deliberation, and to offer better platforms with information and services. Gaventa argues that work is required on both sides of the equation. It is by deepening democracy and democratic participation by citizens, but also through the state's attempts to seek new forms of expression, that sustainable modalities of participatory governance will be found (Gaventa 2011, 255).

Gaventa (2011) quotes the Hungarian philosopher Ágnes Heller (1958), who discusses the limits of both the techno-centric vision of governance and radical grassroots democracy. Heller argues the need for both representative working institutions and a mobilized and demanding civil society, calling this combined approach 'the optimist conflict model' (Heller 2011, 133). Gaventa argues for the notion of citizen participation as 'ways in which poor people exercise voice through new forms of inclusion, consultation and/or mobilization designed to inform and to influence larger institutions and policies' (Gaventa 2011, 255).

A third issue Gaventa raises concerns rethinking voice and reconceptualizing participation and citizenship: '*new voice mechanisms* are now being explored which argue as well for more direct connections between the people and the bureaucracies which affect them' (Gaventa 2011, 256). These new voice mechanisms resonate closely with the work around voice by Nick Couldry (Couldry 2010). The issue of more direct connections between the people and bureaucracies speaks to the potential for increased accountability of governments and to citizen engagement. It highlights the many new opportunities that the advent of new technologies has brought.

Accountability: the heart of participation in governance?

A key focus of contemporary debates about participation is the challenge of accountability, that is, ensuring that governments remain open and transparent in their service delivery. What could seem like a minimalist approach to accountability often hides structural problems of corruption, mismanagement and fundamental problems in the performance of good governance. Citizen participation in accountability has gained strong ground since the mid-2000s, largely due to the general consensus that all stakeholders seem to buy into about the advantages of citizen engagement in governance processes. It has been further facilitated by the many new modalities and mechanisms that new ICTs have provided opportunities for. As Cornwall argued back in 2000: 'Mechanisms to hold policy-makers and implementers to account open up further terrain for participation in development. It is in this area that a number of exciting initiatives are beginning to create and make use of further spaces for direct democratic involvement in governance' (2000, 64).

The growing need for governments to play an active and responsible role in development was recognized in the late 1990s. This was in the aftermath of early experience with shrinking states linked to the International Monetary Fund and World Bank's structural adjustment programmes of the 1980s and 1990s. These structural adjustments had forced governments to cut public spending, shrink the state and sell off state assets. Ironically, it was also a World Bank report, the seminal *World Development Report 1997*, that in outspoken terms put the state's role back on the agenda in development. Accountability issues and state–citizen relations were central to this report (World Bank 1997). They were also key issues in the *Voices of the Poor* report (Narayan et al. 2000), which made a loud call for a stronger presence of citizens' voices in determining the direction of development. A few years later, the World Bank Institute handbook on *Social Accountability in the Public Sector* drew attention to a series of threats to good governance and social accountability in the public sector, flagging corruption, clientelism and state capture as the dominant ones (World Bank Institute 2005).

Good governance programmes became a top priority of development programming in the first ten to fifteen years of the new millennium. Mechanisms for ensuring citizens a space and a place to be heard have become part and parcel of such programmes. Many bilateral development agencies, such as the DFID, Irish Aid, Hivos, DANIDA and Sida, have prioritized these, as have private foundations such as Harvard's Accountability Program. However, criticism and concern can also be heard regarding the risk of development agencies contributing to the domestication of participation and a continuation of indirect colonial rule, or enhancing the dynamics of exclusion in 'participatory governance' where the control and decision-making power remain beyond the ordinary citizen (Junge 2012; Ribot 2011).

In parallel with the state institutionalizing mechanisms that account for their spending and other activities, civil-society-driven initiatives have developed a multitude of modalities to provide people with opportunities to hold their governments to account. The German media scholar Norbert Wildermuth explores this in his research on civil society-driven ICT platforms in Kenya, which asks whether such social accountability mechanisms adhere to the core principles of the participatory paradigm within communication for social change (Wildermuth 2014, 372). Wildermuth outlines six stages of strategic action in the 'multitude of communicative approaches to ICT for social accountability'. These range from the *public educational* stage, where open access to government data secures public knowledge on government activities, through a series of stages by which citizen engagement is made increasingly possible by aggregating data, generating systematic evidence bases for accountability-related advocacy campaigns, and providing *more deliberative spaces* for citizens to voice their concerns. The two most participatory stages are those of *public mobilization* and *participatory decision making* (Wildermuth 2014, 380–1).

Wildermuth's stages of strategic action in ICT for social accountability resonate with some of the original steps on Arnstein's ladder of participation, albeit focused more exclusively on communication approaches and ICT experiences. Wildermuth places his modelling of communicative action within the concept of *e–participation*, differentiating it from *e–government* and *e–governance*. While e–government is traditionally associated with a highly instrumental use of ICTs, and is about improving the efficiency of the flow of information between government and state institutions, e–governance is more open, dealing with state-led communication with citizens. It is within e–participation that Wildermuth places his six stages of strategic action, as civil-society-led actions to enhance social accountability.

In reality, e–participation can seldom stand alone, and where it does it becomes obvious that the initiatives lack sustainability, popular appeal, funding and impact. As is demonstrated in the example of Brazilian PB, citizen-led and state-led initiatives on accountability may well intersect at the incorporation of a variety of stakeholders and of top-down and bottom-up processes.

Participatory Budgeting in Brazil

The iconic PB originated in Porto Alegre, the capital of the southernmost state of Brazil, Rio Grande do Sul. More than three decades later, this is still seen as a key reference in the international experience of participatory democracy, and is an experience that inspired hundreds of cities and later many organizations, communities, development projects and even national governments to attempt similar efforts. Let me briefly describe its history, key activities, decisive moments, results and lessons.

A political and cultural transformation began in the late 1980s, after the end of a military dictatorship that had governed Brazil since 1964, with long-standing traditions of authoritarianism and clientelism. Massive mobilizations against the dictatorship throughout the 1980s had led to the emergence and growth of many social movements, alongside the appearance of many new political parties, of which the Workers' Party (PT) was the most significant. The country adopted a new constitution in 1988, and municipal elections were held the same year. For the first time in the young party's history it gained power in a number of big cities. The Frente Popular – a coalition of progressive political parties – won in Porto Alegre, and the PT's Olivio Dutra became mayor. A massive recruitment drive resulted in many people from the social movements and community-based organizations in the town finding themselves employed overnight as civil servants in the new municipal government. The political project was to pursue a participatory governance model, with PB as the flagship.

In addition to being a political project with aspirations to achieve participatory democracy, PB in Porto Alegre was just as much a complex administrative reform project with clear aspirations to move away from clientelism and corrupt procedures and practices. The organizational set-up developed around a range of committees, councils, assemblies and forums (Fedozzi 2001). Some of these involved direct citizen participation in electing delegates, while others contained representation of CSOs, in particular community-based organizations and neighbourhood associations.

PB aimed to establish a strong relation with and solid spaces for dialogue and interaction between the popular movements and ordinary citizens, on the one hand, and the executive power of the municipality, on the other. It began operating in 1989, when the first annual budget of the municipality was agreed and investments in infrastructure and services were prioritized on the basis of the deliberations and decisions made in the new institutional set-up. This was and continued to be a tricky and constantly conflictual process, given the fact that while it was the executive branch (Prefeitura) that developed the rather complex system of participatory democracy around municipal budgeting, it was the legislative branch (Câmara de Vereadores) that possessed the formal political power to adopt it. PT and the Frente Popular made up a minority in the Câmara. The popular participation in the budgetary process, however, established a fait acompli to the extent that the Câmara had no other choice but to pass the budgets (Santos 1998, 467).

The key objective of the PB was to encourage broad participation and establish a sustainable mechanism for joint management of public resources. This was to happen through joint decisions on how to allocate the budget, and was to be enhanced through accountability mechanisms to ensure effective implementation and citizens' trust in the system. Two of the central planning instruments in this process were the regional and thematic plenary assemblies: the Forums of Delegates and the Council of the PB (COP). The sixteen regions of Porto Alegre and the five key thematic areas (transportation and circulation; education, leisure and culture; health and social welfare; economic development and taxation; and city organization and urban development) were discussed in two rounds of plenary assemblies, in March and June each year. In between these assemblies there were preparatory meetings. The meetings and assemblies had a triple goal: first, to define and rank the regional or thematic demands and priorities; second, to elect delegates to the Forums of Delegates and councillors to the COP; and, finally, to evaluate the executive's performance. The COP became the most participatory institution. The citizens who were elected became acquainted with the municipal finances, discussed and established general criteria for resource allocation, and defended the priorities of the regions and themes (Santos 1998, 473)

Since its launch in 1989, the initiative in Porto Alegre has undergone several processes of institutional learning and innovation. There were initially many limitations to the initiative, including the lack of experience of the community leaders and the executive, but also the political and organizational culture each brought with them – a culture of confrontation and clientelism. Finally, but fundamentally, the budget allocated for investment started very small. In 1989 only 3.2 per cent was left for investment, but by 1992 the new administration had managed to increase this to 17 per cent. This was due partly to policy changes and increases in federal and state transfers linked to the new constitution, but also to improved expenditure control and municipal fiscal reform. In evaluating the first ten years of PB in Porto Alegre, Santos concluded that 'PB has become more transparent regarding its core character: a democratic political struggle centered on different conceptions of fair distribution of scarce public resources in an extremely unequal society' (1998, 482).

PB has come to be seen as the iconic example of participatory democracy in Latin America. It was a three-pronged challenge to promote participation by citizens in decision-making on distributive justice, the effectiveness of decisions and accountability, both in the municipal executive and of the delegates elected by the communities to the COP and the Forums of Delegates. It succeeded, and the example spread to 180 cities in Brazil, 120 of which were among the 250 largest in the country (International Development Bank n.d.), and beyond, for example to Paris in 2014. Many of the principles of PB were also incorporated into the Kenyan Constitution of 2010, where decentralization of public spending has resulted in the largest devolution process to district level responsibility for public spending in the history of Kenya – and in civil society mobilizing to enhance the participatory process in order to hold local government accountable.

In Porto Alegre, the strong commitment in the early years, especially during the three consecutive five-year PT mandates in 1989–2004, meant that PB continued to be an institutionalized practice. After a change of government in 2004, however, the nature of PB in Porto Alegre changed. It was opened up to a stronger presence of and role for the private sector in one of three non-binding 'co-responsibility partnerships' (Junge 2012, 410). The executive experienced an exodus of PT members (Junge 2012, 411), many of whom either set up an NGO or joined one. The US anthropologist Benjamin Junge, in his ethnographic study among these NGOs, reports the existence of what he calls 'shadow pseudopublics', a kind of parallel government. Their growth, alongside the changing nature of the PB organized by the municipal government, contributed to what Junge called 'a destabilization of the narrative of active citizenship hegemonic in earlier years, implanting a market-oriented, individualistic ethos in its place' (Junge 2012, 407). Nonetheless, while it was difficult to sustain a single particular approach, despite changes in the politicians in power, the core element of PB continued.

Junge challenges the 'idealistic predisposition' of both Fedozzi and Santos by outlining important limitations of PB. These include: placing too much significance on the participation of a small percentage of citizens; counting nominal participation, even one-time show-ups at annual meetings of the neighbourhood associations, as if they were equivalent to sustained, deliberative participation; ignoring what happens to participants outside of formal spaces of participation, such as the implications for home life, gender relations, and so on; ignoring people who have fallen out of participation; ignoring the appearance of clientelist logics in spaces of PB participation; downplaying the fundamental dependency of PB on the good will of the mayor and the city council; and ignoring the relationship between the 'civil' spaces of PB participation and the 'uncivilized' and seldom-addressed parallel system of local authority – drug lords and drug traffic (Junge 2012, 421).

Despite Junge's criticisms, there was popular support for the system – 56.5 per cent of participants in the regional and thematic assemblies declared that they had benefited from PB (Santos 1998, 494), and an estimated 8 per cent of the population participated in the PB process (Santos 1998, 486). The credibility of the political contract lay in both the effectiveness of the decision-making and the accountability of the executive and the representatives of civil society in the COP. However, PB was and continues to be a negotiation, a power struggle between the administration in government and the aspirations of the ordinary citizens and their organizations and movements. They all want a say on a daily basis. As Santos highlights: 'the PB decision model tries to reconcile the principle of democratic representativeness of the mayor and his executive with the principle of participatory democracy of the citizens organized in grassroots associations and assemblies' (Santos 1998, 502). This results in constant conflict, and it is the constant process of reconciliation that contains the frustration and dilemmas, on the one hand, but also the opportunity to make visions come true, on the other. It is this tension that Santos describes. PB is in many ways a culmination and a realization of the utopias of Brazil's social movements of the 1980s. It was the result of long-standing activism and deliberation outside of the formal system and institutions. Suddenly, activists and the large confluence of community-based associations achieved political power through the PT that so many of them had become affiliated to in the 1980s. This gave them an opportunity to try out the blend of democratic representativeness with participatory democracy in practice.

PB therefore became a system-driven initiative, but a system that employed a whole new generation of activists who became municipal workers. They fought institutional inertia, cultures of clientelism, legislative resistance and the implications of national policy as well as restrictions on budgets – and still pushed through principles of participation that gave those outside the system access and power. Arnstein's visions of citizen power from her 'ladder of participation' and Peruzzo's 'power-participation' were tested in the experience of PB. From the experience in the years that followed came replicable versions that were transformed into participatory methodologies and practices to be incorporated into development projects across the world.

PB has become a seminal learning process in how to tackle relations, and the often large gaps, between people and institutions in society, which as Gaventa and so many others have outlined is a key challenge for participatory governance. Santos (1998, 500) argues that *a techno-democratic culture has emerged*. Evidence increasingly shows Brazil becoming in many ways a Latin American laboratory for citizen participation experiments, not just with PB but in many sectors – a more recent example being the health sector (Cornwall and Shankland 2013). I return to Brazil in chapter 6.

In recognizing the many lessons learned about citizen participation from PB in Porto Alegre, the underlying questions are: What role does communication play? Which participatory communication processes inherent in the PB case enhanced participatory governance? Dialogic spaces were created where citizens could do more than voice their concerns. The municipal system was very deliberate in how it chose to communicate with citizens. It was a relationship of give-and-take between citizens searching for influence and a system pursuing an administrative ideal. The next section reviews in more detail the key principles of participatory communication as they pertain to different arenas of social practice.

Participatory Communication

The notion of participatory communication is associated with two classic locations of action: *participatory communication in development projects*, which is tied closely to development cooperation; and *community-based participatory communication*, which is linked to more informal citizen initiatives. While the former is typically associated with more system-driven communicative practices, the latter has a more informal character, traditionally associated with the large field of community media, alternative media, tactical media, radical media, citizen media, social movement media and the many other denominations that have come to characterize citizen-driven, bottom-up participatory communication focused on social and structural change. I return to this in more detail in chapter 4. It is important here to emphasize that participatory communication is not a communicative practice reserved for either institutions *or* social movements. It occurs in both settings, as the case of PB illustrates.

Participatory communication in development projects

The role of participation in development projects ranges from providing basic services effectively to the pursuit of advocacy goals, but can also be that of monitoring progress towards goals through forms of self-reporting and community involvement in monitoring processes. Finally, participation can be used to facilitate reflection and learning among local groups in a development project, thus also for evaluation purposes (Tufte and Mefalopulos 2009, 5).

In his typology of how participation guides the strategies applied to development projects, Paolo Mefalopulos distinguishes between four perceptions: *passive participation, participation by consultation, participation by collaboration* and *empowerment participation* (Mefalopulos 2008, 91ff). This covers a continuum of citizen engagement, where the primary stakeholders' participation ranges from a minimal or non-existent involvement in a development project to a range of forms of organized interaction with the primary stakeholder, viewed from the perspective of the project administrator responsible, to the situation where joint decision-making occurs and where the primary stakeholders are considered equal partners. Mefalopulos' four perceptions resonate with Arnstein's ladder of participation (Arnstein 2011) as well as with Peruzzo's model of participation, but contain the distinctive feature of tying the levels of participation to the agenda for carrying out the development project.

In connecting this typology with forms of communication, Paolo Mefalopulos and I linked the distinction between monologic and dialogic variants of communication with the three generations of communication for development which I outline in chapter 1 (Tufte 2004). The first generation of communication for development equates to monologic, one-way communication and the third generation to two-way or dialogic communication. A project cycle can be distilled into four phases. First, *participatory communication assessment* is a process where communication methods and tools are used to investigate and assess the situation. Second, *(participatory) communication strategy design* is a process based on the findings of the research on defining the best way to apply communication to achieve the intended change. Third, *implementation of communication activities* is about determining where the activities planned in the previous phase are to be carried out. Finally, *monitoring and evaluation* runs through the whole communication programme, monitoring progress and evaluating the final impact of the intervention (Tufte and Mefalopulos 2009, 20).

The typology of participation in development projects outlined here, the two distinct forms of communication – monologic and dialogic – and the four phases in a project cycle all offer conceptual entry points for strategizing communication for development and social change from a participatory perspective. However, I would argue that the overarching distinction is *the one between institutionalized participatory communication and participation outside of institutions* (Tufte and Mefalopulos 2009). The categories outlined primarily offer ways to approach system- or institution-driven development projects, and thus they can assist from a technical point of view in optimizing strategic communication planning in development cooperation. However, they do not move beyond the arena of development projects. The role of participatory communication outside of institutions, which is thus closely tied to community-based communication, offers such a wider perspective. This is discussed next.

Community-based participatory communication

This field of participatory communication contains a strong legacy from the Latin American experience with media and communication for development. It is a more than fifty-year-old academic field and practical discipline to which Latin American scholars have made key conceptual contributions. These range from seminal thinkers such as Paulo Freire, Antonio Pasquali, Juan Díaz

Bordenave, Mario Kaplún, Luiz Beltrão and Luis Ramiro Beltrán in the early years to Rosa María Alfaro Moreno, Jesús Martín-Barbero, Jorge González, Rossana Reguillo and Cicilia Peruzzo in more recent times. Most recently, a new and growing generation has been working on these issues, including Leonardo Custódio, Ana Suzina, Florencia Enghel and Paola Sartoretto.

I would argue that it is possible to synthesize two common denominators. First, there is the strong commitment to seeking bottom-up, community-based, grassroots-oriented strategies of empowerment, social critique and social change. Core concepts such as voice, participation, social mobilization, *conscientização*, dialogue and horizontal communication have been instrumental to the long-standing commitment to empowerment and social change. These have emerged primarily from the environments in and around the social movements in Latin America. As we have learned, this knowledge production and social practice were closely connected with the fight against military dictatorships, but also with fighting the historically massive socio-economic polarization found in many Latin American countries.

Second, there is the cultural dimension of this grassroots-oriented approach to participatory communication, which was seen in the multiple forms of social and cultural mobilization linked to the social movements of the 1980s, and in the work on alternative values and, for example, challenging the political culture of clientelism. According to the Colombian scholar Arturo Escobar:

> The grassroots movements that emerged in opposition to development throughout the 1980s belong to the novel forms of collective action and social mobilization that characterized that decade . . . these processes of identity construction were more flexible, modest and mobile, relying on tactical articulations arising out of the conditions and practices of daily life. To this extent, these struggles were fundamentally cultural. (Escobar 2006, 902)

The experience of PB in Brazil combines these two distinct forms of participatory communication. If Porto Alegre's municipal 'project' of engaging citizens in budgeting processes is viewed as a development project, I would argue that most of the stages in the continuum of citizen engagement outlined by Mefalopulos can be found. Participation by consultation was obviously the hallmark of the initiative, but participation by collaboration was clearly also seen in the partnerships between the municipality and community-based organizations, and empowerment participation was often the outcome of the positive experiences with PB. Passive participation was a reality among the many who chose not to engage in the variety of opportunities all citizens were given to engage in the budgeting process. Seen from a community perspective, awareness-raising through participation was a fundamental outcome for many of the community-based organizations engaged in the PB process.

Culture-oriented collective action emphasizing the construction of new values and identities was perhaps the most important outcome of the PB process. A perception that 'the state' was in opposition to citizens' interests had been widespread in Brazil throughout the period of military dictatorship. To alter such a perspective requires the construction of new values and identities, something that was a core ambition of the PB initiative.

Culture-oriented collective action as a strategy for community-based participatory communication, however, covers a wide area of experience in Latin America and beyond. From the strong legacy of community media – community radio in particular, but also alternative video movements, community television and not least community print media – it has evolved a new dynamic around next-generation digitally based participatory communication, seen in everything from the 'Mídia NINJA' example in chapter 1, to the new online forums for advocacy and crowd-sourced, citizen-driven accountability claims.

Some of these experiences with community-based participatory communication are spilling over into the debates about participation in the public sphere. This is happening increasingly as the public sphere multiplies into a variety of forms and spaces, as I touch on next.

Participation in the public sphere

This discussion has gained increased prominence and relevance in recent years due to the mediatization of society. While debates about deliberation, voice and the public sphere have long been associated with Habermas, there have also been articulate critiques of his conceptualization of a singular sphere for idealizing it as a space for dialogue and rational argument within neutralized power relations. Oskar Negt and Alexander Kluge (1972) and Nancy Fraser (1997), among others, have articulated alternative visions of the public sphere. Both articulate the concept of counter-publics as a different ideal of the public sphere, where inequality, private issues and power struggles are not excluded but help to determine the issues and dynamics of the public debate, which often occurs in multiple spheres. Thus, it is most important in this context to flag how new media developments have increasingly opened up for debate the multiplication of public spheres, the new impetus of interactive communication, dialogue and voice sparked by ICTs, and the potential for more participatory and democratic development linked to these new opportunities.

Take, for example, the US sociologist Todd Gitlin, who coined the term 'public sphericules' as a metaphor for the multiplication of spheres, which the Internet in particular facilitates. He connects these debates to democratic development, raising a multitude of questions that highlight the challenges posed by new media developments to processes of citizen engagement (Gitlin 1998, 173). Josée Johnston offers us an example of where critical perspectives on the role of the public sphere in citizen engagement unfold. Drawing particularly on the case of the Zapatistas in Mexico and their communicative strategies, Johnston identifies three dimensions of participation in relation to the public sphere. First, the Zapatistas sought to create subaltern counter-publics focused mainly on enhancing their own democratic self-determination. Second, in radical democratic practices, they constructed these counter-publics as a means of interacting with the official public and expanding their discourse into broader political, social and cultural settings. Inherent in this double strategy is a third dimension: the fundamental vision of a deliberative democracy. This is no different from Habermas', but is conceived and practised very differently (Johnston 2011: 390ff).

I further developed Gitlin's notion of sphericules in my own fieldwork in Tanzania (Tufte 2013). The notion of *civil society sphericules* offers a way to connect Johnston's typology to the discussion on the role of civil society. I return to this discussion in chapter 4 when discussing how media and communication contribute to the articulation of what Roger Silverstone calls 'civil spaces'. The most important conclusion to draw here is that participation in the public sphere is closely tied to strategic considerations of how citizen perspectives and visions about society can be articulated and pursued. As such, participation in the public sphere is a core common denominator for both social movements and organizations, and the institutions involved in communication for development and social change.

Reclaiming Participation as a Project of Transformation

The cases expounded in this chapter illustrate a number of lessons that can be learned about participatory communication and that help to identify the strong points and challenges associated with its use.

1. Participatory communication can be used as *both a means and an end* in itself. In the way it was installed as dialogic spaces in the PB institutional framework in Porto Alegre, it became both.
2. Participatory communication has, in our increasingly networked,

mediatized and globalized society, come to mean *multi-level change processes*. The local experience is far from isolated, and will practically always be connected to and influence other levels of society, in addition to individual change.

3. As has been demonstrated here, participatory communication serves *the purpose of service delivery* and *to advocate a cause*. While its most severe critics have been outspoken about the limitations of mere service delivery, most initiatives contain both the politically transformative aspiration inherent in advocacy and the aim of improving a service for the ordinary citizen.

4. It has become evident that for participatory communication to survive as a social practice requires *management, leadership and organization*. Otherwise, the participatory aspect may well wither away, as it can be difficult to sustain.

5. Perhaps most importantly, developing a change in political culture based on values of participatory governance, civil society inclusion and accountability is a time-consuming process. The example of PB is a case in point. It illustrates that while a change in political administration can happen overnight, the fundamentals of culture and values only change slowly. *There is no fast track to a culture and practice of participatory governance*.

Assessing the nature of participation and strategizing participatory communication initiatives thus requires clarification of a number of issues. What are the overall aims of the initiative? Does it have a transformative perspective, or is it more a question of ensuring the successful implementation of a project? Furthermore, what is the knowledge-producing aspect of the initiative? Does it, for example, entail co-creation or similar techniques in the narrative it pursues? Or is the content of the initiative a predefined given, involving little or no participation by the target audience? Participation can be interpreted in many ways, but as the British sociologist of international development Sarah White clarifies: 'If participation means that the voiceless gain a voice, we should expect this to bring some conflict. It will challenge power relations, both within any individual project and in wider society. The absence of conflicts in many supposedly "participatory" programs is something that should raise our suspicions. Change hurts' (White 2011, 68).

4   Movements and Media, Communication and Change

New Practices, New Theory

In the aftermath of the recent uprisings that swept the globe, several media and communication scholars engaged in communication for development and social change have highlighted the need to take a closer look at social movements. John Downing calls for studies of media activism and communication practices within social movements (Downing 2014), Silvio Waisbord calls for further research into the relations between strategic communication and social movement media (Waisbord 2014), while I have called for further research into social movement media and communication experiences and their conceptual connections to communication for social change (Tufte 2013). I show in this chapter that many of the concerns of social movements, with regard to citizen engagement, leadership, the organization of activities, information dissemination, the use of storytelling and performance, and expected outcomes, are very similar to those of the more institutionalized communication for development experiences. I argue that these fields of media and communication practice, which otherwise live quite separate lives within media and communication studies, are complementary and face similar conceptual and practical challenges. While we note a growing interest in social movements amongst a growing number of social scientists, we should recall the approach to social movements that Alberto Melucci argued: 'movements are not occasional emergencies in social life located on the margins of the great institutions . . . In complex societies, movements are a permanent reality' (Melucci 1994, 116)

Emerging interdisciplinarity

Research into media, communication and social change has become a broad and highly interdisciplinary and transdisciplinary field of inquiry. The novelty lies in the fact that political scientists, anthropologists and sociologists are increasingly recognizing the importance of media and communication practices in everyday life, and to social and political change. In addition, broader sections of media and communication scholars are becoming interested in the role of media and communication practices in processes of change.

Political scientists are approaching media and communication studies by tying it to questions of democracy and issues of the organization of resistance, rebellion and transnational activism (Chadwick 2006; 2013; Kavada 2014; 2012; Segerberg and Bennett 2011; Bennett and Segerberg 2013; Olesen 2005). Anthropologists are increasingly concerned with media and communication ecologies and practices (Spitulnik 2011; 1993; Vidali 2014) but also with in-depth studies of media activism and activist media (Barassi 2014). There is such a growing interest among anthropologists that Oscar Hemer and I have argued that one of the most significant developments in this field is that it constitutes an 'ethnographic turn' in communication for development and social change (Hemer and Tufte 2016). Sociologists are also increasingly inquiring into the role of media and technologies in social movements and processes of change (McDonald 2006; Castells 2009; 2012). Media and communication scholars are engaging with a wide array of issues, which include but are not limited to discourse analyses of blogs (Denskus and Esser 2015), analysis of activist media practices (Milan 2013), citizen journalism practices (Rodríguez and Miralles 2014), practices and expressions of creative and performative activism (Duncombe 2007), media activism (Della Porta and Mattoni 2013), analysis of the mediated representations and messages emanating from social movements (Chouliaraki 2006; 2012; Madianou 2012), surveillance studies (Fuchs 2012; Leistert 2013; Jansson and Christensen 2014), analysis of production dynamics (Watkins, Tacchi, and UNESCO 2008), audience/user and consumer studies around digital cultures, activism and social movement media, studies of media and communication platforms and their role in ensuring transparency and accountability (Wildermuth 2013; 2014), relations between media activists and established media houses (Mollerup 2016) and the political economy of the Internet (Jørgensen 2013; Fuchs 2014a; 2008). Adding to this largely Anglo-Saxon body of research is a rapidly growing Latin American and Spanish literature (González 2014; 2012; Renó, Martínez Hermida and Campalans 2015; Gumucio-Dagron 2014; Galindo Cáceres 2008; Custódio 2016). Media and communication for social change as articulated in social movements is currently drowning in publications and attention, but it is also pointing in many different directions.

Mediated mobilization

Despite the strong interdisciplinary interest in the role of media and technology in social movements, scholars and observers are divided according to their different approaches to technology. Like so many other books in recent years, Christian Fuchs' neo-Marxist critique of Manuel Castells' 2012 book, *Networks of Outrage and Hope*, is an illustration of these differing opinions (Fuchs 2014a). Fuchs argues that Castells delivers a highly techno-optimistic interpretation of how new social media can be appropriated for social change purposes. The Fuchs–Castells polemic followed the debate between Shirky (2011) and Morozov (2011), which articulated similar divisions. On one side, Shirky (2011) unfolded his techno-optimistic approach and his emphasis on the 'almighty power of social media as a means of collective action' (2011, 7). In contrast, Morozov (2011) expressed deep pessimism, warning against the risk of *slacktivism*: 'a feel good activism that has zero political or social impact'. Fuchs argues that it is material conditions – economic, political and social realities – that determine social and political action, not a particular technology.

Outside of the Anglo-Saxon mainstream discourse we find many other voices. González' critical stand on ICTs for social change is a case in point (González 2012; 2014). One interesting thing about González is his methodological approach to historicizing the use of technology. Another is his highly critical stance, speaking out about the 'profound stigmatization' associated with the techno-optimistic imaginary. I return to some of these issues in chapter 5.

Optimism, and even the tendency to turn social media into a 'fetish of collective action' as Gerbaudo (2012, 8) argues some scholars do, is in sharp contrast to the critical stance of Morozov. While Morozov navigates within a given of access to and use of these technologies, González takes the perspective of viewing social media from the margins of society, from among the realities of the marginalized, poor urban and rural communities of Latin America, where there are serious limits to access.

In the midst of these polemics, the US media scholar Leah Lievrouw (2011) explores how alternative and activist new media have been perceived over time. She identifies five genres, one of which she calls 'mediated mobilization'. This she understands as the use of digital media to 'cultivate interpersonal networks online and to mobilize those networks to engage in live and mediated collective action' (Lievrouw 2011, 25) What is particularly important in Lievrouw's approach is that she identifies social movements and their uses of media as 'fundamentally interventionist in purpose, practices and ethos' (2011, 68). This interventionist perspective allows closer comparison with the traditional field of communication for development, which is also perceived as interventionist within the modernization paradigm of communication for development. This opens up a discussion on how to conceive interventionism and problematizes whether this notion is at all appropriate when discussing communication for social change.

Lievrouw argues that it is possible to distinguish between three levels of mediated mobilization in social movements. At the society-wide level, mediated communication is about helping movements to intervene in the workings of social and political institutions, changing norms and values, and *reconfiguring the distribution of power and resources* (2011, 175). This resonates with the most political versions of participation outlined in chapter 3. At the mid-range level, mediated mobilization is about *organizing the practices and structures within the social movements* themselves, a challenge that Anastasia Kavada has also written substantially about in her studies of Avaaz.org and other transnational civil society initiatives (Kavada 2014). Lievrouw argues that it signals a shift from a more intensive form of movement organization to a more extensive form, where the new 'cultural logic of networking' (Juris 2008) represents a move towards an increasingly flat and flexible form of social movement organization. This 'flatness' of the organization is contested by other social movement media scholars, however, as I discuss later. Third, at the micro-level, Lievrouw views the interventionist nature of mediated mobilization as *a space for 'prophetic' and 'prefigurative' activities by activists* (Lievrouw 2011, 176), a sort of modelling of individuals that contributes to the cultivation of collective identities. This resonates with the traditional modelling of behaviour known from behaviour change communication within the DevCom tradition of communication for development and social change.

Lievrouw's interpretation of mediated mobilization finds strong resonance with some of the key debates about the characteristics of communication for social change as practised within the institutionalized forms of this field. Her three levels resonate with the three generations of communication for development that I have identified. In addition to the modelling of individual behaviour, Lievrouw's characterization of social movements aligns with communication for social change on issues of organization and the sustainability of interventions, in its focus on advocacy communication and influencing policy and power relations, and in the attention paid to changing norms and values in society. These are all well known and intensely debated in communication for development. It will therefore prove useful to analyse further the experiences of social movements with communicating for social change, and compare these to the experiences of the institutionalized communication for development practices of NGOs, UN agencies, governmental organizations and so on.

The common challenge that cuts across the different media and communication practices is how the citizens of today can appropriate them to construct themselves as actors. Inspired by Alain Touraine, I pursue his call for a new social thought focused on discovering the subject and placing the struggle to become an actor in society at the centre of the social sciences. How do these different approaches reconcile with this call? In what follows, I explore the dynamic relationship between actors and their communicative actions in the context of social movements.

Theorizing Social Movements

Before analysing the communicative actions of social movements we must first assess how social movements are defined. They have been perceived quite differently over time. There are three distinct phases in the classic chronology. The ideologically driven social movements of the industrial age constituted the first generation of social movements. They were national entities, embedded in material demands. The second generation, which came to be known in Touraine's phrase as 'new social movements', emerged in the 1960s and 1970s (Touraine, Duff and Sennett 1981). These were not ideological but instead focused on wide-ranging issues such as atomic energy, nuclear arms and the environment or on group identities such as gender, sexuality or ethnicity. A third generation of social movements emerged with the development of larger-scale, transnational movements in the 1990s, many of which identified as transnational rights-based movements. The Global Justice movement is an iconic example (Juris 2008; Milan 2013).

Later, following social mobilizations from Iran to Iceland in 2009, and in particular after the Arab Spring in 2011, social movements experienced a new momentum. Although they are a continuation of the third generation, many of the more recent social movements signalled something new and different. The Australian sociologist Kevin McDonald calls them *experience movements*, defines them on the basis of 'grammars of action' and argues that a whole new grammar has emerged (McDonald 2006). I illustrate what this grammar entails later, using the example of the Spanish social movements. Massive mobilizations and occupations erupted in Spain in May 2011, which later became known as the Indignados movement. However, let me first outline the schools of thought that have informed many of the scholars who theorize on social movements.

The theorizing around social movements reflects some of the key strands of social science. From a Marxist perspective, the nationwide movements of the industrial era in the nineteenth and early twentieth centuries were struggles for basic rights around jobs, working conditions and voting rights. They were strongly associated with class struggles and strongly driven by ideological standpoints. The labour movement was the central social movement of those times. The explanations of such movements were thus ideological, and emphasized their ability to articulate and mobilize for collective action.

Collective behaviour theory, a strand of interactionist sociology, explains social movements from a psychological perspective as a behavioural process. Social movements are seen as collective behaviour and characterized as sudden, spontaneous, disorganized outbreaks of crowd behaviour. Collective behaviour theory emerged in the Chicago School of the 1920s and 1930s but had its roots in European mass psychology at the turn of the century. Later, Ralph Turner and Lewis Killian, in their book *Collective Behavior* (Turner and Killian 1957), rejected the suddenness, but still emphasized the collective aspect of such behaviour.

These theoretical distinctions raise two key questions. The first, already being articulated in the 1950s, is whether the articulation of social movements is primarily about collective behaviour and collective action. Turner and Killian argued that this is so, drawing on the histories and legacies of large-scale crowds, mobs and protests that have acted together around key concerns, often related to social class. The other question is whether social movements are sudden, spontaneous and disorganized, as argued by the early collective behaviour theorists, or, as the Italian sociologist Alberto Melucci argued, they are to be conceived as an ongoing dynamic articulating social change (1994, 116).

A contrast to the conceptions of collective action and spontaneity as drivers of social movements emerged in the rational-choice-oriented *resource mobilization theory*. This mainly North American tradition includes scholars such as Doug McAdam, John McCarthy, Sidney Tarrow, Charles Tilly and Mayer Zald. They argue that 'the most effective social movements are those whose leaders and organizers are able to recognize the political, organizational, economic, and technological *opportunity structures*' (Lievrouw 2011, 49). This line of thought quickly came to dominate US social movement research and remains influential today. It explains the dynamics and development of social movements as based on rational choices that are driven by navigating among opportunity structures. Rational analyses of costs and benefits drive the process forward. However, resource mobilization theory does not consider the often highly emotional character of social movements. Given rational choice within political, organizational, economic and technological opportunity structures, where do emotions fit into the equation? If we recognize the significant presence of emotions such as anger, anxiety and outrage, but also expressions of togetherness, humour, optimism and hope – all clearly present in many contemporary uprisings – this poses a serious challenge to the explanatory potential of resource mobilization theory. Rather than the Habermasian ideal of a rational public sphere based on reaching consensus, Chantal Mouffe's notion of 'agnostic democracy' (Mouffe 2000) recognizes that conflict, and the outpouring of emotions associated with it, should be expected to influence the formation of the public sphere and our democratic society. Recognizing this centrality of conflict – and emotions – in Mouffe's theory of the public sphere speaks to the point that emotions, and their central role especially in protest movements, ought to be analysed in much more depth.

New social movement theory (NSM) emerged from the student, anti-war and cultural movements of the 1960s and 1970s. In contrast to the rational choice organizational strategies and the focus on opportunity structures and the cost–benefit analysis of resource mobilization theory, these NSMs arose as 'unconventional' forms of social activism (Lievrouw 2011, 46). They were characterized as part of the overall transition from an industrial to a post-industrial society. Touraine (2009), Klandermans (1994) and Eyerman (1992) were among the social scientists analysing these transitions in society and arguing that highly educated, 'white-collar' knowledge workers are central to the new social movements. Identity issues such as sex, age, ethnicity or gender mark the actors in these movements, and the shift away from the traditional movements. Nevertheless, as the Italian political scientists Alberto Melucci and Mario Diani emphasize, the NSMs are still oriented towards collective behaviour, although Melucci later stated that: 'collective behavior presented movements as "action without actors" while resource mobilization and other structural accounts like Marxism saw movements as abstract "actors without action"' (Melucci 1989, 18–22)

What cuts across all these social movement theories is action, understood in intentional terms as the power to represent – be it a social class or a group with a particular identity such as women, or ethnic or sexual minorities. This intentionality of action goes hand in hand with the perspective of the interventionist approaches already mentioned. Like Kevin McDonald, we can argue that all these strands of theory stand on common conceptual ground in the form of a Western paradigm of *action as representation* (McDonald 2006, 213). McDonald argues that the genealogy of this understanding takes us back to the European Renaissance and the separation of inner beings, emotions and bodily experience from public representations of people. Like Hobbes, he argues that the nation state was the first modern collective being with the power to represent an entire collective – a group of beings. Thus, in building his argument for a fundamentally new understanding of social movements, McDonald insists that the common denominator in all previous understandings of social movements is centred on the power to represent a community, a group, a nation or a people (2006, 210–14). This entails the need for leadership, and for structures of representation of ideas and arguments. What gets lost in this struggle for representation is the bodily experience. Exploring this adds a whole new perspective to our perception of how both social movements and institutionalized communication for social change can go about articulating social transformation.

Experience movements

'Experience movements' constitute a fundamentally new approach to comprehending social movements in society. It moves beyond seeing action as representation, and looks beyond action understood in intentional terms (McDonald 2006, 214). From a series of case studies of current or recent social movements, McDonald emphasizes the importance of 'embodiment as practice', where embodied experience is a 'mode of presence and engagement' that goes beyond a claim for representation. This converges well with the practice approach within social science. In this convergence between the increasing emphasis on practice in everyday life as the entry point for understanding actors and their action, on the one side, and the framing of most contemporary social movements as experience movements, on the other, I believe we can find a useful starting point for a common understanding of new generations of communication for social change and empowering communication activism.

This proposed approach reflects a 'citizen perspective' on communication and social change, in the sense that it calls for a conceptual and analytical openness and a deepening of inquiry into understanding the lifeworld of citizens and the emotions and motivations that enhance their engagement and action. This fusion of 'everyday practices' with 'embodied experiences' converges as fields of action in the post-Arab Spring era and signals a new way of conceiving citizen engagement in contemporary social sciences.

It also speaks to another understanding of subjectivity and action, and resonates strongly with Touraine's call for a rediscovery of the subject, placing the struggle to become an actor as central to the social sciences. The practice approach opens up opportunities to pursue this analytical pathway, and many of the contemporary social movements are powerful examples of experience movements that illustrate that 'at the heart of struggles for freedom lie experiences of encounter and the vulnerability necessary to feel, suffer, wonder and create' (McDonald 2006, 226). I use the example of the Spanish Indignados movement in what follows to reflect on this.

With the experience movements comes *a shift from solidarity to fluidarity*, as McDonald argues (McDonald 2006, 15). This constitutes the grammar of action that arose with the new social movements, in which struggles became more ad hoc or fluid, topically speaking, while at the same time remaining a struggle for each individual to become an actor, to find a way to produce meaning, find a role, engage and project themselves towards a blurred future in a globalized world afflicted by permanent crisis. This reflects the 'epochal shift' that Martín-Barbero has spoken about (Martín-Barbero 2010), and which lies in close proximity to the point I have made, that we are living in a time of risk and uncertainty, with ontological insecurity as a condition of life (Tufte 2011). In this context, the struggle Touraine speaks of, for ordinary citizens to become actors in society, becomes part and parcel of the contemporary challenges facing social movements. The individual fear, uncertainty and insecurity, coupled with the structural determinants articulating these feelings, help to explain the strong orientation towards emotion, and positive emotional experience, that the contemporary social movements offer.

It can also help explain why the practice of communication for development often has difficulties in getting people to change behaviour. Articulating agency in the ways seen in a lot of communication for development practice is simply insufficient. This is another way of saying that context plays a huge role when communicating for change, especially for behaviour change. For example, if campaigns on HIV testing in sub-Saharan African do not work, it may not be because of the unclear message or the lack of reach of the campaign. It could well be about the disempowered feeling of the target audience, say youth, that would regard it as an immense burden, stigmatizing and maybe even a death sentence to risk being tested positive. It is easier to live with uncertainty than face such an overwhelming situation (Tufte 2006).

From this analysis a model of understanding emerges that marks a shift away from the old forms of social practice based on action as representation. All the former theories of social movement contain the idealized model of a bourgeois public sphere accompanied by expectations of rational deliberation by secular, disembodied actors. From this new perspective, many of the contemporary social movements are seen to be offering an experience of *'embodied intersubjectivity'* (Csordas 1993, 146). This contains a strong emphasis on *embodied experience*, on the senses and on social practices such as dance, music and drumming, which allows our theorizing of social movements to 'break out of often repeated debates framed in terms of individual versus the community, opening out forms of individual autonomy that do not correspond to the rational, disembodied individual' (McDonald 2006, 18).

The new movements are less articulate about their sense of 'us' and instead concerned about assembling many people's similar experiences of displacement, strangeness and 'encounters with the vulnerable self' (Shildrick 2002). Again, these insights from analysing contemporary social movements can help us to understand the shortcomings in communication for social change. For example, a lot of HIV/AIDS communication is based on 'action as representation', crafting relevant and precise messages. It does not manage to develop a 'grammar of action' that the target audience can engage with. Such campaigns have fallen short in their ability to work constructively with the highly embodied experience and generalized feeling of the target audience – the feeling of being disempowered vis-à-vis the challenge of the pandemic. The result has often been an inability to act.

This example emphasizes that in order to articulate action, it is important to place *the embodied subject at the centre of action*. This is an opening for a discussion on how communication for development might learn from the new social movements. Rather than replacing the old conception of structure of representation – associations, parties and so on – with networks, McDonald argues for them to be replaced by *grammars of embodiment, as experiences and as modes of presence and engagement in the world* (Csordas 1993, 135). This may well be the crux of the matter, of the true gap between communication for development based on the old grammar of civic action and the new grammars of embodiment and experience. The cases in chapters 6 and 7 illuminate this hypothesis but, meanwhile, let us examine the example of the social movement Los Indignados in Spain.[1]

Los Indignados: Mobilizing for Social Change

As already outlined, the way in which communication for social change has been practised by social movements has shifted over time. The remaining sections of this chapter explore Los Indignados in Spain, its unfolding as a social movement, its nature, actors and actions, and in particular whether and how media and communication practices enhanced this movement for social change. After a brief introduction, I use the case to develop five

---

[1] This case of Los Indignados is based on a thorough review of the following publications: Anduiza, Cristancho and Sabucedo (2013); Castañeda (2012); Castells (2012); Fuchs (2014b); Gerbaudo (2012); Hughes (2011); Postill (2014a; 2014 b); Turner (2013); Laraña and Díez (2012).

analytical perspectives that have emerged from the social movement's media and communication experiences, and that I argue connect well with insti-tutionalized communication for development experiences. These analytical perspectives will help to frame the next generation of challenges for the field as a whole.

Spain has long experience of social mobilizations. Like many other coun-tries in Europe, it suffered severely from the consequences of the financial crisis of 2008. The crisis led to massive layoffs, deep cuts in education, social and cultural spending, and increased foreign debt, while banks were bailed out using public funds. The youth unemployment rate reached 41 per cent in 2010, a factor that profoundly challenged family lives and youth identities.

In the course of the winter of 2010–11 a confluence of initiatives eventu-ally led to the setting up of the web platform ¡Democracia Real Ya! ('Real Democracy Now'), which on 1 March 2011 called for a large demonstration to be held on 15 May in Plaza del Sol, the most important square in Madrid (¡Democracia Real Ya! 2014). Inspiration came from events in Tunisia and Egypt, as well as *Indignez-vous!* ('Time for Outrage') (Hessel 2010), a short book by a 93-year-old French former senior diplomat and co-founder of the United Nations, Stéphane Hessel, which reached an enormous audience worldwide – primarily in France but also in Spain (figure 7).

Across Spain several young unemployed university graduates took their own initiatives, formulated their own statements and posted them online. These expressed frustration, anxiety, outrage and lack of trust in decision-makers, but were also visionary and contained hope. Cross-cutting the initial outcries was a generalized call for youth to mobilize in rebellion against the government. An initiative against the new law on information security, the Ley Sinde (see chapter 6, n. 3, for a further elaboration of this law), sparked heated debate about surveillance and government policy. Furthermore, there was a mobilization of radical student and youth movements (Juventud Sin Futuro, 'Youth without Future'), along with a large number of other move-ments. The reasons for mobilization were many and varied – over 400 organ-izations eventually contributed to the mobilization effort. It was an informal gathering with shared feelings of discontent and frustration and with strong motives for expressing these not just online, but through a physical presence. The trajectory of growing discontent was also a significant demonstration of a loss of trust in the established political parties.

The demonstrations, scheduled for one week before the municipal elec-tions, took everybody by surprise. More than 30,000 people gathered at Puerta del Sol, and 20,000 at Plaza Catalunya in Barcelona. There were also demonstrations in more than fifty cities across the country. A small group of demonstrators decided to stay overnight in Puerta del Sol, and this initiative

Figure 7. The call for 'real democracy now' mobilized many people for street demonstrations

Source: Wikimedia Commons

was posted online. The next day the authorities attempted to remove the demonstrators, but this backfired and attracted thousands of new supporters who had read about the police action on social networking sites and the Real Democracy Now website. Overnight camps also sprang up and grew in support in Barcelona.

The camps in the public squares (figure 8) rapidly evolved into what can best be described as 'small cities', densely populated but organized sites with committees for everything. The committees discussed political topics, and formulated proposals that they then uploaded to YouTube and other sites. Other committees organized logistics in the square, or cultural and social activities. University lecturers came to speak with the activists, and libraries and other cultural activities were organized. A key activity during the occupation was a daily general assembly, where all the major decisions were taken by consensus. No leadership emerged and the floor was open to all. Thus, activities that had initially been prompted and articulated online peaked in the demonstrations across the country of 15 May and the following weeks, where activities were concentrated around the occupied squares.

Throughout the mobilizations, continual and active use was made of Facebook, Twitter, YouTube, email listservs, blogs, radio, the press and

Figure 8. *Acampada* in Cadiz, June 2011

Source: Wikimedia Commons

television for mobilization, public deliberation, political advocacy, and the organization and coordination of activities. It was generally a highly inclusive process of citizen engagement. Initially, the participants were mostly youth, but others rapidly joined, making it a truly broad movement. There was a strong synergy between many different organizations with different causes, combined with a wider public that identified with the sentiment of outrage. The many different actors all expressed their individual feelings while also joining in the common outcries that were orchestrated in the course of the demonstrations and assemblies. There was a lot of creativity in the statements that were expressed, and sometimes even performed.

At times the movement was threatened by anti-system activists who disrupted the public events with violent acts. This led the movement to reaffirm non-violence as an important principle. The movement had a clear policy against spokespersons and leaders, which was demonstrated by its horizontality and in the fact that all decisions were taken by consensus. However, as I analyse in what follows, despite the rejection of formal leadership there was still a degree of orchestration, coordination or 'choreography' of the social mobilization.

The camps continued on and off throughout June, and the last were removed in early July. July 2011 was then characterized by a number of marches, all of which came together in a huge demonstration in Madrid on 23 July, which attracted over 250,000 people. Following this immense mobilization, initiatives continued, mainly organized around neighbourhood committees which developed similar debates and proposals on a wide variety of community issues.

In parallel with the events unfolding in Spain there was an intense transnational dialogue, and the US Occupy movement can in many ways be seen if not as an offspring, then at least as a natural international spread of the calls for action that dominated Spanish activism for large parts of 2011. A new peak in demonstrations was seen around the global mobilization on 15 October. In the largest demonstrations to date, there were 500,000 people in Madrid and 400,000 in Barcelona, as well as millions more in 1,000 cities in 90 countries worldwide. After this, the Spanish mobilizations diminished while the Occupy movement in the United States and elsewhere gained momentum.

What was the result of all these mobilizations? Castells is clear in his book *Networks of Outrage and Hope* that 'the most important change happened in the head' (2012, 236). Meanings and emotions were strongly expressed, and the mobilization sparked a profound rupture in government–citizen relations. This contributed to a questioning of the role of citizens in national development processes, reinvigorated many of the participating organizations, such as the Plataforma de Afectados por la Hipoteca, and in 2014 even led to the establishment of a new political party, Podemos, which grew exponentially over the course of that year. These events contained many of the core characteristics and qualities of a new generation of communication for social change. These are analysed in the next sections.

Organizing for Social Change: From Collective Action to Connective Action?

The Spanish case was one of mass civic engagement, protest and rebellion, but also contained many examples of performance, media and cultural production. In all its multiplicity of expressions, emotions, deliberations and contestations, there was a clear political agenda. How can the organizational principles underlying such a social movement be assessed? The political scientists Lance Bennett and Alexandra Segerberg offer a useful set of concepts in their book *The Logic of Connective Action: Digital Media and the Personalization of Contentious Politics* (Bennett and Segerberg 2013, 13). They develop a typology for what they call 'connective action', which defines the forms of digitally networked action that result from large-scale personalized and digitally mediated political engagement. From case studies in the USA, Germany and the UK, they identify three ideal types of action involving media in contemporary contentious politics. These help us to understand the distinct organizing principles that lead to political engagement. The three ideal types of action are:

- **organizationally brokered collective actions**. These are coalitions of heavily brokered relations among organizations that seek a common collective action framing. Such action is based on resource-intensive mobilization and formalized relations with followers with the aim of cultivating commonly defined emotional commitments to the cause. While the Indignados movement had many organizations supporting and engaging around the common effort to take to the streets on 15 May 2011, they were not the ones brokering the collective action. That was a loosely organized collective of individuals that came together around the online platform Real Democracy Now. In contrast to Los Indignados, organizationally brokered collective actions are seen in traditional organizations such as political parties and trade unions. The category represents collective action as we historically know it from the political arena.

- **organizationally enabled connective action**. This is a form based on loosely tied networks of organizations sponsoring multiple actions and causes around a general set of issues in which followers are invited to personalize their engagement on their own terms. This might be seen in some large NGOs that have moved beyond traditional collective action, engaged with digital media and opened up to personalized engagement in their causes. Bennett and Segerberg give Oxfam and World Wildlife Fund as examples. Again, Los Indignados have little to do with this typology, as they do not constitute an organization or a network of organizations as understood traditionally.

- **crowd-enabled connective action**. Rather, the Indignados movement aligns itself with this third typology, consisting of dense, fine-grained networks of individuals in which digital media platforms are the most visible and integrative organizational mechanisms. The actions of face-to-face activists gain scale and publicity through these media networks. A lot of recent experience of social movements and bottom-up citizen-driven initiatives falls into this category, actions where crowd-sourcing and similar logics of aggregation and mobilization are used. The Indignados movement is one of them. As Anduiza, Cristancho and Sabucedo write about Los Indignados: 'We have, apparently, no clear leadership, no involvement of main political organizations, no specific demands, no triggering event, no presence in traditional broadcast media, and still extremely high turnout levels' (2013, 4).

The concept of *connective* action (Bennett and Segerberg 2013), in which communication through digital media plays a crucial role, is useful to help us understand the intriguing nature of the Indignados movement. In this case, traditional leadership, resource mobilization and organizational roles were replaced by loose organizational linkages built around personalized action frames, driven forward by emotions (indignation). With these characteristics the Indignados movement challenged the traditional conception of collective action.

Bennett and Segerberg's model helps to bring together the experiences of social movements and those of communication for social change. They enable the integration of experiences into a joint reflection on the way to conceptualize the organization of digital media practices in political communication. While this does not tell the whole story of how social movement and communication for social change initiatives seek in their different ways to engage citizens, it is a forward-looking typology which captures the most innovative developments, lays out analytical pathways and constructs conceptual bridges between these fields of action that have developed independently of each other.

Emancipatory Communication Activism

While the first analytical perspective focused on the organization of communication action, this second perspective deals with the more media-centric dimensions of social movement media. As outlined in chapter 2, many scholars have explored the development of alternative media and their role in processes of social change. Stefania Milan (2013) cuts across a number of these scholars in her efforts to conceptualize the media and communication infrastructures of resistance. She aligns her work with that which coined terms such as radical media (Downing 2001), citizens' media, alternative media (Atton 2002), tactical media (Garcia and Lovink 1997), civil society media (Hintz 2009; Hadl and Hintz 2009) and social movement media (Downing 2011). The commonality revolves around media-centric and citizen-driven processes of enhancing social justice.

Milan defines emancipatory communication practices as 'ways of social organizing seeking to create alternatives to existing media and communication infrastructure' (2013, 9). Milan sees media activists as pursuing the aim of independent communication infrastructures, while at the same time these alternative infrastructures serve as a communication backbone for many other social justice struggles, thus opening up the broader pallet of contemporary development challenges. Milan's work, however, is centred on a specific case study of alternative media, focused on an analysis of the cultural system of actions that 'radical techies' and community broadcasters perform. She argues that her study contributes to a better understanding of contemporary social movements and especially the mobilizations that emerge and live online (2013, 179). Milan identifies four key contributions to her own work to increase understanding of the elements and processes of collective actions.

First, there are new dynamics of collective identities in interplay with the emerging individualism. This approach also connects with the logics of aggregation that Juris writes about (Juris 2012), where the collective identity emerges from many individual narratives and actions. This dynamic is at the heart of the form of voice seen in the Indignados movement. Second, the 'anti-organization' forms of organizing speak to the leaderless horizontality that characterizes many of the social movements, including Los Indignados, but is also questioned for being neither as leaderless nor as horizontal as the movements claim. An interesting point highlighted by Milan is the transitory nature of the activism, something which speaks to the overall dramaturgy of social movements which I discuss later. Anti-institutional repertoires of contention are in line, for example, with the work of Holston (2008) on insurgent citizenships in Brazil's social movements (see chapter 5). Finally, Milan's point about helping to emphasize the relevance of cultural processes and cultural explanations in the emergence of contemporary mobilizations connects well with Jorge González' (2012; 2014) conceptualization of cyberculture and the notion of mobilization and engagement 'from below', which is profoundly embedded in cultural practices and processes. (This is elaborated further in chapter 5.)

In line with the features of the 'experience movements' I have argued for, Milan makes a point about affinity-based clusters: 'We will gradually see an increase in affinity-based temporary clusters and in the groups that creatively mimic familiar but apolitical models of organization' (2013, 181). The Indignados movement is a good example: people came together around identity issues – issues of relevance where they could mirror their own life situations, aspirations, tastes, interests, dreams and visions for the future. However, like Gerbaudo and many others, Milan tends to focus almost exclusively on social media practices. Although this is a novel field of research, the interdependency and interrelationships that exist between online and offline activities must also be contemplated when theorizing about movements and media, and communication and change.

Mediapolis and the Symbolic Construction of Public Space

The third analytical perspective is that of the symbolic construction of public space, which explores the dynamics between online and offline practices. Citizen engagement as manifested in the Indignados movement is informed by a variety of perceptions of public space. Three perspectives can help us in this analysis: first, analysing public spaces as civic spaces of both contestation and deliberation; second, assessing the performativity by which public spaces are constructed to articulate emotion and enhance togetherness; and, third, understanding public spaces as ritualized space, where rituals help to create a sense of order and structure.

Theories of counter-democracy (Rosanvallon 2008) and counter-public spheres (Fraser 2007; Negt and Kluge 1972) can help us articulate *public space as a civic space*. They theorize public space as that in which citizen engagement unfolds in opposition to dominant discourses and spaces. Todd Gitlin's notion of 'sphericules' (Gitlin 1998) adds another dimension by emphasizing the multiplication of spheres which has come about with the advent of the Internet. I have further developed Gitlin's notion in suggesting the concept of 'civil society sphericules', which recognizes the symbolic construction of public space that civil society engages in. While the Internet risks accelerating processes of fragmentation of the mediated public space, it also creates new opportunities. There are many examples of civil-society-driven media platforms that enable the construction of a mediated public space where information is shared and dialogue enhanced (Tufte 2014a).

These ideas of citizen-led public spaces resonate well with the 'new cosmopolitan critical theory of the emerging global civil society and its contradictions', which Roger Silverstone sought to develop (Silverstone 2007). Silverstone develops a new theory of the public sphere in which the logics, dynamics and opportunities of the media take centre stage. He provides us with a conceptual framework that is able to situate and understand media and communication practices in the context of the globalized world, preceding later mediatization theory such as Hjarvard (2013). Inspired by Hannah Arendt's work on the 'polis', Silverstone calls this space 'mediapolis'. Mediapolis is

> the mediated spaces of appearance in which the world appears and in which the world is constituted in its worldliness, and through which we learn about those who are and who are not like us. It is through communications conducted through the mediapolis that we are constructed as human (or not), and it is through the mediapolis that public and political life increasingly

comes to emerge at all levels of the body politic (or not). (Silverstone 2007, 31)

Silverstone is concerned with how mediated spaces represent or constitute public life, the degree to which these spaces are inclusive or exclusive and whether they enable or disable public debate. In the case of the integrated on- and offline spaces which the Indignados movement created, it managed with modest means to create a mediated space overnight using Twitter accounts, websites, radio, television and the printed media, all integrated with each other and with the core physical space of the movement – the camps in the squares of Madrid and Barcelona, and across many other cities of Spain. As Silverstone argues, mediapolis, even as embryonic and imperfect as the Indignados version was, is a necessary starting point for the creation of a more effective civil space. The mediated space of appearance is at best a space of potential and possibility (Silverstone 2007, 33).

The second perspective was to see public spaces as *performatively constructed*. In pursuing a definition of 'mobilization' Gerbaudo (2012), like Silverstone, draws on Hannah Arendt (1958), using Arendt's notion of collective action to emphasize the importance of issues of togetherness and assembly. He also makes a pertinent historical link to Emile Durkheim, who used the example of cultural practices among Australian tribes to explain what occurs around physical assembly, emphasizing the 'collective effervescence' of the encounter. This is an interesting historical explanation of the purpose and meaning of assembly, and the emotional situation that is created.

We can, however, expand on this cultural analysis of the performatively constructed public space by emphasizing another concept with which anthropologists have worked a great deal: ritual. By drawing in anthropologists such as Victor Turner (1995) and Arnold van Gennep (1960), media scholars have developed analytical insights into the particularity of the mediated spaces created in everyday life (Larsen and Tufte 2003). Inspired by Goffman's notion of ritual, approaching everyday media use as ritualized media use is a way of understanding particular moments in everyday life – what Klaus Bruhn Jensen identified as time-ins and time-outs (Jensen 1995, 57–8). Time-in culture is the practical, action-oriented everyday life where structure and agency, in Giddens' terms (1986), are incorporated into social action. Jensen defines time-out as 'a separate social practice . . . which can be identified by social agents as such. It places reality on an explicit agenda as an object of reflexivity, and provides an occasion for contemplating oneself in a social, existential or religious perspective' (1995, 57).

Bent Steeg Larsen and I (2003) further analysed the everyday use of television, where situations of togetherness were established through particular rituals. The emotional density established around television took two forms: it established a sense of community and sociability between those in the room, while similarly establishing a sense of imagined community, in Benedict Anderson's famous phrase (Anderson 1991, originally published 1983). Thus, constructing togetherness, a feeling of community or simple unity, requires an element of performativity but also one of ritual. Rituals also help to create a sense of order and structure regarding which performances and emotions can be enacted and where.

The temporary *and* mediated cities that Los Indignados created in the central squares of many towns in Spain – and complemented with online transmissions and communications – created both unity and togetherness. The integrated on- and offline symbolic space created a distinct space, a time-out from everyday life in Spain. A mediated 'city within the city' was created in the public square through performance and ritual. It evolved as a civic space, a mediapolis with rules of its own, a unique organization and a system of communication, schedules and the distribution of power and roles. It emerged as Los Indignados' construction not only of a public space but also of an imagined community.

Contesting Horizontalism: Choreography of Collective Action

What role does leadership play in Los Indignados and similar social movements? While the movements themselves argue very strongly that they are horizontal in structure, and opposed to hierarchies of leaders and layers of distributed power, a growing number of scholars contest this claim. The Italian media scholar Paolo Gerbaudo is one who perceives the existence of 'soft leadership' through what he calls a *choreography of assembly*. 'Choreography' is Gerbaudo's label for the construction of a sense of unity as a core element in the process of mobilization and assembly (Gerbaudo 2012). The assemblies were pivotal for the Indignados movement, and the choreography around these assemblies indicated a process where social media activists helped to stage a symbolic and material gathering, assembling both online and in the public square.

The role of the body and the senses is central to the way in which McDonald's concept of 'experience movement' characterizes contemporary social movements. This is seen in the way the Indignados movement and others create a sense of emotional intensity through the choreography of assembly. The choreography of assembly has both an emotional scene-setting dimension and a dimension of 'scripted action' (Gerbaudo 2012, 12). This achieves three goals: it directs people towards specific protest events; it provides participants with suggestions and instructions on how to act; and it constructs an emotional narrative to sustain their coming together in the public space. The public space becomes practically synonymous with the occupied square, with its magnetic gatherings and powerful emotional attraction (Gerbaudo 2012, 13).

Linked to these choreographed dynamics between media and locality, and between the virtual and the physical, the social movements of today contain soft leadership, Gerbaudo argues: 'influential Facebook admins and activist tweets become "soft leaders" or choreographers, involved in setting the scene, and construction of an emotional space within which collective action can unfold' (2012, 5). In arguing that they are far from leaderless, Gerbaudo challenges the discourse of horizontalism (Juris 2008), which is informed by notions of networks (Castells 1997; 2009; 2012) and 'swarms' (Hardt and Negri 2000; 2005). Gerbaudo's notion draws on Bauman's sociology of complex and liquid forms of leadership (Bauman 2000).

Gerbaudo is sceptical about the 'ideology of horizontalism' (Juris 2008): 'I am convinced that this idea tends to obscure the forms of organizing underlying contemporary collective action and the forms of hierarchy, or the "hierarchy of engagement" which continues to exist also within informal organizations like contemporary social movements' (Gerbaudo 2012, 19). Drawing on Melucci (1996), Gerbaudo argues that the ideology of horizontalism obscures the asymmetrical relationships between those who mobilize and the mobilized. He criticizes the US anthropologist Jeffrey Juris (2008) and his analytical approach to the anti-globalization movement. Juris focuses on the networking logic as a key element in the success of the movement, but Gerbaudo is convinced that his 'reliance on almost metaphysical concepts such as "openness" and "horizontality" constitutes an ideological obstacle to understanding the dynamics of the contemporary space of participation' (Gerbaudo 2012, 25).

Although focused on spaces of participation, Gerbaudo surprisingly makes no connection to the history of participatory communication developed in the Latin American tradition of the 1960s and 1970s. This was highly attuned to the dynamics of spaces of participation, as I explain in chapter 3. While Gerbaudo focuses on the literature on networks and new social movements, the theories of the 1970s, particularly Frank Gerace on horizontal communication (Gerace 2006) and Luis Ramiro Beltrán's 'A Farewell to Aristotle' (Beltrán 2006), contain critical and embedded reflections on horizontality. Paulo Freire (2001) also contains lengthy reflections on the power relations between change agents and the communities involved.

When Gerbaudo argues for the construction of a process of mobilization that is based on notions of 'assembling' or 'gathering' rather than networking, he draws on Bauman (Arendt 1958; Melucci 1996; Laclau and Mouffe 1985). Such was apparent in the case of the Indignados movement, where there were many statements from people who appeared in the early days just for the sake of assembling, listening and expressing their own opinions. The whole set-up of that movement was focused on gathering in the main squares of cities, and organizing assemblies where the many challenges of contemporary Spanish life could be debated.

Gerbaudo also argues against the spontaneity of mobilizations, defending the hypothesis that 'collective action is always structured by the forms of communication responsible for "setting the scene" for its display' (2012, 21); that is, they are choreographed. This speaks explicitly to a communicative intentionality, where a strategic aim informs the communicative practice of a social movement. This ties in closely with similar concerns about communication for development as practised in many organizations.

Gerbaudo argues that there is an intellectual impasse that is 'the result of that abstraction from material and local contexts of interaction which the language of networks carries within itself' (2012, 25). Citing Kevin McDonald (2006, 37), Gerbaudo argues that many network-analysis approaches are one-dimensional, ignoring 'the body and the senses', the materiality, and therefore allowing development to be about voice and networking, and appear 'disembodied and too located in a culture of simultaneity'.

The sorts of situations analysed here, those of social movements mobilizing for social change, constitute highly localized material situations. They have erupted as moments of tension, compressed in all senses of the word, involving many people, many agendas and many emotions coming together in processes of social mobilization. They constitute situations of rupture, of breaking routines and rituals, creating a social and political momentum, an emotional state of mind, a togetherness which indeed seems choreographed in the manner in which aims are deliberately pursued. They are said to be horizontal and leaderless, but there is nonetheless a highly explicit communicative intentionality embedded in the actions of mobilization, and in the communicative practice surrounding it. As such, it is no less strategic than the work of organizations and institutions carrying out more traditional communication for social change activities. To understand these situations, they need to be subject to grounded analyses of their history and development, and of the interconnections between online and offline activities.

Understanding the nature and character of these dynamics and relations is crucial to deriving a more general social theory of the media (Couldry 2012) and for theorizing the role of communication in processes of social change.

Constructing Shared Meanings, Identities and Narratives

Already in the mid-1990s Johnston and Klandermans were articulating a critical vision of techno-determinism and arguing that the use of ICTs in processes of social and political mobilization required a holistic view: 'the process of mobilization cannot be reduced to the material affordances of the technologies it adopts but also involves *the construction of shared meanings, identities and narratives*' (Johnston and Klandermans 1995, in Gerbaudo 2012, 9). This softer and more reflexive position is our fifth analytical perspective on social movements. It opens up opportunities for a more comprehensive understanding of what their communicative practices entail for the actor, or the citizen. Narratives are first and foremost constructed through communication. Many narratives unfolded in the mobilization of Los Indignados, with the individual narratives shared during assemblies as testimonials, or bits and pieces of a jigsaw puzzle, adding up to the meta-narratives of an unjust system that marginalizes large segments of the population.

Narratives are similarly constructed in the communication for development initiatives of traditional organizations, for example in their many entertainment–education (EE) initiatives. They construct narratives in the form of radio and television dramas, theatre, social media series and cartoons. All these narratives, from social movements to organizations communicating with their audience, feed into the construction of shared meaning and identities. They can potentially become powerful 'voices from below', communicating shared values and representing identities, values and visions.

The sharing and circulation of narratives, however, is one thing. Even more important is the construction of meaning among those who listen, use or in any other way engage around these narratives. Thus, understanding the storytelling process and the stories conveyed is fundamental. Equally important, however, is exploring the uses of these narratives, analysing the communicative practice which comes with making use of particular media flows, genres or technologies. Many scholars have called for user studies to explore how new technology is used by social movements, citizens, communities and decision-makers (Costanza-Chock 2012; Downing 2014; Gerbaudo 2012; Kavada 2014; Tufte 2014a; 2015; Wildermuth 2014). It is almost a case of déjà vu sparked by a new generation of technologies, very much in line with the now classic studies of the 1980s and 1990s of the construction of meaning in media programming (Ang 1985; 1991; Lull 1988; Morley 1986; Tufte 2000), and the social uses of technologies

– most notably television (Jacks et al. 2006; Silverstone and Hirsch 1992; Silverstone 1994; Tufte 2000; Moores 1996).

Characteristic of many studies exploring social movements and their media and communication practices is the emphasis on the peaks, or *condensed moments*, of mobilization, occupation and assembly. The diachronic aspect, that of the gradual awareness-raising and mobilization of a population, is more often ignored. Both the synchronic and the diachronic dimensions of these movements must be explicitly assessed, ensuring that we historicize action through the latter analysis. Some interesting work in this regard has been carried out by Jorge González (2012; 2003) and Jesús Galindo Cáceres (2008).

The British anthropologist John Postill has added an interesting layer of complexity to the analysis of protest movements and the role of social media by exploring their multilinearity. Postill argues that by uncovering the multiple concurrent time lines of protest movements we can gain insight into the highly diverse temporality of digitally assisted protest, without overlooking the ubiquity of clock-and-calendar time (Postill 2014a).

Another approach to contextualized studies of social movements and their unfolding dynamic of events and routines is to explore them from *a dramaturgical perspective*. My proposal is to look at the dramaturgy of social movements. Their actions unfold in a very similar way to that of storytelling. There is a dramaturgical flow – to achieve public visibility and political impact, they have dramatic peaks, moments of concentrated action, occupations, demonstrations, visible concentrations of energy, emotion, voice and contestation. This is often followed by long periods of less visibility and action, and more of reorganization, negotiation and mobilization, and then new peaks followed by troughs. The social movements had no intention of remaining in the public squares of Madrid or Cairo forever. These occupations were peaks of social mobilization, emotional tension and political pressure, deliberately orchestrated but open-ended, as they, the activists, did not know how the drama would unfold.

No movement can keep up such pressure and, in the further unfolding of social movements, we see today that social media have become instrumental in maintaining the sense of unity and collectivity. We also see new episodes of their struggles unfold, for example when the Indignados movement, after an intense six months of mobilization in 2011, diffused into community work in neighbourhoods, and into specific cause-driven movements and organizations. Then, in 2014, a new political party, Podemos, was launched and gained rapid support, winning five seats in the elections to the European Parliament in May 2014 and threatening the Socialist Party as the second-largest party in Spain. Much of Podemos' strategy and structure resonated closely with that of Los Indignados. Thus, the dramaturgy of the Indignados movement has reached a new phase and is still unfolding.

Consequently, the complexity of understanding movements and media, and communication and change, must include: in-depth user studies of media and communication practices, an emphasis on the diachronic dimension of ongoing social movements, studies of their multilinearity and, last but not least, the dramaturgy through which they unfold.

Communication for Development and Social Movement Communication: Common Challenges

In summarizing this chapter, the key insights crystallize around two issues. First, we have analysed social movements conceptually, illustrated by the case of Los Indignados in Spain. This analysis identified five types of communication for social change outcome where social movement experiences with media and communication converge with those of the more institutionalized practices of communication for development and social change. The five types of challenges or outcomes are as follows:

1. *New forms of organizing discontent, resistance and political action* were seen. Mediated communication played a decisive role in the mobilization practices of the Indignados movement.
2. *New ways of practising communication activism* aligned with the rapidly emerging online media and communication infrastructures for resistance helped spark a strong political momentum.
3. *The symbolic construction of public space with a dynamic synergy between online and offline practices* opened up space for new forms of public deliberation.
4. *The role of leadership in social movements took on new dimensions.* The activists claimed they were operating as leaderless movements, but in practice – and embedded in innovative communication practices – they developed new, subtle forms of leadership.
5. The actors in the movements found *new pathways to construct shared meanings and narratives, and to articulate identities* in a social process that was fundamentally a highly embodied and emotional experience movement.

The second key issue emerges out of these insights. By analysing the way social movements strategize and use both new and old media in their work, it becomes evident that many of their communication characteristics and challenges are similar to those of more established organizations communicating for and about similar social change causes. The issues are defining goals, ensuring equity in participation, constructing the narratives of the initiatives, sustaining interventions and, not least, understanding whether or how the organization and communicational interventions are engaging the target audiences.

There are, furthermore, two features that we have identified as characteristic of this new generation of social movements: one is linked to the movements being 'experience movements', where embodied experiences have become a mode of presence and engagement that goes beyond claims of representation. To communicate successfully for social change today, in a social movement but equally in established organizations, requires a conceptual and analytical openness to understanding the lifeworld of citizens and the emotions and motivations that enhance their engagement and action. The second feature is the way online and offline media and communication practices fuse into a difficult-to-separate reality of communication practices. All this reaffirms that the next-generation challenges of communication for social change, be they articulated by a social movement, an NGO or a governmental or UN agency, will be tackled most successfully and sustainably by a new social thought that takes the actors as its point of departure.

5   Cultures of Governance: Enhancing Empowerment and Resilience

This chapter revolves around three issues: epistemologies of development; stakeholders in development, particularly focused on civil society; and, finally, the discovery of new dynamics of development unfolding in urban peripheries across the world. Together these influence the perception and formation of cultures of governance. The first section uses three scholars – Portuguese sociologist Boaventura de Sousa Santos, Ugandan philosopher Mahmood Mamdani and US anthropologist James Holston – to frame the chapter's focus on what 'cultures of governance' entail and how they are articulated. In the next section, Mexican cultural sociologist Jorge González' concept of cibercultur@ is unpacked and related to notions of civic culture and citizenship. Cibercultur@ is practically synonymous with what I call 'cultures of governance'. This section explains how cibercultur@ can be both an object of study per se and an intervention strategy, both of which support bottom-up processes of creating 'emergent local knowledge communities'. The third section discusses four different perceptions of technology, arguing that technology can be perceived as a technology of citizenship, a social vector, a technology of choice and a political technology. The conclusions reaffirm cultures of governance as a culture-centred approach to communication for development and social change that can enhance processes of empowerment and resilience for local communities. Let us first turn to the overall conceptual framing of a cultures of governance approach.

Towards Global Cognitive Justice

Boaventura de Sousa Santos has been deeply involved for many years in the World Social Forums that have taken place in Porto Alegre, and since travelled the world. Santos makes a strong argument against 'one-size-fits-all' development, and in particular for a reconstruction of epistemologies based on a more just relationship between different kinds of knowledge beyond those of 'the Western left': 'First, the understanding of the world by far exceeds the Western understanding of the world. Second, there is no global social justice without global cognitive justice. Third, the emancipatory transformations in the world may follow grammars and scripts other than those developed by Western-centric critical theory, and such diversity should be valorized' (Santos 2014, viii).

In arguing for *a global cognitive justice* Santos argues for the acknowledgement of other forms of knowledge such as lay, popular, urban, peasant, indigenous, women's and religious, to name just a few. It is the valorization of such alternative discourses and practices and their transformative potential which lies at the heart of such a reconstruction of epistemologies of development and change (Santos 2014, 42).

While Santos helps us rethink epistemologies of knowledge production and social change, the Ugandan philosopher Mahmood Mamdani has delivered insightful analyses that deconstruct the institutional features and characteristics of processes of development. His seminal book from 1996, *Citizen and Subject*, delivers a critical analysis of the institutional legacies left more or less intact from colonial times in contemporary African development dynamics. State institutions reproduce the power relations between state and citizen that originated in colonial times, where civil society remains a weak and marginal player in development processes. Moreover, Mamdani shows the parallel and often opposing discourses that prevail between modernists and communitarians (Mamdani 1996, 3). Eurocentric modernists use a rights-based discourse to argue for a strengthening of the otherwise marginal civil society seen in many African societies. They propound a liberal solution, attempting to situate local politics within civil society and drawing heavily on references to the East European uprisings of the late 1980s. On the other side, Africanist communitarians defend traditional cultures, systems and organizations. The opposition between these systems is, Mamdani argues, 'a paralysis of perspective' (1996, 3) and, in the midst of this paralysis, the dominant state prevails and civil society struggles for influence and power:

> To grasp major shifts in the history of the relationship between civil society and the state, one needs to move away from the assumption of a single generalizable moment and identify different and even contradictory moments in that historical flow. Only through a historically anchored query is it possible to problematize the notion of civil society, thereby to approach it analytically rather than programatically. (Mamdani 1996, 3)

Mamdani's interest lies in deconstructing the structures of power and the shape of resistance in contemporary Africa. He seeks to transcend the opposing perspectives of modernists and communitarians without denying them. From case studies from rural Uganda and urban South Africa, he argues the need to rebuild the institutions inherited directly from the pre-independence colonial hegemony. His analysis is helpful for critically reflecting on the institutional logics and dynamics in processes of development and social change and helps us assess the institutional and power dimensions of development and change.

Finally, the North American anthropologist James Holston uses a comprehensive ethnography of city- and citizen-making in Brazil to illustrate the contradictory realizations of citizenship that characterize democracies across the world:

> today's globalizations of capital, industry, migration, communications, and democracy render cities more strategic: by inscribing these global forces into the spaces and relations of daily life, contemporary cities make them manifest for unprecedented numbers of people. City streets combine new identities of territory, contract, and education with ascribed ones of race, religion, culture and gender. Their crowds catalyze these new combinations into the active ingredients of political movements that develop new sources of rights and agendas of citizenship concerning the very conditions of city life. (Holston 2008a, 23)

Holston makes a strong call to historicize the present, delving into the trajectories of agents of change, citizens' movements and institutions to show how the emerging forms of insurgent citizenship in Brazil have been in the making for many decades. This offers us a cautionary tale in response to the contemporary obsession among both governments and social movements that change is something that happens quickly. It seldom does.

Together, these three scholars help us to focus our attention on the issues at the heart of any development process: how to perceive development and rethink the epistemology of knowledge production and change; the need for an analysis of the interrelations between key stakeholders and the institutional features influencing the power play of resistance and social change; and, finally, the need for grounded empirical studies of dynamic sites of social change, such as urban neighbourhoods, and a strong call to 'historicize the present' in order to understand citizen-making better.

Culture-centred development

Framed within the dynamics of development outlined, I propose the notion of 'cultures of governance' as the core epistemological approach applicable to communication for development research and practice. I see this approach as in close alignment with the 'new social thought' articulated in chapter 1. By proposing this notion I wish to deepen further the argument made in chapter 1 in favour of culture-centred development. This aspect of governance speaks to the recurrent focus in this book on citizen engagement, processes of empowerment and particularly *the ability to control the direction of one's own life trajectory*. It is to do with voice and agency and much less to do with governments.

In conceptualizing cultures of governance as a cornerstone of a culture-centred development process, I rely heavily on González' notion of cibercultur@ (González 2003; 2012; 2014). This concept helps bring together the three issues of rethinking epistemology, analysing power play and calling for grounded studies. Together, this package speaks to a new social thought in the social sciences. Oscar Hemer and I use this approach as a means to substantiate what we have elsewhere termed 'the ethnographic turn' in research and practice of communication for development and social change (Hemer and Tufte 2016).

Cibercultur@ must be deconstructed as the composite neologism it is – as a notion that draws our attention to the interrelations between information, communication and knowledge. It shows that to enhance emergent local knowledge communities that wish to stand a chance of governing their own destinies, a radical, in every way embedded, historical and dynamic approach to change and empowerment is required. González' approach offers us an embedded cultural sociological approach that focuses on research and social action, and on the interrelations between processes of information dissemination, communication practice and knowledge production. In so doing, cibercultur@ offers us an opportunity to formulate a conceptual approach and a research agenda for the study of communication and social change.

As we have seen recurrently, the general emphasis in studies of communication and social change is on immediate and observable change. This limits communication for development's ability not only to address, identify and capture, but also to understand the deeper-lying processes of social change that communication interventions contribute to. *An obsession with the present and with observable change has permeated communication for development research and practice* over many years. Such a focus has been embedded in and tied to the logic of the short-lived projects that governments, NGOs, community-based organizations, UN agencies and other similar institutions embark on. They have been driven by strong demands from donors or from decision-makers to produce *visible results* in the short run, be it in awareness-raising, behaviour change or social change. Similar reasoning can be found in social movement research and its intense focus on the most apparent, visible and tangible outcomes of social movements and their mobilizations. Much social movement research focuses on the immediate, short-term outcomes of mobilization, be they the number of people mobilized in public squares, the de facto fall of a tyrant or the subsequent call for an election.

This obsession with 'immediate, observable change' is reinforced by the new social media and their ability constantly to monitor, document and communicate every little step of an intensely lived mobilization in the life of a social movement or the outcome of a specific activity in a more traditional communication for development intervention. This focus on immediacy and observable change begs the questions: What about the longer-term change processes that are neither immediate nor very observable? How are citizen engagement and empowerment articulated, developed and sustained over time? What is the trajectory by which a community, large or small, develops an ability to drive and direct its own process of development? Can intangible indicators be assessed? And, in this context, can media and communication be attributed a role, be it as technologies or, more importantly, facilitators and articulators of social change?

Just as Melucci argued long ago that movements are not occasional emergencies in social life (Melucci 1994), so we can argue that any mobilization or social change process takes time to achieve an impact. In research about communication and social change we desperately need to recognize that we know far too little about the dynamic relations between communication practices, information dissemination, knowledge production and the long-term social change process. A 'cultures of governance' approach to communication and social change offers an analytical framework that can help alter that lacuna.

Cibercultur@

The long-term and intangible processes of change and the roles of media and communication practices within them constitute the most apparent missing dimension in both research on and practice of communication for development and social change. In order to enhance the culture of governance, much more emphasis must be put on the diachronic dimension of change, and on understanding the complexities of this longitudinal dimension.[2] The ability to look back on past processes of change constitutes a resource for the present and the future.

---

[2] For further elaboration on the diachronic dimension in communication for social change see Tufte (2015), in which I argue that there are three ways of working with memory and develop three perspectives on how memory can strengthen a diachronic dimension. I distinguish between public memory as rhetorical strategy, memory as political and the challenge of translation in memory work, arguing the need to explore how to translate memory into a discourse that is workable and feasible for the present and the future.

Cultures of governance is my name for a socio-cultural condition of society. It refers to the resources and dispositions that citizens develop and draw on to push societal change in a direction that is in accordance with their aspirations. It is a condition and concept that is grounded in the notion of cibercultur@ (González 2012; 2003; 2014). González has worked on large-scale empirical studies of cultural practices since the early 1980s, mainly in Mexico but also in Spain and more recently in Brazil.

Cibercultur@ is a composite neologism that integrates the Greek word *kyber*, the Latin word *cultur* and the spiral form of the sign '@'. *Kyber* originally meant rudder, a sense used in cibercultur@ to express the ability to direct, steer or govern a process. *Cultur*, or culture, signifies the act of cultivation, taking care of or paying attention to. Integrating cyber and culture signifies the ability to govern a process ourselves. Finally, the @ represents diversity – it has graphical similarity to the helicoid, which is a three-dimensional spiral. González uses it to represent a positive feedback loop, 'an open and adaptable process that generates a range of emergent answers' or rather 'an emergent capacity to solve problems using the intellect' (González 2014, 38).

Cibercultur@ is a culturally embedded theorization of the relationship between information, communication and knowledge. This ties in with the perception of technology as a social vector, which opens up the more explicit connection between information and communication, and knowledge production. By understanding technology as a force for social energy, its use and impact on society are then determined not only by access, but also by political, economic and institutional constraints. The ability to access technology – and thus access information and communicate about it – is far from enough. The information–communication nexus must necessarily be connected to the dimension of knowledge. Otherwise, it can easily just result in confusion, bewilderment, uncertainty or disorientation: 'Knowledge is not just about accessing or handling information created and diffused by others, about others . . . Knowing is . . . a complex process of neurological, psychological and social activity that increases our capacity to differentiate and integrate lived experience' (González 2014, 31).

As a strategic weapon, knowledge is essential for gaining control over our lives and increasing our quality of life. It maximizes the power of any community to construct and establish relations over non-relational experiences. 'As an emergent property, it has a highly practical function, supporting an endless process of resilience' (González 2014, 31). In other words, processes of empowerment, and enhancing the capacity and ability to govern or control your own life, require knowledge. The overall normative and strategic objective embedded in cibercultur@ is to understand and support processes by which information and communication practices enhance *emergent local knowledge communities*. This means moving far beyond the technocratic and techno-centric perceptions of technology that prevail in our time, to put technology instead in its relevant contexts and view it as a social force in society.

Confronting an uneven and unfair social order

The work of González and his close friend and colleague in Colima at the time, Jesús Galindo Cáceres, along with their team, constituted a leading contemporary cultural research environment. Their aim since the early 1980s has been to understand the dynamic interplay between social and cultural formations and practices, information and communication systems and dynamics, and empowerment and social change. Drawing on scholars such as Pierre Bourdieu, Daniel Berteau, Henry Trueba, Humberto Maturana and Francisco Varela, Gilberto Jimenez, Immanuel Wallerstein and last but not least the Italian anthropologist Alberto Cirese, González has since the mid-1980s developed and refined a conceptual approach to and methodology for studying the ways we produce knowledge *and* the ways in which the practice of local knowledge production can be enhanced. However, although influential in the Ibero-American academic world, only a limited amount of this work has been translated into English (González 2014).

One of the fundamental starting points and basic assumptions for González is his stand on development. He argues clearly that poverty is by no means a 'natural' condition,

> but an outcome of a set of powerful relations and tensions that historically de-energize large groups of the world population, not because they are less talented or cognitively inferior, but because of their position in a set of social and historical relations . . . A number of strategic actions are conveyed to cope with these conditions, but the unresolved, permanent situations in everyday life push citizens in these impoverished regions to believe that it really is their individual problem. A large part of human social activity is engaged in designing strategies for re-energizing through different 'tactics' (Certeau, Giard, Mayol 1998) confronting a deeply uneven and unfair social order enacted at all scales. (González 2014, 27)

Drawing on Wallerstein, González situates and understands the lived experiences of all disconnected localities as part and parcel of the same world system: a system of flows of capital, people, images and information. González argues that the individual lived experience of being isolated and disconnected from social organization is the pre-eminent social representation of capitalism. It keeps many local communities fixed in marginalized and isolated positions in which they have difficulties claiming their rights and making their voices heard. This unfolds as two agendas for cibercultur@: cibercultur@ as research and thus an object of study, and cibercultur@ as intervention.

Cibercultur@ as an object of study

First, González proposes a basic research agenda, providing an analytical framework to design research that increases our understanding of *how* local communities produce knowledge, form identities and handle specific challenges in everyday life. As an object of study, cibercultur@ involves the study of the history and formation of the *material ecosystems of culture* and the study of relations between the *symbolic ecologies of a specific society and their technological vectors*.

González takes a specific interest in the dynamic relations between meaning, norms and power seen from the perspective of those excluded from the social space: the economically exploited, politically dominated and culturally directed (2014, 39). He remains focused on populations excluded from 'the benefits of globalization', and that have become the black holes of informational capitalism (Castells 2010), or 'the reverse side of globalization' (Bauman 1998). As such, the project González has embarked on is about understanding but also enhancing local knowledge production. This resonates with my own work in Brazil, in which I explored processes of globalization, but specifically cultural globalization. My interest was in understanding how local communities, that is, specific families in the town of Porto Alegre, produced knowledge, formed identities and handled specific challenges in everyday life at a time when rapid media development was under way in the region. Cable television was being rolled out, and the working hypothesis was that it would offer new opportunities for these Brazilian families to connect with the world.

Our research group viewed technologies as a social vector, exploring the information-communication and knowledge production processes in four different families with different ethnic, socio-economic and geographical backgrounds (Jacks and Tufte 1998). We explored how these processes unfolded by following González' research protocols on how to study the formation of audiences over time, producing diachronic and synchronic descriptions and analyses of these processes. We historicized the present by conducting interviews about the family histories, their mobility and incorporation of new technologies over the past four generations – from the introduction of electric light, to buying cars, their first radio, television and video up until their first purchase and use of the Internet. However, rather than being techno-centric we were practice-focused, interested in understanding the social practices of the use of these technologies over time in everyday life, as well as their symbolic value. With González we explored the symbolic ecologies of gaucho families in Porto Alegre and their techno-logical vectors. This diachronic exploration of identity formation and media use was complemented by ethnographic studies of their everyday life with particular focus on their social uses of the media, describing and analysing the symbolic ecologies these families navigated (Jacks et al. 2006).

In the integrated analysis of the knowledge produced about their family histories, and further connected to the studies of urban development – of city and neighbourhood, media developments and programme supply – we were able to describe the history and formation of the material ecosystems of culture to which four families had been exposed, integrated with the for-mation of audiences and with a particular interest in seeking to understand how their media use, social practices and processes of cultural identity for-mation were interrelated, coming together as symbolic ecologies with spe-cific technological vectors. Thus, although not at the time framed as being about cultures of governance, our study focused on how these families were connected to the world and how media were involved in sustaining such connections. Thus, it became a study of emergent local knowledge commu-nities, studying four particular families, identifying their family ideologies and the trajectories of their disposition, and as such understanding their engagement as citizens with the world around them.

Cibercultur@ as intervention

Cibercultur@ seeks to confront and challenge processes of isolation, igno-rance and inability to develop local and situated knowledge. The aims are to enhance the production and organization of local knowledge, and to connect disconnected localities that have similar experiences of global forces to knowledge-born networks. Cibercultur@ thus serves as part of an over-all 'intervention strategy', moving from a basic research agenda to a more applied one, strategizing to enhance processes of empowerment, creating local knowledge and thereby supporting long-term processes of resilience.

Cibercultur@ should not, however, be confused with otherwise strategic and intervention-oriented research, which tends to be functionalist and highly solution-oriented, like the 'first-generation' communication for development practices outlined in chapter 1. The interventionist agenda of cibercultur@ is problem-oriented and emphasizes the study of deeper societal processes. It seeks to understand profoundly and describe what culture-centred development entails in practice, and consequently strategizes to enhance such processes. Cibercultur@ is an approach deeply committed to social change, but more in line with the approach to knowledge and change that also guided Paulo Freire. In one of his final texts, Freire discarded 'aggressive rationalism, where, once deified, reason knows and can do everything'. Instead, he argued for 'intelligence about the world as our required knowledge basis in our strategies for change' (Freire 2004, 5). The production and uncovering of emergent local knowledge communities that are at the heart of cibercultur@ seeks exactly this and connects well with Freire's thoughts on 'capability': 'Intelligence about the world, which is as much apprehended as it is produced, and the communicability of that intelligence are tasks for the subjects, who in the process, must become more and more *critically capable*' (2004, 5).

Freire's emphasis on capability resonates with one of the paradigms that today challenge the growth focus of Western notions of development – the 'capabilities approach' developed by the Indian economist and philosopher Amartya Sen in the 1980s and 1990s. Sen defines development as 'a process of expanding the real freedoms that people enjoy' (Sen 1999, 293). Four elements characterize his approach: (1) development understood as a process, not an outcome; (2) a focus on freedom of choice in all spheres (personal, social, economic and political); (3) putting people at the centre of development; and (4) people themselves defining what they value. The capabilities approach of Sen, Freire's pedagogical philosophy and González' cibercultur@ converge well. Cibercultur@ becomes not only a conceptual substantiation of Sen's capabilities approach but equally an operationalization of the culture-centred development that I argue for in chapter 1, drawing on Freire, Dutta and others. It also addresses the power plays in development, to which Mamdani gives particular attention.

As a strategy for development and empowerment, cibercultur@ draws on the dynamic interplay between knowledge production, information and the creation of networks to communicate and use knowledge and information for specific purposes: 'To develop cibercultur@ means … to enact the capacity for building and using dialogically every technique submitted for social reflexivity built and shared within horizontal networks' (González 2014, 40). The aim is the creation of local knowledge and, by connecting through networks to others, to create situated knowledge from the bottom up.

Narrating and communicating other possible worlds

González' interest in developing cibercultur@ as a concept is grounded in an interest in marginalized, exploited and silenced populations. His own empirical work has in recent years focused on indigenous populations in remote areas of northern Mexico as well as studies among the landless peasants of Brazil and their social movements. Developing a 'culture of governance' approach reinforces the point of focusing on some of the many not-yet-citizens, people who are excluded from citizenship rights. Many people still have a long way to go to achieve the status of citizens. As an intervention, cibercultur@ can help us with 'narrating the threads and communicating the *value* and meaning of landmarks of social memory, definitions of the current situation, and the feasibility and density of other *possible worlds*' (González 2014, 39). There is a clear aspirational dimension driving such research, and seeking social change through such interventions.

By understanding the reality on the ground we can get a better grasp of 'the process of becoming' (Dahlgren 2003). Dahlgren, González and many others depart from a normative base; they are interested in the social and cultural processes by which cultures of governance develop and empower people to take decisions, engage in public debates or, as González emphasizes, create local knowledge. González sees cibercultur@ as a tool for developing self-determined answers to and actions on relevant problems by means of collective intelligence (2014, 41).

According to Dahlgren, citizen participation is understood in terms of 'meaningful action and the cultural prerequisites for such action' (Dahlgren 2003, 152). Furthermore, Couldry (2006) makes a strong argument in favour of studying 'cultures' of citizenship, rather than 'cultural citizenship'. The formation or articulation of civic cultures as part and parcel of processes of empowerment seems to be a common denominator. As Couldry puts it: 'whether citizens feel they have a voice, or the space in which effectively to exercise a voice, is crucial to their possibilities of acting as citizens' (2006, 326).

What we see here are research agendas around civic culture and cultures of governance (cibercultur@), some more media-centric, some more socio-centric. Dahlgren makes a helpful distinction between focusing on the public sphere and on civic culture: 'If the more familiar concept of the *public sphere* points to the politically relevant communicative spaces in daily life and in the media, *civic culture* points to those features of the socio-cultural world – dispositions, practices and processes – that constitute preconditions for people's actual participation in the public sphere, in civil and political society' (Dahlgren 2003, 154). In exploring these preconditions and understanding how they are formed and developed, we can get a sense of the nature and state of the civic culture of a society. Civic culture as conceptualized by Dahlgren has many similarities to cibercultur@ as conceptualized by González. However, civic culture has a less articulate orientation towards social justice and the social inclusion of marginalized communities, something which is a basic assumption of González' work.

Performing a new civility

Holston adds to the social-change-oriented research agenda by connecting the *location* of citizenship and civic culture with the realities of the rapidly growing cities in Africa and the enormous and multiple, decades-old peripheries of Latin American cities. Holston's work delves into one of the biggest cities in the world, São Paulo, exploring everyday life and the practices of resistance in the large eastern periphery of the city (Holston 2008). His interests connect well with González' theorization of 'city nodes' that concentrate millions of people and immense volumes of capital (González 2014, 39).

When assessing living conditions and the ability to be and act in the large urban centres, Holston argues that a bird's-eye view of their history and development is dehistoricizing. Simply viewing these immense neighbourhoods from a plane, on television or in passing from a nearby highway cannot capture or recognize them 'as a place where Brazil's past and present disrupt each other, much less does it consider this disruption an important agent in constructing a different future' (Holston 2008, 34). Holston is interested in the *performance of a new civility*, which he detected as emerging in Brazil. It fits well, I would add, with similar emerging civilities elsewhere in the world. The place where government power worked explicitly and strategically with the performance of a new civility is most famously Bogotá, where the municipal authorities under Antanas Mockus made it a central policy. One of the best-known examples was the use of hundreds of clowns to perform a new civility in among the traffic of Bogotá. However, similar connections can be made to the social movements I unpack in chapter 6. Thus, the process of catalysing the performance of new civility can be either bottom-up or top-down.

Perceptions of Technology

To enhance cultures of governance requires an explicit emphasis on what González calls 'the trajectories of disposition' of the citizens and communities in question. This sparks associations with Putnam's political sociology, something Dahlgren is well aware of and also discusses. In the world of political sociology as defined by Putnam, it is the concept of *social capital* that serves to define and explain some of the dispositions, practices and processes that determine civic and political engagement. Civic culture tends to have features similar to those of social capital. Dahlgren speaks about the 'civic' being 'a reservoir of pre- or non-political potentiality' (Dahlgren 2003, 155), a reservoir positioned within the lifeworld of the Habermasian conceptual framework and shaped by many factors, be they for example education or the media. Paraphrasing Cruikshank (1999), Dahlgren calls these factors *technologies of citizenship*, technologies that can both empower and disempower.

As we can see, civic cultures become dispositions, practices and processes that are both conditioned and articulated by a range of technologies of citizenship. Dahlgren (2009) further expands his analytical framework of civic cultures, emphasizing the dynamics by which values, affinity (community), knowledge, practices, identities and discussion come together to configure 'the storehouse of assets' that characterizes civic culture (Dahlgren 2009, ch. 5). Without this resource, he argues, empowerment and political engagement cannot prevail. However, Dahlgren remains within a rather narrow object of study, that of media as journalistic practice. Although he seems to follow a similar pathway to González, he is more focused on media-centric concerns, that is, the behaviour of journalists and the transformation first and foremost of the media sector and the public sphere.

González' research agenda is more broadly embedded in everyday life and bottom-up processes of empowerment and social inclusion. He speaks of *technologies as a social vector* (González 2014, 30). This approach has little to do with technology, computers or the materiality of media and technology: 'To develop cibercultur@ really means redesigning collectively – and from the bottom-up – a different attitude to and way of relating to technology and social problems' (2014, 40). It becomes a normatively based research agenda that seeks to 'address information needs, to generate and evaluate knowledge and to coordinate communication actions that can break the vicious circle of technological dependence and subaltern representations that conform to symbolic ecologies . . . It will entail a coordinated effort to reweave the unbalanced social bonds' (2014, 40).

Compared to Dahlgren's notion of civic culture, González' work with cibercultur@ offers a broader cultural perspective and a broader object of study. Where Dahlgren remains within the world of media as the 'technology of citizenship', González' notion of 'technology as a social vector' approaches technology as more deeply engrained in the social practices of everyday life. Thus, recalling the model I developed in the concluding section of chapter 2, which positions communication for development and social change between media-centric and socio-centric approaches to communication and social change, Dahlgren can be seen as the more media-centric analyst of civic cultures, while González is taking a socio-centric approach much more deeply embedded in social practice, and offering a strong diachronic as well as a synchronic approach to his study of the material and symbolic trajectories, practices and dispositions of marginalized communities.

Technologies of choice and belonging

Technology as discussed here cannot be reduced to the affordances offered by a particular ICT. Rather, what is at stake is technologically mediated social practices. As the central concept, I employ González' notion of viewing *technologies as a social vector*. The social practice of using technologies for all the elements González speaks about – dissemination of information, communication practices and production of knowledge – comes with a number of social and cultural qualities. I argue later that a number of different perceptions of technology are relevant to the production of emergent local knowledge communities. In unpacking perceptions of technology I emphasize two key perceptions of the role of technologies in processes of change, perceptions where technologies:

1. increase the ability to choose pathways of change, which draws on Dorothy Kleine's work and is closely associated with Amartya Sen's capability approach to development and social change (Kleine 2013);
2. illustrate the ubiquity of power, being a political technology that can enhance Governmentality processes (Leistert 2013).

Studying and exploring cultures of governance means articulating both a socially committed research agenda and appropriate strategies of intervention whereby a new civility can emerge through the further development of local emergent knowledge communities. It becomes an interdisciplinary but culture-centred concept of development that speaks to both researchers and practitioners. It also becomes a practice that unfolds in a dynamic interplay between technologies understood as social vectors and capabilities, but also as 'Governmentalities'.

Perceiving technologies as social vectors signals an approach to development that is neither techno-centric nor linear in its perception but rather connects with the ideas of Sen and his capabilities approach. However, it is the notion of 'technologies of choice' that is most directly connected to Sen's approach. Kleine (2013) explores explicitly how Sen's capabilities approach could be used to empower people to make choices in their lives. In developing her 'choice framework' Kleine builds on Ruth Alsop and Nina Heinsohn's World Bank policy research paper where they develop their notion of 'degrees of empowerment' (World Bank Institute 2005). While they define these as the availability, use and effectiveness of choice, Kleine goes a step further, adding what British Bangladeshi social economist Naila Kabeer has worked a lot with – 'the sense of choice', or the knowledge that choice exists. Consequently, four degrees of empowerment appear in Kleine's framework: the existence of choice, the sense of choice, the use of choice and the achievement of choice (Kleine 2013, 44). Kleine emphasizes the ability to choose – an action-oriented approach about making the best choices in the personal, social, political, cultural and economic spheres.

Although reluctant to use the notion of empowerment, stating that 'Empowerment . . . has gone from bad (being underdefined and overused in academic discourse) to worse (being underdefined and overused in policy and public discourse)' (Kleine 2013, 31), Kleine connects the process of making choice to processes of empowerment. By tracing the etymology of the concept back to work on gender relations and community participation (Moser 1991; van Eyken 1991) she puts particular emphasis on community development, and as such is in sync with González' focus on emergent local knowledge communities.

A critique Kleine makes of Sen's capabilities approach is that it tends to be overly rational: 'People make sense of their lives in diverse and complex ways, and this is ultimately part of what it means to be human' (Kleine 2013, 25). It is this missing cultural embeddedness that runs the risk of focusing too exclusively on the rational, leaving emotion and irrationality, beliefs and imagination aside. We have seen how contemporary social movements speak exactly to this, claiming embodied experience through performance. Paraphrasing Kevin McDonald (2006), I call such movements 'experience movements'. Kleine strikes a similar chord in reclaiming the role of emotions, irrationality, beliefs and imagination in processes of social change.

Sen's capabilities approach is fundamental to opening up a reinterpretation of 'freedom of choice'. However, Sen has also been criticized for not paying enough attention to social constraints (Koggel 2003) or power (Hill 2003). Another criticism is Sen's weak articulation of individual and collective choices (Kleine 2013, 29).

In moving beyond these weaknesses in Sen, and consequently also in Kleine's insistence on conceiving the technologies as 'technologies of choice', cibercultur@ offers a more holistic proposal for how to empower citizens to engage and act from below, embedded in cultures of governance. Rather than being 'technologies of choice', González' notion of technologies as a social vector is a more sustainable approach that factors in the power dynamics of everyday life as well as cultural dynamics to the way of conceiving of technologies as social vectors articulating processes of empowerment.

Political technology and the ubiquity of power

The German media scholar Oliver Leistert adds yet another perspective by speaking about mobile media as *political technologies* (Leistert 2013, 59) because of their ability to enhance the management of government, but also to articulate counter-rationalities and counter-conducts. Leistert delivers quite a harsh critique of social movements and the struggle for change as echoing the insistence on dividing the political and non-political spheres. Social movements seem to reproduce this matrix, which is a reproduction of the separation of the spheres of civil society and the state. The example of PB illustrates the opening up of what Leistert has called an 'unidentifiable, temporary space of possibilities, or a temporary autonomous zone' (2013, 56). Experience in Brazil, however, shows a pathway beyond the temporary space, given that the social movements managed to gain power, win the municipal election and subsequently unfold their ideas from within the formal system of governance. What began as a bottom-up development of a culture of governance became a system-driven governance process whereby the attention sought by local knowledge communities was institutionalized. Bottom-up and top-down processes and hierarchies converged. It was not an easy process to sustain, but it survived and continued to grow (see chapter 3).

An important point Leistert continually returns to in his study of the political rationality of mobile media is the Foucauldian notion of power, a ubiquity of power in all spheres of everyday life, but also the point that 'power and resistance are mutually inclusive forces: power only functions where there is resistance, and resistance only functions in fields of power' (Leistert 2013, 58). Again, the dynamics and tensions of the relation between social movements and the formal governance system in Porto Alegre are a strong illustration of these forces.

During protest and collective action, Leistert argues, uses of mobile media can be seen as empowerment processes, independent of government programmes. They become political technologies influencing government rule, but at the same time empowering counter-rationalities and counter-conducts as they, for example, facilitate coordinated collective distributed action (2013, 59). What happens in these processes is a 'reconfiguration of subjectivations': 'Counter-rationalities and counter-conducts are sites of desire production which challenge the predominantly economical conduct of governing' (2013, 60). Such processes have been seen in many social movements in recent years. Counter-conducts have been seen as productive in constituting subjectivities through the performance of dissent. Examples include the Indignados movement in Spain and the Occupy movement in the USA.

Mobile media alters the performance thanks to its capacity to organize, mobilize and coordinate – which I provide examples of in chapter 4 and elaborate on in chapter 6. However, one major challenge in these processes of mobilization and resistance lies in the highly individualized dimension and use of technology, something Natalie Fenton and Veronica Barassi have drawn attention to: 'Political participation is frequently defined by and takes place in relation to and in coordination with others. Foregrounding creative autonomy and the power of individuation may well be appropriate analytical tools for social media, but to do so negates the collective dimension of political participation and thereby dissipates the political properties of the participatory communicative act itself' (Fenton and Barassi 2011, 187). As Leistert rightly highlights, it begs the question of how a technology of individualization can be changed into a technology of collective action (Leistert 2013, 65). This question is addressed in the case studies in chapter 6.

Tensions and challenges in supporting processes of resilience in a glocal reality

This chapter has unpacked how a 'cultures of governance' approach to social science becomes a way both to understand and to intervene in social realities on a normative ground and in support of an endless process of resilience-building, mainly with regard to marginalized communities. It is an approach to communication and social change that insists on 'joining the dots' between information dissemination, communication practices and knowledge production, reiterating that their interconnectivity and interdependence are fundamental in order for emergent local knowledge communities to prevail. Technologies in this context are seen as social vectors, and their uses can potentially encompass the roles of enhancing the capabilities of citizens to make choices in everyday life, articulating processes of belonging and of resistance against the 'conduct of governing'.

In order to support emergent local knowledge communities, a cultures of governance approach thus insists on connecting any information dissemination or communicative practice with local cosmo-visions and thus with the 'other knowledges' that Santos speaks of (2014, 42). It becomes an approach to communication and social change that could well challenge the one-size-fits-all approaches to communication and social change inherent in working with generic models and strategies. When, for example, emergencies such as Ebola or Zika, natural disasters or war and conflict lead to speedy communication interventions from international organizations, this tends to reinforce the established power relations and structural strengths and weaknesses in a society. Global matrixes meet local realities, often leading to tension, misunderstandings and conflict. Thus, when working with emerging local knowledge systems and with a long-term perspective on social change, it is important to recognize that these local communities are dependent on global forces but at the same time genuine to a locality. This global-local interdependency is at the heart of contemporary development and is the reality in which communication for development and social change interventions also operate.

6   Communication Movements

The elections in December 2015 provided evidence of the historic victory of the new political forces in Spain. The leftist political parties Ganemos Madrid, Barcelona en Comú (previously Guanyem Barcelona) and Podemos had already won big victories in municipal and regional elections in May of that year. Now the mayors of the three largest cities in the country, Madrid, Barcelona and Valencia, were elected from these brand-new political parties. Two of these mayors are women. Madrid's mayor, Manuela Carmena, is a 71-year-old lawyer who had a record of opposing Franco. She was the candidate of the coalition Ahora Madrid, which brought together Ganemos Madrid, a citizen platform inspired by Guanyem Barcelona, EQUO, Podemos and PUM+J. Barcelona's mayor is Ada Colau. She was the candidate of Barcelona en Comú, having previously led the Plataforma de los Afectados por la Hipoteca (PAH), the housing movement that gained substantial momentum and obtained significant results in the aftermath of the Indignados movement's mobilization in 2011. The mayor of Valencia is Joan Ribó, a former school teacher and university lecturer who represents the Coalición Compromis (the Commitment Coalition), which is a Valencian political party committed to Valencianist, progressive and green politics.

These political winds of change were articulated using new methods of mobilization and funding crowd-sourced directly from citizens through social media. They represent radically new political visions and discourses, and are new arrivals in party politics with a recent history strongly embedded in social movements and the trajectory of the Indignados movement. Their political projects emerged from bottom-up processes, organized in a way hitherto unseen in party politics. The electoral victories achieved in 2015 enabled the social mobilizations of the Indignados movement to insert themselves highly successfully into the vertical power structures of society.

In retrospect, how can this political victory be assessed? What was the cause? Can it be considered a success vis-à-vis the indicators of success of social movements per se? What about their communication for social change endeavours more specifically? Does becoming part of the vertical power structures clash with the long-standing insistence in many social movements on horizontal leadership, organization and policy formulation?

Or can we use González' notion of 'cibercultur@' to argue that new systems of information, communication and knowledge production are succeeding in Spain? Are they also succeeding elsewhere, such as in Tunisia, Turkey, Brazil or Kenya? Is a new culture of governance permeating the formal structures of politics in the growing number of countries that have experienced profound and widespread popular uprisings in recent years? Most crucial for those of us working in the field of media and communication for social change: what roles have the media and communication strategies and practices of the social movements had in enhancing these processes?

These questions suggest at least three analytical perspectives in need of further inquiry. First, what do some of the cases mentioned here tell us about the ability of social movements to achieve social and political change? Second, more detailed analysis is required to pin down the role of media and communication in articulating the social change that these movements are pursuing. Finally, the communication practices of these movements must be analysed in order to identify any innovations in their practice of communicating for social change vis-à-vis the way communication for social change is carried out in established institutions.

Communication Movements and Political Repertoires

According to John Postill, there is innovation in the Spanish case, mainly in how media and communication are integral technologies and practices to the process of enhancing citizenship. The Spanish case illustrates that 'the 15M movement, including its political offshoots, has contributed to the emergence of a new language and praxis of citizenship in Spain' (Postill 2014b, 2), and it has done so at a time of rapid technological change. Drawing on the sociologist Jorge Benedicto (2006), Postill argues that Spain had been living with a 'transition culture' for thirty years, in which civic rights took precedence over social rights. Both Postill and the Spanish media scholars Alejandro Barranquero and Miriam Meda González (2015) argue that this transition culture was based on an agreement by the political left in Spain not to engage in cultural and social mobilization. Culture was depoliticized for many years, as the need for national stability outweighed the deeper process of democratization (Barranquero Carretero and Meda González 2015, 142).

In the aftermath of the 2008 financial crisis, however, a *movement of movements* emerged in Spain, which Barranquero argues can be interpreted as *communication movements* because of the central role of communication in defining their political agendas, the way in which they articulated their information and organization strategies and their transnational networking (Barranquero 2012; 2014; Barranquero Carretero and Meda González 2015) Barranquero and Meda argue that the Indignados movement was based largely on communication demands such as *transparency* in public and private expenditure (*gestión*), greater *pluralism in the media*, and (*apuestas*) *a neutral and accessible Internet* (Barranquero Carretero and Meda González 2015, 142). The protests against the Ley Sinde[3] were among the first demonstrations in the spring of 2011. Like Barranquero and Meda, I argue that two issues define whether a social movement is a communication movement: (1) a media- and communication-centric political agenda as a central plank of the overall agenda; and (2) being highly tech-savvy in the use of digital technologies and online networks.

The political scientist Vicente Ordóñez focuses less on the communicative aspects and more on the nature of the political repertoires and the tools used in pursuit of the aims of Spain's social movements. Ordóñez emphasizes the different political repertoires used in the actions taken by civil society, which follow the path of civic disobedience, but also an institutional path of claiming power through participation in the system. In his analysis of the PAH, Ordóñez identifies five *political tools*. First, there were blockades and sit-ins, which draw on the history of the autonomous anti-nuclear movement in Germany in the 1970s and 1980s, but also on the anarchist tradition within Spain. In both cases human shields were created in the act of protesting against the power holders. Since 2008 and 2009, and especially 2011, there have been many examples of blockades and sit-ins, often as an integral part of the growing practice of creative activism.

A second tool, used to renegotiate mortgages, was the occupation of banks (figure 9). The PAH often managed to assemble dozens or even hundreds of people who were either activists or directly affected by evictions. Third, direct action was paramount and achieved significant results, as it had for the German anti-nuclear movements that inspired the PAH. The PAH managed to stop more than 1,000 evictions using direct action (Ordóñez 2015). Fourth, there were *escraches*, a type of demonstration where activists go to the homes or workplaces of those they want to condemn or publicly humiliate in order to persuade decision-makers and governments to take a

---

[3] The Ley Sinde, or the Sinde Law, is a provision of Spain's Sustainable Economy Act designed to address Internet copyright infringements. The bill was made law on 30 December 2011 despite substantial protest against it. One of the larger demonstrations took place during the Goya Awards ceremony in February 2011, when hundreds of people loosely organized by the Internet group Anonymous attended the red-carpet event wearing Guy Fawkes masks to call for the resignation of Ángeles González-Sinde, the minister who gave her name to the law. See https://en.wikipedia.org/wiki/Ley_Sinde.

Figure 9. Protest action in front of the BBVA Bank in Malaga, 7 June 2012

Source: Wikimedia Commons

certain action. The fifth political tool was the formation of anti-elite political parties (Ordóñez 2015) such as Guanyem Barcelona and Podemos, which, as already mentioned, were big winners in both municipal and national elections in 2015. Conclusively, in addition to civil disobedience, which is characteristic of any social movement like the PAH, the Indignados movement paved the way for social movements not only to enter party politics, but also to take power across the cities and regions of Spain. The demands for space, visibility and participation were enhanced through a 'politics of the street', but this gradually expanded to include claims on power through involvement in party politics.

In analysing the role of communication in the empowerment and impact of the PAH anti-evictions movement, Mariona Sanz Cortell identifies the wide range of its media and communication practices (Sanz Cortell 2015), from the weekly face-to-face assemblies to the establishment of email groups, instant messaging platforms and a variety of communicative actions in line with the repertoire of political action outlined here. It was seen not only in the joyful civil disobedience actions, where singing and dancing were integral elements, but also in the uses of social media. The PAH, for example, established more than 200 local committees or groups, the vast majority of which had their own Twitter accounts or Facebook pages (Sanz Cortell 2015, 42). For those who lacked skills, training was organized so that, for example, some of the older women active in the PAH could learn to tweet. In its relations with the press, the PAH was collaborative and proactive, being both open with and interested in its contacts. This was reinforced by the active production of more than 110 videos, which were made available on its main website (Sanz Cortell 2015, 50).

The PAH became a showcase for communication movements in Spain. This was primarily linked to its creativity and innovation, and the central importance of media and communication to the organization's networking and mobilization. However, it was also seen in the way the PAH addressed capacity-building for ordinary citizens to become active media users and producers and thus challenge the exclusivity of the established media sector in Spain, a sector that is far from in sync with the concerns of ordinary citizens. In empowering citizens in communication terms, that is, in using and producing media and communications proactively, such competencies and such forms of popular participation have had an impact not only on the social movement and its political agenda, but equally on the formation of a new and more dynamic media scene in the country. In this way, contemporary social movements such as the PAH, in their pursuit of popular participation and ultimately a social and political impact, end up becoming communication movements.

Glocal movements

Most of today's social movements fit well with the notion of *glocal* movements, that is, movements that link local development challenges to the global ones, thereby linking the micro-narratives of specific challenges and themes to the macro-level stories of development and social change. The confluence of movements described by Barranquero, Diaz and Laraña, among others, notes that the self-identity of many of these movements contains a strong element of being part of something bigger, a transnational or even global movement that is fighting for citizen inclusion in processes of development and social change. Ruben Diaz, for example, argues, like Barranquero, that Los Indignados were a movement of movements that came together around common causes in the 15M mobilization, but at the same time contained a multiplicity of histories of activism that stretched from the anti-globalization movements to cyberactivism, anarchism, civil rights, environmentalism, neighbourhood movements and beyond (Diaz 2014). Thus, the local movements connected clearly with many of the contemporary global development challenges and actively networked with other movements in other countries that were pursuing similar agendas.

This confluence of many movements was also seen, for example, in the political coalitions and parties that emerged in 2014 and 2015, which were extremely diverse in their thematic orientation, but nonetheless uniform in their overall critique of the contemporary neoliberal development paradigm.

In this movement of movements, the globality is clear: the massive transnational networking and coming together across national agendas speaks to this. Common thematic traits are seen in, for example, their concerns over urbanism and environmentalism, and about the inability to resolve problems linked closely to the financial crisis and economic inequality, most notably youth unemployment. There is clearly an activist identity that considers itself to be part of a global movement in addition to being part of a national one (Diaz 2014). In addition, there is more than just digital interaction among these movements across the globe – there is also face-to-face interaction. For example, the Gezi movement in Turkey and the Vinegar revolution in Brazil have held a number of joint seminars to exchange experiences and build networks and collaborations on joint actions. Such links can also be seen, for example, between the Occupy movement in the United States and the Indignados movement.

Beyond the common global traits and the transnational networking, however, there are also highly localized situations and challenges. The Gezi uprisings in Turkey in June 2013, for example, were prompted by the concrete urban challenges surrounding the future use of a public park in Istanbul. The mobilization quickly spread across the country, and transformed into massive demonstrations focused on issues of urban development, sustainable cities, urban gardening and housing policy, but also on a number of other, deeper socio-economic issues that questioned the policies of the government.

Local characteristics are much more prominent in all movements. The São Paulo and Rio uprisings in June 2013 and again a year later were about public transport and local infrastructure projects linked to the 2014 FIFA World Cup and the 2016 Olympics in Rio. In Greece the massive mobilizations in 2011 were related to the financial crisis and austerity measures. Later, however, once Syriza had won the 2015 general election, the citizen uprisings were in sync with government policies connected to transnational concern about the EU. It became a symbolic fight between Greece as David and the EU as Goliath. Greece challenged the EU's financial policies and largely lost. It was a highly local Greek conflict, but with widespread support from citizens across the EU member states. In sum, while these movements – acting outside but increasingly also within the political system – are specific to their local context, they are also part of a global trend. It is a trend whereby new forms and dynamics of enhancing citizenship and articulating cultures of governance are carved out in innovative, dialogic and creative spaces through the practice of citizen communication and engagement.

The Dramaturgy of Social Change

Social scientists often embed their analyses in language that seeks to capture the performance, creativity or musicality of the social movements they are analysing and theorizing about. I argue here that approaching social movement and social change analysis from a dramaturgical perspective can capture these dynamics. It is also a useful way to capture the links between long-term social change agendas, with their long-term strategies, and short-term insurgencies, with their here-and-now tactics. The notion of dramaturgy helps us connect the small story of a particular event with the larger narrative of development and social change.

In connecting the analysis of social movements more integrally with media and communication analysis, Todd Gitlin was one of the early scholars to use metaphors from the creative arts. He was therefore interested in the dramaturgy of the movements. Gitlin used the language of the creative arts in part to understand the actual creative practice of a social movement, but also to grasp its dramaturgy, putting the components that constitute the social movement in a dramaturgical formula. Drawing on dance studies, Gitlin used dance metaphors to analyse the interactions between movements and media. He likened their relation to that of two dancers in a 'movement–media dance' where the media needed stories, and preferred the dramatic, while the movements needed publicity to recruit activists, maintain public support and have a political effect (Gitlin 1980).

Developing *the dance metaphor*, the Italian political scientist Alice Mattoni and Italian media scholar Emiliano Treré propose a three-level conceptual framework for studying social movements and the media. In identifying micro-, meso- and macro-levels of change, they connect *media practices* to the micro-level of change, *mediation processes* to the meso-level and *mediatization* to the macro-level. They focus on 'activist media practices', which they define as 'routinized and creative social practices in which activists engage . . . interactions with media objects . . . and interactions with media subjects' (Mattoni and Treré 2014, 259). This media practice approach has proved useful for studying media in everyday life, but it fails to capture political processes and global media events, for which purpose the notions of 'mediation processes' and 'mediatization' are useful.

Drawing on Silverstone and in particular on Martín-Barbero, Mattoni and Treré define mediation as 'a social process in which media supports the flow of discourses, meanings, and interpretations in societies' (Mattoni and Treré 2014, 260). It is thus both a circular and a situated process that intertwines with a series of social activities; it is both a means, whereby people use media, and an end, where media users constitute flows of media production, circulation, interpretation and recirculation. An activist on Plaza del Sol in Madrid uses social media to stream what is happening at the assembly on the square, but also becomes part of those flows. This understanding of mediation processes offers us insights into the extent to which social movement actors 'engage with the reconfiguration and remediation of media technologies and meanings, and act according to patterns of appropriation and subversion, with regard to both mainstream and alternative media, digital and analogue technologies' (Mattoni and Treré 2014, 261). Finally, the concept of mediatization focuses our attention on the ways in which media influence social and cultural institutions in society.

Mattoni and Treré add further distinctions to their framework – short-, medium- and long-term change – and operate with different actors: individual actors operating at the micro-level, collective actors operating at the meso-level and social movement 'families' operating at the macro-level (Mattoni and Treré 2014, 256). To illustrate these dynamics, Mattoni and Treré, like Gitlin, link the three analytical levels to aspects of a dance, thereby also making a connection to dance studies. This dramaturgical approach to the study of media, communication and social movements captures the interplay and the dynamics between the micro-, meso- and macro-levels that we wish to capture and understand. According to Mattoni and Treré:

- *dance steps* reflect the media practices that individual actors develop before, during and after their mobilization;
- *a dance* describes the more general media–movement dynamic and is tied to the notion of mediation;
- the *dance style* indicates the specific stage that a social movement is in at a particular moment in time (different times, different styles), as the specific styles relate to the forms of mediatization at work in society.

Media practices, mechanisms of mediation and processes of mediatization thus reflect the dance steps, the specific dance and the overall dance styles.

However, one issue that Mattoni and Treré do not consider in their analytical framework is the spatial dimension of these dynamics. Mobilizations and sit-ins in public squares have been highly visible aspects of most of the recent social movements, and the strategic role of these spaces in the creation of community and the articulation of strong emotional experiences has been clear. To understand the spatial dimension of social mobilization, I introduced the work of Gerbaudo in chapter 4. Gerbaudo sees *public spaces* as performatively constructed. In arguing that the leadership of social movements is a soft leadership, he unpacks how a *choreography of assembly* becomes crucial to staging a protest in a public square.

It is the choreography of what goes on in the public space that is Gerbaudo's object of study: an organization, orchestration or, better, a choreography of social relations in time and particularly in space – that of the public square (Gerbaudo 2012). He draws on the work of Foster (2003), among others, on the choreographies of protest. In her analysis of non-violent direct action, Foster argues that dance studies per se constitute a form of social theory, and offer a perspective on individual agency and collective action that gives the body a central role (Foster 2003, 397). The creative use of the body in creative actions of social mobilization gained massive momentum in uprisings such as the Occupy movement, the Indignados movement and the Vinegar revolution (figure 10).

Similar thoughts can be found in the work of Stephen Duncombe. In characterizing the actions of social movements and drawing in particular from his own activist experience of the Occupy movement in New York, Duncombe speaks of their *creative activism*, analyses their actions

Figure 10. Protests in Brasilia, June 2013

Source: Wikimedia Commons

as performances and reveals the creativity and efficiency in their efforts to mobilize and protest (Duncombe 2007; 2013)

What comes across in the way these social scientists integrate social movement theory, communication theory and social theory about mediation, activism and performance is that they all connect by using the creative arts, in particular dance, to tie together the actors and actions and their dynamics of articulating social change. However, what also comes across is that the way many social scientists and communication scholars work in this field seems to privilege the individual over structures and norms. In the case of the dance metaphors, the dance itself can follow a range of practice from individual improvisation to being completely choreographed and following normative expectations (ballet vs modern, for instance) as well as structural constraints (ownership of troupe, size of stage, etc.). Thus, power dynamics need also to be considered when analysing complex, dynamic and dramatic social change processes.

Weaving together topics and tactics

While many social movements are clear about both the tactics of the moment and their strategies over time, a dramaturgical approach to their communication and social change practices helps us connect the peak moments of insurgencies with the broader process of long-lasting struggles for social change. A dramaturgical approach opens up the possibility of integrating two analytical pathways: exploring the topics, the issue at stake and the tactics, including the strategies, for development and social change. It helps us to visualize and understand how 'topics and tactics' are spun together in a web of social dynamics and a highly contextualized narrative progression. Exploring the development topic at stake indicates a focus on the content, the narrative of development, suggesting the need to analyse the deeper-lying development challenges that a particular social movement seeks to address. It also requires close attention to the cultural, socio-economic and political contexts that determine the situation and the character of the development problem. Exploring the tactics emphasizes a focus on the 'how to' of articulating a social change process, and thus is more focused on the actions of change, the mobilizations and the orchestrations of protest. Nonetheless, it also includes the study of the often more comprehensive strategy in which the tactics are embedded.

Let us look first at the development topic from this dramaturgical perspective. Dramaturgy indicates a story being told. An implied drama curve connects the immediate dramatic highlight of a narrative – in this case the peak moments of insurgency – with the long-term process of social change. Thus, for example, the immediate anger over price rises on public transport or a general outcry about the terrible condition of public hospitals are not just incidental moments of anger, but suggest connections to deeper development challenges such as fighting for a proper public health system or a decent public transport system. The immediate narrative of protest is connected to the longer-term development agenda. This larger agenda is usually an ongoing struggle that has its ups and downs. Social movements and organizations pursue this long-term agenda over time, but with peak moments such as those experienced in recent social mobilizations. As mentioned previously, Alberto Melucci speaks to this interrelation between short-term, urgent demands and longer-term development objectives underscoring the point that movements rather constitute a permanent reality in everyday life than a provisional emergency (Melucci 1994, 116). The longue durée of social movements and the sparks and outpourings of anger seen in the peak moments of mass social mobilizations are interconnected processes. Melucci distinguishes between the periods when social movements are active and visible in the public sphere, and the latent periods when social movement activity declines and becomes less prominent (Melucci 1989).

A dramaturgical analytical framework helps us to capture the drama and dynamics of this 'permanent reality'. Most of the recent social uprisings assume this connection, without which the analysis of their activities would be extremely superficial. Why, for example, did the Indignados movement in Spain mobilize as it did and at that specific moment in time? Similar questions can be asked about, for instance, the Gezi uprising in Turkey, the Syriza movement in Greece or the Vinegar revolution in Brazil. Early and often premature explanations in the media indicated that many revolutions and insurgencies 'arise from nowhere' and 'take governments by surprise', but it is widely recognized today that each has its own particular history and trajectory, and that all are rooted in long-term struggles.

The connection between the peaks of social mobilization and longer-term development objectives does not imply that social change must be a linear process. Instead, it signals that the struggles for social justice and human rights have their ups and downs. In pursuing longer-term development objectives, something that is often seen as a game-changer in a deadlocked situation is the engagement, motivation or emotion of experience movements, which intelligent tactics help to articulate (McDonald 2006). *Logos*, in the form of long-term, well-planned, pre-tested and reasoned strategies, and *pathos*, in the form of emotional outputs around public performances and demonstrations, go hand in hand in sparking social change, a process that more often than not tends to be not linear, but circular and repetitive, with built-in redundancy – just like a good story, a fairy tale or a soap opera.

Changing opportunity structures

To capture the bigger picture and the long-term dimension, the late Charles Tilly (2008, 95ff) provided a useful theorization grounded in his in-depth studies of historical social movements in London in the eighteenth and nineteenth centuries. According to Tilly, a new form of popular politics came into being in Europe and the USA in the period 1760–1839, and widespread use of the term 'social movements' emerged (2008, 119).

Tilly connects specific performances and their repertoires to overarching claims typically based on identity, standing or programmes. He identifies three core elements of social movements that demonstrate this deep inter-connectivity. First, he understands *campaigns* as a 'sustained, coordinated series of episodes involving similar collective claims on similar or identical targets'. Campaigns are often understood in development cooperation today as shorter interventions, but Tilly understands them as long-term efforts to achieve a specific development objective (2008, 121). *Repertoires* are understood as the way participants in campaigns regularly use performance to make collective claims. These performances can range from associations and coalitions to public meetings, petition drives, street demonstrations and rallies to public statements and lobbying (2008, 121). Many of the current studies and examples already mentioned focus on developing such repertoires, typically by carrying out a number of performances to make their collective claims. The third element is the display and collective enactment of worthiness, unity, numbers and commitment (WUNC). For example, Sanz Cortell's (2015) study of PAH's anti-eviction campaign applies Tilly's display and collective enactment of WUNCs. Although Tilly's conceptual framework was developed from analyses of social movements of the past, the core principles are still valid – as Sanz Cortell's study shows. Tilly also analysed more contemporary processes of transformation in popular politics, such as Mexico's political development, to illustrate how political opportunity structures changed due to a number of factors that came together around campaigning, repertoires and WUNCs (Tilly 2008, 88).

Charles Tilly's social movement analysis helps us connect the micro-narratives of change that many individuals and movements came to the public squares with to the more profound critique of development, which remains an underlying discourse in most of these uprisings. The narratives of individuals and sub-groups, often sparked by frustrating personal experiences, are almost always connected to more generalized aspirations, be they deeper struggles for better health, education and green growth, or against corruption, environmental degradation and global warming. Often, what appeared to be a collection of highly heterogeneous movements was in fact a movement of movements, where common ground had been found around critiques of the neoliberal economic growth model that is supporting a modernization process at the expense of marginalizing groups in society. The lack of connection between governments' policies and the reality of their citizens, the distance between the political class and the people, and the lack of listening are the issues that unite.

The proliferation and transformation of media and communication infrastructures and the transforming social practices aligned with this process are challenging the dominant political science framing of social movements. From their being understood within the logic of maximizing political opportunity structures, a new analytical framework is emerging that better captures the interplay between media, power and social change. This framework is making a conceptual space for media as everyday practices, as social and cultural processes, and as actors influencing institutions in society, as Mattoni and Treré's (2014) three-level framework argues. The Belgian media scholar Bart Cammaerts (2012) has offered another inspiring contribution to this field by proposing 'mediation opportunity structures' (MOS) as a conceptual approach to the necessary contemporary incorporation of media and communication studies into the analysis of social movements and social change. He suggests MOS as a non-media-centric and situational concept that captures the dynamic interplay between structure and agency. The concept opens up opportunities for studies of mediations as cultural processes where negotiations of power occur in asymmetrical but not totalizing contexts, and where the double articulation of mediation has both a symbolic and a material dimension. With the Chilean media scholar César Jiménez-Martínez, MOS is applied to an analytical model for the study of the Vinegar revolution in Brazil and activists' opportunities to engage in social mobilization and social movements (Cammaerts and Jiménez-Martínez 2014).

Many of the contemporary examples of social movements show that the current expansion from traditional political opportunity structures, to include and even emphasize mediation opportunity structures, underscores the centrality of media practices, mediation and mediatization to the opportunities for citizens to articulate their voice and have an influence through social mobilization and collective action. We are now seeing social movement theory expand its focus to contemplate the significant role of media and communication in processes of social change. Similar communication challenges can be identified from the perspective of institutions such as NGOs, United Nations agencies and even governments communicating for social change. Communication challenges emerge when, for example, defining the aims and agendas of a movement, ensuring equity in participation, constructing coherent and joint narratives, sustaining interventions and understanding whether and how the organization or movement is engaging with its target audiences. All these challenges constitute common ground for the use of communication by both social movements and more established institutions, but the role of and opportunity for the citizen, alone or in collectivities, to act and participate differs significantly. An example of this is analysed in chapter 7, in which I unpack the communication for development and social change practice of UNICEF.

Experience movements and their archetype dramas/icons of change

One of the most significant aspects of the social uprisings of recent years has been the emotional outpouring, seen in the *condensed moments* when multitudes have assembled physically, and in the multiplicity of demands, discontent and new visions. Many words have been used to characterize the intensity of these moments: rage, outrage, desperation, insurgency, deception, but also feelings of optimism, community, hope and belief in an alternative vision for society. From the violence of the Black Blocs, a radical social movement active in the uprisings in Brazil – not to mention that of the police and the military – to creative performances in a variety of forms, emotions have taken a variety of forms and directions. One interesting point is how these experience movements have dramatized their cause in pursuit of results. As Helen Dixon, the founder of the Nicaraguan feminist movement Grupo Venancia, noted: 'It has to go through your body' (Dixon in Stenersen 2014, 204). Political action literally has to be felt in order to be real. This resonates with McDonald's emphasis on the bodily experience in his definition of social movements as experience movements (2006). I discuss this in chapter 4.

In many of the social movements of recent years, iconic experiences have been catapulted into national and global circulation, remediated as archetype dramas from those movements, often in visual form – a photograph, drawing or graphic illustration – combined with a message such as 'We are all Khaled Said.'

Crafting stories was central on many levels, and many individualized stories became iconic narratives about the specific social movements, from Mohamed Bouazizi setting himself alight in Tunisia on 17 December 2010, to the woman with the blue bra succumbing to police brutality in Cairo on 17 December 2011, or the 'lady in Red' with a white bag, the colours of the Turkish flag, sprayed with tear gas on 28 May 2013 during the Gezi uprising in an unprovoked attack. While these iconic individuals with their colours and dramatic experiences allow individual identification to flourish, they were all tied to the more collective elements of crowds mobilizing. These 'narratives of uprising' were also closely linked to the 'narratives of public protest', most notably the coming together of dissatisfied citizens in squares in Madrid, Cairo and Istanbul, or in front of buildings such as the huge sports arenas in Brazil or the Wall Street of Hong Kong. Consequently, the articulation of these narratives, combined with massive social mobilization and the integral use of social media, produced opportunities to remediate particular experiences into the infinite space of social media networks.

Creativity and the active use of all forms of media helped these narratives quickly spread far and wide. While there were a variety of reasons across the globe for these demonstrations to occur, and vast multitudes took to the streets, a common element in these processes was their struggle for visibility, of their feelings and story, along with a strong urge to pass on a message and make private opinions and feelings a public concern. These individualized dramatized narratives were often at the heart of the highly emotionally charged movements. They resonated strongly with the centrality Hannah Arendt gives to storytelling and artistic expression in her reflections on how to make the private a public concern. According to Arendt:

> Compared with the reality which comes from being seen and heard, even the greatest forces of intimate life, the passions of the heart, the thoughts of the mind, the delights of the senses, lead to an uncertain, shadowy kind of existence unless and until they are transformed, deprivatized and deindividualized, as it were, into a shape to fit them for public appearance. The most current of such transformations occurs in storytelling and generally in artistic transposition of individual experiences. (Arendt 1958, 50)

The three examples from Tunisia, Turkey and Egypt managed to achieve this, and in so doing made individual dramas the exponents of a deeper collective cause.

From social movements and social media to party politics and parliamentary power

The Indignados movement is a fascinating example of a communication movement that embodies nearly all the features described in this chapter.

First, it is a communication movement that inhabits an alternative vision of the mediascape in society and builds the capacity of its activists to engage with this vision. Second, it navigates the permanent and creative use of new and old communication technologies, embedding these new media practices solidly in everyday life and in the everyday struggle of activists. The movement is *glocal* in its scope, acting locally on global development challenges, but also engaged in transnational networks by which local activists become part of a global movement. The movement emerges bottom-up from people's lived experience of a variety of social, economic and political challenges, but is at the same time globally connected with many other activists and movements in a joint vision of a different development. The dramaturgy of the movement connects the insurgencies that lasted for only a limited time in 2011 with wider topics of development and the long-term strategy of practising citizenship and doing politics in new ways, as demonstrated by the entry of Indignados activists and movements into the party political system in Spain. Finally, it is an experience movement that has made maximum use of the emerging mediation opportunities and structures to challenge and develop civil society in Spain, breaking with the country's autonomous tradition of extra-institutional civic action and cultivating a culture of governance that has both a cultural and a systemic impact.

These features of the Indignados movement illustrate how its topics and tactics are woven into the contemporaneous emergence of new opportunity structures for pursuing social change agendas. These features drive the current social movements that are also characterized by their strong emphasis on bodily experiences, which qualifies them as experience movements. Taken together, these features and characteristics of the Indignados movement confirm the challenges facing a novel communication for social change agenda outlined in the concluding section of chapter 4. First, valuable experiences have been gained from the Indignados movement, as well as the other recent social movements and uprisings, with regard to what I call *the grammar of change*, a concept that integrates concerns about and the challenges of organizing, leading and sustaining social change processes.

They are furthermore *weaving together new spaces between the off- and online as a means of reclaiming a sense of unity and community and to carve out new possibilities of agency.* The physical public squares were crucial meeting points, but these were tied to many other places across the country where similar processes of taking to the streets occurred. The experiences that happened in these public squares articulated strong feelings of community, togetherness, aspiration and hope, confirming the centrality of the bodily experience to mobilization efforts. They connected with the precariousness felt by so many due to the financial crisis, experiences that articulated fear, uncertainty and insecurity, or what I have called elsewhere *human insecurity* (Tufte 2011, 126ff), as a kind of composite concept that aggregates many of these feelings – a state of both mental and material insecurity. The anger, insurgency, protest, dissent and critiques that were a common experience for many were, in the construction of a common space, followed by feelings of aspiration, optimism and hope.

Additionally, parts of the Indignados movement, such as the PAH movement, *built capacity and reinforced media activism as a way to strengthen the political and socio-centric agendas, as well as the media-centric agenda of what I consider to be a communication movement.* Media activism speaks to the representational side of the setting up of your own media – be it through blogs, websites, online and print newspapers, television stations, and so on – but has also been about carving out opportunities for agency through communication.

Finally, they are *formulating new narratives about a vision of development* and echoing the harsh critiques of the model of development they are experiencing in their everyday lives: poor service delivery, evictions and deteriorating urban livelihoods in marginalized neighbourhoods; environmental degradation, and an undemocratic media and corrupt political culture that favours the elite networks of power holders.

Towards a New Grammar of Change

In conclusion, this analysis has identified a number of elements of what might be called a new grammar of change: new logics of action, new actors, new narratives and new strategies to articulate them and make them heard. To explore this new grammar of change, it delved into the recent Spanish experience of social movements, but also drew on recent experiences from Brazil, Turkey, Nicaragua, Greece, Kenya and Egypt. Each experience is unique, with its own context and its own features, but there are also similarities in their communication for social change efforts through mass mobilization, and their media and communication activism to formulate and communicate visions of development and act collectively on them. Many of these movements are inherently communication movements, which have media- and communication-centric political agendas as part of their overall agenda, but at the same time are highly tech-savvy in how they use digital technologies and online networks.

Despite these new opportunities and the significant momentum in the social mobilization we have seen, a number of challenges must be faced before these communication movements can qualify as social movements. First, there is the challenge that many movements face – that of sustaining a claim-driven process, where they are able to articulate processes of making their own claims and thus become subjects that are defining and driving their own change process, rather than being invited to offer their opinions and respond to agendas set by others. Second, many face the challenge of how to position their struggle. Social movements have by definition emerged from outside of the political or parliamentary system. But should they remain there? What factors determine whether to remain outside of such systems or to seek to become part of them? What happens to the character of a movement if it decides to participate in the parliamentary system? The Spanish case was paradigmatic in the sense that it broke with thirty years of autonomy and 'outsiderness' to pursue power through party politics. Third, should social movements insist on remaining bottom-up, with all the complications this usually implies? Democracy takes time. Becoming less bottom-up, which happens with representational systems, might speed up decision-making and the implementation of new ideas, but at the expense of the participatory dimension of the change process. Fourth, and tied to the latter, many movements face the dilemma of having citizens – the activists engaged in their movements – set their goals, aims and agenda or setting up institutions to do this. Can the principles of bottom-up participation and being claim-driven, and so on, persist if institutions set the agenda?

The list of challenges can be expanded further, but the bottom line is that it begs two questions that bring us right back to square one when dealing with communication for social change. The first is about how we perceive change, and at what level we see it occurring. If we take Jorge González' efforts to articulate cibercultur@, or a culture of governance, as the foundation for any further change process, then we are talking about the fundamental building blocks of society, a grounding that emphasizes the development of a genuine culture of decision-making and of politics that is built on community-based systems of information, communication and knowledge-sharing.

The second question is about the role of media and communication in processes of social change. We have explored the social movements in some analytical depth, seeking to understand what it is that they bring to the table that is innovative or can contribute to establishing a common ground for communicative practice that the established field of communication for development and social change – the NGOs, UN agencies and even governments – can also draw on in pursuit of positive social change agendas. This question moves beyond the agenda of developing an alternative media sector to address today's development challenges and make communication, as both a means and an end, an integral part of the development debate. The discussion has thus moved far beyond the fear of being too media-centric. Rather than debating specific media institutions, texts, genres or discourses, the question becomes how to deal and work strategically with the obvious communication-centrism of today's social change processes. Social movements have displayed innovation in the dynamic interplay between media, communication and social change. The question is whether more established institutions can develop opportunities by which similar social change processes can be enhanced.

This chapter has analysed the features and characteristics of contemporary social movements and their use of media and communication. One of the fundamental issues is that social movements are contributing to the general debate about communication for social change and revealing pathways for the discourses and actions of ordinary people to be heard, cultivated and put into practice. Contemporary social movements are developing spaces that resonate with what Silverstone once called *mediapolis*, a mediated civil space which, like Hannah Arendt's visions, should be understood not as a city state with a physical location, but 'as the organization of the people as it arises out of acting and speaking together; its true space lies between people living together for this purpose' (Arendt 1958, 198). Arendt characterizes this space as a 'space of appearance', a space that does not always exist and where you do not necessarily live: 'To be deprived of it means to be deprived of reality, which humanly and politically speaking, is the same as appearance. To men the reality of the world is guaranteed by the presence of others' 1958, 199).

I now wish to take some of these discussions further in chapter 7, where I discuss the practice of communication for social change of one of the largest organizations active in the field: UNICEF.

7   Invited Spaces: Institutions Communicating for Social Change

The role of media and communication in the practice of communication for development and social change within international development cooperation is far from a neutral, technical business. Although it is often packed with technical language and discourses about refining strategies, improving effects, increasing outcomes or enhancing impact, the field of international development cooperation is composed of a complex mix of organizations with a variety of aims and objectives, and ways of working. Pradip Thomas warns us that the social change objectives suffer in some of the dynamics and processes at stake:

> The commoditization of behavior change communication has reached epidemic proportions. The accent on symptoms rather than causes has led to the normalization of short-term, project-based CSC [communication for social change] initiatives and to a perpetuation of individual-based projects abstracted from context. The obsession with results-oriented projects, outcomes, and numbers has led to a skewed understanding of what communication in social change is all about. (Thomas 2014, 17)

Far from just requiring a well-defined aim and a good communication tool box, it is a field informed by values, ideologies, power struggles and agendas that are often difficult to identify, being more implicit than explicit. I explore these underlying agendas in this chapter. First, I draw attention to the overall perceptions of development that influence the practices of communication and possibilities of agency. Second, I argue that a political economy-based analysis of the field of communication for development is crucial to understanding the possibilities and limitations of actual communication practices. Finally, and more elaborately, UNICEF, the UN agency for children, and its communication for development work (C4D, as UNICEF calls it) is described and critically assessed. UNICEF is responsible for some of the most comprehensive communication for development initiatives in the world, spanning the local, national, regional and global.

The analysis reveals some of the challenges UNICEF faces in its necessary adaptation to new civil society dynamics, digital media developments and so on. The assessment illustrates the potential for using social media to engage youth in public debate but problematizes UNICEF's ability to capture and capitalize fully on the deeper dynamics of change. The focus is on UNICEF's response to the innovations that social movements – or *communication* movements – bring to the field of communication for development.

Perceptions of Development, Practices of Communication, Possibilities of Agency

As already outlined, values, ideologies and specific policy agendas inform the practice of communication and social change. We saw that most models of communication for development are derived from the institutionalized practice of communication for development, which is again tied up with an organization's logic of thinking. Organizations tend to narrow their attention to their own singular impact, leaving aside considerations about broader, deeper and more complex questions of development and social change. Furthermore, many communication for development models assume an implicit imperative for communication for development to have predefined goals. Institutionalized communication for development is so focused on predefined goals that it does not contemplate the unintended outcomes that were not explicit in the design or in the established indicators of the planned evaluation. Third, while strategic communication as a means to reach the predefined goals allows a highly systematic approach, and thus the ability to track observable outcomes, it at the same time contains its own limitation – it has difficulties capturing synergies, off-track outcomes, intangible change processes and longer-term outcomes beyond the planned period of monitoring. Finally, and most importantly, there is a normative framing of development, which assumes a commitment to the common concerns of social justice, equity and human rights, albeit with variations. These point to the same commitment, that which Touraine has framed as a 'return of the political' (2007), articulating a pro-poor, pro-social orientation in their communicative intentions. Thus, although it has a progressive, explicitly normative socio-political agenda, the technical approach appears rigid, which often limits the capture of the socio-cultural and political dynamics that communication processes can spark.

This leads consequently to a questioning of how this tension between vision, idea and aspiration, on the one side, and the technical approach to the realization of it, on the other, translate into practice when organizations such as the UN system, NGOs and government entities seek to translate their goals into a communication practice. To answer this, let us recall that all such organizations are influenced by the game-changers identified previously as influencing the field of communication and social change. These include new media developments, the growing critique of the dominant Western and economic growth-centred development paradigm, the proliferation of civil society, and not least the emergence of a new generation of social movements. From this blend of contexts and opportunities springs a potentially highly critical stance on the neoliberal development agenda, along with an increased openness towards social change from the perspective of the subaltern and rooted in often radical participatory approaches to development. Once again, however, while the discourse of communication for social change reflects such positions, is such talk reflected in the communication for social change practice among organizations such as NGOs, UN agencies and government institutions?

Furthermore, the growing culture-centred approaches to development presented and discussed in chapter 5 have put anthropological inquiry centre stage in communication for social change. The communities in which systems of information, communication and knowledge production must be based are today networked, digital and transnational. This complexifies the enhancement of 'cultures of governance' seen in the social movement analysis in chapter 6, something which again potentially poses great difficulties for organizations marked by politicized agendas as well as time and budget constraints.

Finally, a number of significant contexts have been identified as influencing current communication for social change practices within international development cooperation, in particular the recent wave of social movements and their social-change-oriented communication practices. The analysis of these movements in chapters 4 and 6 produces food for thought for the established fields of communication for development and social change. For example, we identified some of the new narratives and visions of development that social movements emphasize: the construction of new spaces of participation and the building of capacity to reinforce media activism as a means to strengthen both political and socio-centric agendas. At a more concrete level, the social movement analysis addresses the logistics of change – the concerns and challenges linked to how to organize, lead and sustain social change processes.

While these challenges feed into the critical assessment of institutionalized communication for social change, there is another fundamental analysis that must also be addressed in order to understand its possibilities and limitations: the political economy of the field.

Towards a Political Economy Analysis of the Communication for Development 'Enterprise'

A growing number of scholars are questioning 'what communication in social change is all about' (Thomas 2014, 17). One of them is the Indian media scholar Pradip Thomas, who calls for a clearer analysis of the knowledge interests and power plays at stake in the field. He is also worried about the growing corporatization of the enterprise of communication for social change, which again is closely tied to the privatization of international development cooperation as a growing number of foundations, such as the Bill and Melinda Gates Foundation, the Bill Clinton Foundation, the Soros Foundation, the Rockefeller Foundation, the Wellcome Trust and the new Facebook Foundation become key players. The US media scholar Karin Wilkins and the Argentinian media scholar Florencia Enghel critically assess this development within international development cooperation. In analysing the framing of the Proof Campaign supported by the Bill and Melinda Gates Foundation, they argue that it serves the agenda of privatized development within a neoliberal project (Enghel and Wilkins 2012).

Florencia Enghel goes a step further by developing a framework for a political economy analysis of communication for development. Inspired by Vincent Mosco (2009) and his conceptual framework for the political economy of communication more generally, which emphasizes commodification, spatialization and structuration, Enghel suggests a way forward to explore 'DevCom' as a field of study, a professional practice and an institutional project (Enghel 2015, 12). She outlines five distinct ways in which a political economy approach to development communication could be productive:

1. It could help *move the focus beyond the narrow attention so often seen on effects* to focus instead on the social totality, which entails unpacking the synergies, tensions and contradictions that are inherently part of the outcome.
2. It could help inform a future-oriented perspective that is grounded in an *insight into the recent history and development of the field.*
3. *Changing power balances* could be exposed regarding the relation between media and information industries, on the one hand, and governments and funders, on the other.
4. *A focus on praxis* could lead, for example, to closer attention to the dynamics between academic research and practice.
5. Finally, as well as these four perspectives there is a general advantage of a

political economy approach – that it would help to map out and analyse the structures and processes in the field.

As noted, Mosco's concept of the processes of *commodification, spatialization* and *structuration* of communication (Enghel 2015, 18–19) can assist with organizing such an analysis and thus in unpacking the values, ideologies and fundamental visions and aspirations reflected in the policy and practices of specific organizations.

Videoletters

Florencia Enghel's doctoral dissertation (Enghel 2014) contributes important theoretical and empirical insights to the long-called-for critical review of this field. The qualitative study of international development communication in practice examines the use of Videoletters in Bosnia as a means of reconciling relations between people forced apart through exile or migration by the civil war. She identifies the contextual and institutional factors linked to the situated practice of international development communication and reveals the processes of mediation established among the key actors. Her case sheds light on the obstacles that challenge the design, implementation and assessment of international development communication interventions that take citizens into account as subjects of rights within a framework of global justice. It also brings to the fore issues of ethics and accountability in both the practice and the project of international development communication. Finally, Enghel's case study 'critically examines the mainstream theorization of development communication, putting forward a working theoretical framework that incorporates attention to justice under global conditions through the lens of proper distance, and to communication as an unequally distributed right and capability dependent on obligations' (Enghel 2014, 15).

Enghel emphasizes in her study that she views development communication intervention 'not as a presumably positive tool, but rather as a practice that may or may not foster justice and strengthen communication as a civic right and a capability' (2014, 15). This comprehensive qualitative study of the full process, from conception of idea to completed implementation and evaluation, is a rare study of the full 'programme cycle' that allows us insights into the complexity of such processes.

Engel's political economy approach is comprehensive and ambitious. In many ways it resonates with other contemporary critiques of the field, such as Pradip Thomas' critical reflection on the field of communication for social change. In elaborating his demands for clarity in theory, he refers to five distinct levels which should be the basis of any theory: a theory of knowledge; a specific understanding of process that feeds into practice; a knowledge of structures; a specific understanding of context; and, finally, a grappling with the flows of power (Thomas 2015, 74).

At the core of both these critiques and suggestions, we find a call for a stronger conceptual foundation in the theoretical and analytical frameworks that inform communication for development and social change, with *strong calls for attention to issues of structure, power, knowledge production, process and context*. These challenges connect well with those outlined in chapter 2, where I identified three areas that require innovations in the theory, concepts and practice of communication for development and social change. First, in order to speak of social change in any depth and tackle structural constraints, socio-economic conditions or human rights will necessarily foster a stronger political perspective, something I explore in the case of UNICEF where an emerging recognition of the role of social movements in contemporary development is shaping new visions of development and subsequent policy agendas. Second, in unpacking the relations between culture, agency and social change, a culture-centred approach is essential to successful practice. This requires a close analysis and understanding of power relations, social hierarchies and opportunities for participation. Third, I argue for the centrality of 'the mediatic', integrating a focus on media as structure and media as content with communication processes.

A common concern of many critical communication for development scholars today is that the field needs to take a step back to review critically its research, its practice and, as Enghel suggests, the institutional project. This will enable us to understand the complex and dynamic relations between communication processes, media and development structures, power dynamics, the way knowledge is produced and the contexts that influence these processes. A stronger critical review of both theory and practice within the institutionalized field of communication for social change is key to unpacking these many elements.

Confluence of discourses

Pradip Thomas' worry about corporatization of communication for social change expands more broadly into concern about the NGO world and the impact of the neoliberal discourse on NGOs in general: 'NGOs, for the most part, tend to replicate the logic of neo-liberalism and participation therefore tends to become the means for extending the project of neo-liberalism through enabling people to participate in a variety of forms of "compassionate capitalism'" (Thomas 2015, 73). He is paraphrasing the Slovenian sociologist and philosopher Slavoj Žižek and his critique of the 'caring capitalists' who buy into 'the goodness encapsulated in a cup of coffee bought from Starbucks', where the corporate strategy is based on principles of Fair Trade and a part of the profits go to starving children in Uganda.

Although Thomas generalizes about NGOs replicating the logic of neo-liberalism, his claims raise a series of concrete questions about the practice of communication for development. Do development organizations generally serve to replicate the logic of neoliberalism? Or is it mainly the private actors in development cooperation that Wilkins and Engel spoke about that serve such an agenda? Are the latter mainly carrying out project-based communication for social change initiatives, while ignoring broader programmatic objectives? Is there therefore a perpetuation of individual-based projects abstracted from context? Have they normalized the 'short-term' as the main scope of their work? What about the long-term development agendas? Are the organizations active in international development cooperation mainly dealing with symptoms and not with the underlying causes of the problems being dealt with?

I have written about the *perverse confluence of discourses in development*, where a growing discursive consensus seems to be hiding conflicts of interest, ideology and values. However, in identifying the three generations of communication for development (see figure 1 in chapter 1), I argue that at least three perceptions coexist. This highlights the fact that rather than being able to draw a uniform conclusion about organizational practices of communication for development, we most often find practice that de facto reflects the confluence of discourses. We will see an example of this in the case study on UNICEF that follows.

The Case of UNICEF

UNICEF is a big player in the field of communication for development. It is a large UN agency with a government-sanctioned international mandate, with all that entails for its complex organizational set-up – a headquarters in New York, seven regional offices, 130 country offices and approximately 300 communication officers who work either full time or part time with communication for development. UNICEF is an intergovernmental agency, with thirty-six government representatives on its governing board. Funding comes primarily, but not exclusively, from bilateral donors.

UNICEF is active in the field of communication for development and social change on many levels and in many ways. It offers C4D capacity-building both internally to its many C4D officers and externally to stakeholders and partners. UNICEF collaborates with bilateral donor agencies, universities, other UN agencies, private companies and a number of other stakeholders to produce new knowledge and research, and to document their interventions, to develop the modules for much of its capacity-building activities and, not least, in collaborations at the country level with a wide gamut of stakeholders in developing C4D interventions. The organization has a complex set-up with many different entry points for exploring and really understanding its work. The place where African youth or children would meet UNICEF is primarily in the context of UNICEF-supported campaigns at the country level, that is, in the areas of HIV/AIDS prevention, Ebola mitigation and prevention, child survival, and hygiene and sanitation. One current successful example is the case of U-Report, a social media platform developed by UNICEF Uganda, which crowd-sources the voices and opinions of youth on a variety of topics. As their main slogan states: 'voice matters'. From the inception of the programme in Uganda to November 2016, U-Report had spread to thirty-one countries.

UNICEF global strategy: adapting to a changing world?

UNICEF's global work on child health is guided by the Convention on the Rights of the Child, a key policy document adopted in 1989 that subsequently became the most rapidly and widely ratified human rights treaty in the world. Furthermore, the Sustainable Development Goals, adopted by the UN General Assembly in September 2015, constitute the most important reference for how a UN agency must approach development in broad terms. With regard to policy documents on communication, there have been a large number of strategies that have informed the work of UNICEF over the years. However, UNICEF's executive director, Anthony Lake, approved an important policy document in August 2014. *Communicate to Advocate for Every Child: UNICEF's Global Communication and Public Advocacy Strategy, 2014–2017* was developed by the Division of Communication (DOC) in collaboration with internal task forces and working groups, and based on comprehensive internal consultation processes. The strategy speaks directly to a lot of the new contextual factors influencing the field of communication for development, and provides an interesting peek into the nuts and bolts of a large global communication for development player such as UNICEF.

In the document, UNICEF argues the need for *a new strategy and a new communication model* that will enable it to work better 'to support shifts in public policy, fuel social engagement, and increase private and public resources for children' (UNICEF 2014, 4). UNICEF acknowledges that this is fuelled by changes in technology and shifts in power, processes that are transforming the way people interact with each other. This resonates with some of the game-changers for communication for development identified in chapter 1, such as the significant developments in civil society and the rapid developments in media and technology. This is resulting in an emerging situation where 'The lines between communication and advocacy are blurring, and citizen-sparked campaigns fuelled by digital media are beginning to drive social movements and achieve political change' (UNICEF 2014, 5). UNICEF is obviously aware that it needs not only to react to these developments but also to be ahead of them. Its current thinking and novel strategic developments contemplate this. This further informs its overall goals of supporting shifts in public policy, fuelling social engagement and increasing private and public resources for children (UNICEF 2014, 4). This overall goal is again translated into three core organizational objectives: to be a leading *voice* for – and with – children; to *reach* 1 billion people around the world; and, finally, to *engage* 50 million people to take action for children (UNICEF 2014, 9–10).

To take up these challenges of voice, reach and engagement, UNICEF argues for a shift in its current communication model, aiming by 2017 to have shifted and improved its way of working to be as outlined in the right-hand side of the model in table 2.

What UNICEF presents in its *Global Communication and Public Advocacy Strategy* signals some important strategic shifts in how it anticipates it should work with communication. For example, the *Strategy* flags the need for compelling storytelling rather than primarily informing; it emphasizes an action orientation, fuelling social engagement rather than mere information dissemination. This speaks to a focus on advocacy communication driving change by moving people to act. Rather than being in the business of knowledge brokering the strategy speaks about 'knowledge leadership'.

Part of UNICEF's shift in strategy also lies in the more explicitly *glocal approach*. This signals a stronger recognition of the dynamic relationship between on-the-ground implementation of activities and global objectives. There is a clear advocacy aspect in UNICEF's plea for glocal approaches whereby local efforts connect with global children's issues: 'Real engagement drives local action – and the link to global movements can amplify the reach and impact of national initiatives' (UNICEF 2014, 10)

In order to make it work, the new strategy requires a stronger internal

Table 2. Shift in current communication model

From working to change policies	To also working to change behaviours, social attitudes and beliefs
From primarily targeting governments, corporates and influencers . . .	To also powerfully communicating with the broad general public
From primarily informing . . .	To inspiring by telling compelling stories
From telling . . .	To also listening, conversing and crowdsourcing (two-way communication)
From disseminating information . . .	To communicating to advocate, to drive change and to move people to act
From focusing mainly on print media . . .	To fully developing content for print, digital, mobile and broadcast media
From knowledge brokering . . .	To knowledge leadership
From press releases . . .	To integrated communication strategies (which include traditional communication)
From 'everything' . . .	To selected strategic priorities, communicated and supported across the organization
From partnership initiatives . . .	To a broader fueling of social engagement

Source: UNICEF (2014, 6)

alignment between divisions and offices in UNICEF that have poor track records of working together: on one side is the DOC, which usually works on communication and public advocacy; on the other side, the C4D Office traditionally works on programme communication. It will, for example, entail leveraging common digital platforms and tools through which both the DOC and the C4D teams will help drive greater citizen and youth engagement.

Recognizing the proliferation of interactive technologies and dialogic communication practices, UNICEF is well aware that it must engage by 'listening and crowd-sourcing stories and ideas' (2014, 10). However, in its own language, UNICEF remains focused on reach and impact, seen in examples such as: 'better understand the local landscape and tailor strategies to specific contexts'; 'we must be faster, sharper and more compelling in our headlines and core messaging'; and 'to maximize our reach and impact, DOC will invest more effort in convening new partnerships' (UNICEF 2014, 10). Having said that, UNICEF also mentions social movements, community-based organizations and grassroots advocacy networks as partners to work more closely with. Thus, it seems to be focused on engaging in proactive communication, but also on ensuring that its 'objectivity and non-political approach' persist and deepen the organization's credibility (2014, 10)

To achieve these shifts will require the fostering of a new organizational culture in UNICEF. Although the model presented here is not completely concrete, it does point towards a change in organizational culture and in communicative practice. It suggests an organizational culture where these new opportunities are embraced, where the organization, as it recognizes in its own policy document, 'cedes total control of the message, questions the status quo and encourages debate and dialogue, both externally and internally' (UNICEF 2014, 11). This goes against the systemic logic of keeping full control of communication initiatives. The increased risk-taking will also require risk management, for example in humanitarian advocacy, where UNICEF recognizes the need to 'balance the risks and values associated with communicating publicly in politically charged situations' (2014, 12).

Overall, what we see in UNICEF's strategy signals a series of *ambivalences*. On the one hand, the strategy is embedded in overall discourses and policies of 'efficiency and effectiveness' in its work. On the other hand, UNICEF is with this discourse seeking a way to navigate a new reality of interactive technologies, a growing and dynamic civil society, and rapid mobilization and circulation of opinions, to which UNICEF must adapt. In so doing, it highlights that it is surrendering some established communicative practices, such as the narrow control of messages. In the language of this policy document, UNICEF considers the required changes to be 'a risk' more than an opportunity – a risk to its credibility and brand as a non-political and objective organization. However, it also acknowledges the need to embrace risk-taking (2014, 11).

In navigating this sea of ambivalence, there is some tension in the way UNICEF strives to measure success. On the one hand, it seeks the clear and measurable indicators imposed by donor demands and international standards. At the same time, however, it acknowledges all the complexities imposed by a new social, mediatic and technological situation. The contextual situation poses difficulties for UNICEF's monitoring and evaluation system, for its ability to capture the depth and complexity of change, and for the role its communication initiatives play. In the advocacy strategy UNICEF mentions the outcomes it wants to measure: voice, reach, engagement and brand. However, the suggested indicators appear narrow and superficial, particularly with regard to evaluating voice and citizen engagement.

What comes through when reviewing UNICEF's global policy documents and strategies as they pertain to communication for development is willingness, but also a struggle to adapt to new contexts and new communication dynamics, where the fundamental communication model in society has moved far beyond a monologic and much closer to a dialogic communication model. It is a situation in which a global organization with a complex organizational set-up is bound to be challenged. The communicative dynamics, combined with many new stakeholders and fast-moving CSOs, make the context UNICEF operates in extremely challenging, and they obviously require more fundamental changes to the global organization. The following sections assess how far an innovative and creative initiative at the country and regional levels is succeeding in pushing UNICEF in this new direction.

U-Report: voices matter

Where do the Ugandan youth meet UNICEF-supported and driven C4D initiatives? Well, if you – like 65 per cent of the adult Ugandan population – own a mobile phone, you can easily connect with a UNICEF C4D initiative, U-Report (Pew Research Center 2015). U-Report is one of UNICEF's major successes with regard to using social media platforms to pursue its development objectives. It consists of a media platform from where those youth who register – known as U-Reporters – are enabled to receive and respond to weekly short message service (SMS) questions about Ugandan social development issues.

They can also send SMS messages on specific matters that concern them, all free of charge. If you click in on UNICEF Uganda's home page you can find your way to the U-Report page and to a video about U-Report. It explains the principles of U-Report and provides video testimonials from young people expressing their satisfaction with being U-Reporters and having the opportunity for their voice to be heard. It also delivers strong encouragement through these testimonials: 'it is important you join U-Report', 'you should be active', 'express your views in the polls'; 'your voice matters' (http://www. ureport.ug/about). As such, U-Report treads a fine line between the objectives of the global advocacy strategy: voice, reach and engagement.

UNICEF set up the platform in collaboration with a number of local partners. This provided a way to source questions and feed the answers received back into local organizations and public offices. Thus, in some cases the partnership is with the Ministry of Health; in others it is with the Girls' Education Movement (GEM), the Scouts or organizations working with HIV prevention. The responses are anonymized, and information and opinions are sourced on issues such as youth unemployment, school dropout rates, child abuse and poverty. Almost 300,000 youth (298,570 as of 21 September 2015), with an average age of 24 years, 36 per cent female and 64 per cent male, are registered as U-Reporters, also known as 'members' on the U-Report Uganda portal. The number of SMS responses to the weekly polls varies, but those I found ranged between 700 and 10,000. The results are fed back to public and private sector organizations and also published as poll results on radio and television or in print. As such, they feed into a national conversation and public debate.

One example of a poll is the one that was SMSed on 21 September 2015:

> What is 1 thing U wld like ur leaders 2 do 4 children? A)End Violence b)End Poverty c)Fight Disease d)End War e)Improve Education f)End Inequality g)other

Within a week, 9,822 'members' had responded, corresponding to a 3.3 per cent response rate. That figure is rather high compared to many of the previous results. Of those who responded, the options that received the largest response were:

Improve Education: 36.5%
End Violence: 17.0 %
Fight Disease: 14.9%
End Poverty: 13.6%

Thus, 36.5 per cent, or 3,585 young Ugandans, pinpointed that improving education was the one thing that Ugandan leaders should 'do for children'. If the campaign strategy of U-Report runs true to form, we will see this topic being discussed on radio programmes and cited in a number of newspaper articles, thereby helping to bring it into the public sphere.

If we correlate the issues generated from the poll with the programmatic priorities on UNICEF Uganda's country programme as well as the East and Southern Africa Regional Priorities of UNICEF, we will find that they converge well. These findings reinforce UNICEF's programmatic focus on questions of, for example, 'education quality and learning outcomes', 'social protection interventions to reduce child poverty and other vulnerabilities' and 'enabling children to survive and thrive' (UNICEF 2014). As such, this is a useful example of what UNICEF considers a successful programme. However, as I unpack in what follows, challenges remain in assessing the ability of such a programme to enhance voice and citizen engagement.

From the beginning of U-Report in Uganda in May 2011 up to November 2016 it had spread to thirty-one countries, including Zambia, Nigeria, Liberia and Chile (figure 11). While the Scouts led the initiative in Uganda, working on a broad pallet of youth-related issues, U-Report in Zambia has focused on offering youth HIV counselling, which has resulted in increasing the likelihood of going for a test by 30 per cent. In Liberia, the U-Reporters were urgently organized in November 2014 and came to serve as a rapid communication system providing information in the midst of the humanitarian crisis linked to Ebola,

Figure 11. U-Report Zambia

Source: © UNICEF/Zambia

delivering information more quickly and to areas that were difficult to reach in other ways. Nigeria for its part is the country with most registered U-Reporters, almost 500,000 or almost half the global number of 1 million reached in July of 2015 (http://www.unicefstories.org/2015/07/10/unicefs-u-report-reaches-1-million-registered-users-worldwide).

U-Report is arguably one of the most popular social media platforms for youth in sub-Saharan Africa, and even beyond. Its growth and success speak to the many opportunities that a new media environment is increasingly making possible even in low-income developing nations – that of using mobile phones as an integral technology and communication system to pursue a development agenda. U-Report speaks to a dynamic interplay between mobile telephony and the general media environment, articulating stories and coverage on the radio and television, and in print. Communication synergies are being articulated and working.

Furthermore, with U-Report, an articulation of common agendas is seen between UNICEF and both governmental and non-governmental organizations and movements. Advocacy gains on educational legislation as well as modification of health behaviours have been flagged as outcomes. In addition, 'system export' from one UNICEF office to another seems to be happening quite fast, with more than thirty countries reached in about five years of existence, signalling one of the benefits of being a global organization.

Together, this shows UNICEF succeeding in using social media plat-forms for development purposes, building on partnerships with civil society and government, and managing to replicate the model in more countries. Replication is an important element for a global organization such as UNICEF. It does, however, also raise questions about the actual outcomes and, as is discussed next, whether such initiatives are successful in their intention to make all voices count.

Whose voice matters? Questions of impact

When engaging with communication for development many of the key players, large multilateral institutions such as UNICEF as well as a long series of NGOs such as ADRA in Malawi, Femina in Tanzania, Soul City in South Africa and many others, put a great deal of emphasis on visibility, voice, empowerment and participation. However, as already mentioned, there is in the global contemporary development discourse an overwhelm-ing consensus on this jargon. I have in chapter 3 and elsewhere (Tufte 2014a) spoken about the perverse confluence around this discourse of participation and empowerment, and criticized how it obscures the genuine and concrete differences in ideology, values and orientation that of course exist across the field of development cooperation. We therefore need to produce grounded and documented studies of the aims and objectives that different communication initiatives have, and what they de facto articulate.

A major point of inquiry emerges from U-Report. The question is: to what extent does the single mobile phone user feel seen, heard and ulti-mately empowered to make informed decisions in life and to take action accordingly? What feeling is de facto associated with the ability to answer a weekly poll? How does taking on the role of a U-Reporter relate to issues of identity and feelings of community? When becoming a U-Reporter, are you then performing the role of a citizen journalist, an opinion leader or a media activist? Are these categories possibly overemphasizing the role, respon-sibility and aspirations of the individual reporter? What forms of digital networking and online community-building emerge in practice? And how does this influence offline communities? Does it enhance the extension, reinforcement and development of social networks? Ultimately, the ques-tion to be asked is: can sustained social change be attributed to U-Report?

Answering such questions about outcome and impact cries out for a far deeper analysis than organizations like UNICEF carry out. Identifying and understanding these change processes would require analysis of the cultural contexts, the sense-making processes, and the issues of identity formation, opinion leadership, role modelling, community-building and, above all, sustained change. Without carrying out this sort of analysis, the processes of participation, citizen engagement and enhancement of empowerment will be very difficult to assess.

Nonetheless, in speaking about U-Report, the representative of UNICEF to Uganda, Sharad Sapra, argues that: 'U-report offers a cost-effective, easy-to-implement means of assuring accountability by tapping community knowledge to learn the local and personal impact of policy and development schemes, health interventions and outbreaks . . . It is a "killer app" for communication toward achieving equitable outcomes for children and their families' (http://www.unicef.org/infobycountry/uganda_62001. html). UNICEF thus emphasizes the potential for 'assuring accountability', 'achieving equitable outcomes' and using this 'killer app' to communicate the opinion of youth back to UNICEF, their partners and governments. It comes through loud and clear on UNICEF's website that this discourse becomes a way in which UNICEF Uganda emphasizes that 'voice matters'. The question, however, remains: whose voice is it that matters? And for whom does it matter? Many of the claims of accountability, equitable outcomes and communicating opinions are just put forward by the organization itself and difficult to document in any depth. In reality, no evidence is put forward to establish a causal relation between the growing number of U-Reporters and the development outcomes of UNICEFs programme. This illustrates some of the difficulties inherent in trying to construct an argument of causality. The challenges associated with unpacking the complex relation between technology and social change include:

- **defining membership**. What are you a 'member' of when you sign up as a U-Reporter? Are you, for example, a U-Reporter when you receive a weekly SMS and answer predefined questions? What rights follow on from the membership title? Can you influence what questions need to be asked? And can you influence the organizations running campaign initiatives? There are thus unresolved issues around use of language and discursive strategies.
- **ability of organizations to 'listen'**. When UNICEF calls its programme 'Voice Matters', it seems to signal the importance of the organization listening to these voices. But what depth of listening lies in having 3 per cent of your 'members' answer yes or no to a predefined question? And what consequences are there for the organization arising from the demands articulated? There seems to be a lack of clarity on the purpose statistics can serve. Yes or no answers from a small group of a country's youth are hardly the voice of youth.

- **whose voice counts**. Then there is the issue of volume: is a 3.3 per cent response rate a success? The poll goes out every week, so it might be unfair to expect constantly high responses. However, what minimum is acceptable, and to whom? What is the profile of those who respond? Can patterns of response be identified, and are the respondents 'the usual suspects'? Furthermore, what is the profile of those who do not answer? Who has the power to influence what has the potential to become a so-called national conversation? The poll questions are formulated by a group of people from the organizations that UNICEF collaborates with. Is that satisfactory? Is it participatory? Is it citizen-driven? It seems *not* to be the ideal set-up to make all voices count, but it is an illustrative example of how a big organization seeking large-scale impact works with these issues.
- **how SMSs link with social change**. There is one final issue regarding the synergies that this online communication platform and the SMS interaction spark. What activities and what debates are de facto sparked? If the intervention further enhances the development agendas of UNICEF and its partners, how does it do so? UNICEF's support to U-Report Uganda is linked to a partnership of nine organizations that together decide, for example, what questions to ask in the polls. To capture all the ways in which communication initiatives lead to outcomes – such as public debate, changes in social norms, increased feelings of empowerment, enhanced community leadership and concrete calls for action – would require designs of comprehensive monitoring and evaluation. This seems not to have been considered in UNICEF's current monitoring and evaluation strategy.

We can conclude that there are a number of systemic limitations in the ways of speaking about the beneficiaries of the projects and in the ways of institutionally presenting outcomes. Although we here are dealing with spaces of participation that are controlled narrowly by the organization funding and implementing the project, what is captured by the monitoring and evaluation strategies could benefit from moving beyond the narrowly defined and observable types of outcomes that are currently used. To comply with a more culture-centred approach and with the multiple dimensions of a mediatic orientation would require assessing both the media and the communication structures achieved with U-Reporter, the actual content produced and the social and communication practices they articulate. Thus, the assessments of U-Reporter could benefit from a broader, more holistic and more comprehensive conceptualization of their monitoring and evaluation policy. The aspirations are there in the communication model UNICEF proposes in the policy, but the transformation of communication strategies on the ground requires further elaboration.

One novel issue yet to be dealt with across UNICEF C4D practice is a key point in the UNICEF *Global Communication and Public Advocacy Strategy*: that of fuelling social engagement. This is dealt with in the next section, where UNICEF, among a growing number of organizations, has taken a strong interest in social movements.

Institutions and their growing orientation to social movements

It can seem ironic and even contradictory to their way of working, but in recent years large international development organizations such as UNICEF have taken the discourse of social movements and in a variety of ways made it theirs. Médecins Sans Frontières (MSF) is among a growing number of large international NGOs to consider itself a movement (*New York Times* 2014). Others include ActionAid, which increasingly works with its activist networks on sparking social movements, and national NGOs, such as Femina in Tanzania, which considers itself to be a social movement in the way it works and communicates with the youth of Tanzania (Tufte 2014a) In parallel with this global trend, senior management in UNICEF have held seminars and written reports about how they can collaborate with and learn from social movements about 'fostering, influencing and leveraging social change for children through local community empowerment' (UNICEF SLDP 2014, 3).

In 2014 UNICEF's Senior Leadership Development Programme (SLDP) undertook a process to explore what lessons could be learned from the way social movements work with communication and social mobilization. On the basis of recommendations from the Cardoso Panel to the UN General Assembly in 2004, UNICEF has acknowledged that civil society is as much a part of today's global governance as governments. Therefore, a constructive engagement with CSOs is 'a necessity for the United Nations, not an option' (Cardoso Panel 2004). Social movements have gained prominence and space as core actors within civil society. Civic engagement and accountability issues are expanding on the global development agenda, something to which social movements have contributed significantly. UNICEF recognizes this and has therefore initiated a process to draw lessons from existing social movements. It conducted a literature review on social movements (UNICEF SLDP 2014, 4–5), explored five key social movements working with children and carried out in-depth interviews with thirty-one key informants, twenty from within and eleven from outside UNICEF. The whole process was guided by four research questions:

1. To what extent should UNICEF engage with social movements?
2. What are the risks for UNICEF when engaging with social movements?
3. How should UNICEF engage with social movements?
4. What should UNICEF do to address potential risks, to overcome internal barriers and to ensure its engagement with social movements is strategic and effective?

This process was preceded by the policy papers UNICEF 3.0 and 4.0. In UNICEF 3.0 the organization recognizes that 'given their informal structure, organic, bottom-up origins, and the individual-driven nature of their mandates, engaging social movements constitutes relatively uncharted territory for UNICEF' (UNICEF SLDP 2014, 9), and in UNICEF 4.0 it asks: 'Is it feasible to create social movements, given the fact that by definition they are created by the users and groups of affected people rather than institutions?' The whole exercise and the preceding policy papers were driven by UNICEF's fundamental and urgent need to position itself as 'fit for purpose', based on a more sophisticated understanding and use of digital media. UNICEF needed to improve its ability to listen to and understand trends at the grassroots level.

UNICEF therefore analysed five social movements working with children's issues: (1) Brazil's Social Movement for Children's Rights; (2) Youth@ COP, the International Youth Climate Movement at the annual global climate change conferences; (3) the V-Day movement on violence against women and girls; (4) Treatment Action Campaign for access to anti-retroviral treatment in South Africa; and (5) the 'Malala' campaign for girls' education. From this analysis UNICEF identified seven key criteria for their success. Their successes were seen to be based on: (1) having reformist or incremental goals rather than seeking radical change; (2) using social media both to mobilize people and to coordinate activities; (3) having the ability to mobilize many people, including 'unlike-minded people'; (4) conducting a rigorous initial power analysis; (5) having a strong leadership; (6) being effective in mobilizing political leaders; but also (7) challenging the system in coordination with power holders (UNICEF SLDP 2014, 6–7). These criteria for success are somewhat different from those found in chapters 4 and 6, where I analysed features of the communicative practice of contemporary social movements. Generally, when compared to what was seen in most of the social movements discussed in the previous chapters, the features characterizing the social movements selected by UNICEF attribute their successes to closer relations with the established system of power holders and their institutions. Another feature was having strong leadership, an issue most of the post-Arab Spring social movements contested. They are also rigorous in conducting power analyses and, last but not least, they explicitly pursue reformist goals.

It therefore becomes very clear that we cannot generalize about social movements, their social change objectives, their perceptions of media and technology, or their choice of communication and other strategies. Rather, we can speak of a multiplicity of movements and organizations all communicating for social change, but radically different in aims and objectives, in communication strategies and in their perceptions of media, technology and communication processes. As a UN agency collaborating with governments and civil society across the globe, UNICEF seems open to being inspired by and collaborating with social movements, but mainly those that have reformist agendas. The pragmatism of UNICEF vis-à-vis how to go about collaborating with social movements comes across even more clearly in what follows.

Risk or opportunity?

Among the interviewees in UNICEF's case study, there was a consensus that UNICEF itself should *not* start or instigate social movements. There was also clear support for it empowering activists and strengthening their technical and organizational capacities as long as they complied with UNICEF goals. Engaging in this manner comes with what UNICEF calls 'risks', in the sense of losing control not only of the messages it wishes to disseminate, but equally of the process whereby information spreads. As illustrated earlier, this reveals ambivalence towards the potential for collaborating with social movements that creatively and dynamically use social media platforms, and at the same time a concern about spreading accurate factual information. This ambivalence reflects a contradiction between the goals expected from information dissemination, on the one hand, and supporting processes of social change communication that, by definition, are social processes that nobody can really control, on the other. Another 'risk' according to UNICEF lay in undermining its often important normative role, or losing legitimacy and credibility if it backed social movements that are unable to improve a situation (UNICEF SLDP 2014, 7).

Despite the ambivalence and risks, UNICEF is seemingly willing to adapt to the changing context in which a series of game-changers can influence the way social change processes occur. A more courageous UNICEF can be seen in the sense that it is taking some of these risks. The study concluded by outlining three recommendations that have not yet been implemented by UNICEF, but nonetheless reflect its reorientation as seen in the *Global*

Communication and Public Advocacy Strategy and in the C4D strategy. The three pillars of recommendations are related to their core principles of voice, reach and engagement:

1. taking the pulse: understanding the context, listening and fostering inclusive dialogue;
2. fuelling engagement through knowledge sharing and strategic alliances; and
3. being fit for purpose: a new toolkit and framework on engagement with social movements.

They point towards a shift in strategic focus, from 'having the solutions' to truly understanding the dynamics of social change. This further entails a shift to relinquishing control and fostering rather than dominating the dialogue. Finally, they point to partnering with organizations that, as with U-Report, possibly 'work at the edges', something that would enable UNICEF to gain new perspectives and form new development pathways to reaching the underrepresented. However, despite these recommended shifts, they still have in common that they are working on the assumption that UNICEF articulates 'invited spaces' and improved representation in public space and spheres. Yet it is also a step further in opening a path for UNICEF to venture down, a pathway where even large organizations might find more dynamic and inclusive ways to work with the social demands that are articulated by citizens from below.

Navigating novel terrains in communication for development and social change

Having now reviewed the case of UNICEF, what can be said about UNICEF's perception of development and social change, its practice of communication and, finally, the possibilities for agency that exist for its constituency – the children of the world?

As I unpacked the case study by reviewing UNICEF's own policy and working documents, I got a sense of how it seeks to operationalize development and communication for development at both the global and the national levels. For example, the 2014 *Global Communication and Public Advocacy Strategy* offered a fairly substantial and concrete view of UNICEF's path ahead, in a world with a strengthened civil society and a novel communications environment. That strategy, supplemented by many others, such as the UNICEF 3.0 and UNICEF 4.0 policy documents, and the C4D Strategic Vision and Policy Framework, reaffirm UNICEF's commitment to reach many children, give them voice and mobilize many people to action, while partnering with all relevant stakeholders to achieve such objectives. However, it has also become clear that collaborating with social movements constitutes quite a challenge to the organizational practice of UNICEF.

Being a multilateral UN agency informs the way the organization works; for example, how to go about using interactive social media platforms to communicate dialogically and dynamically with citizens that speak right back, but also how to go about collaborating with a growing number of social movements. UNICEF interprets these new communication mechanisms and such collaborations as both risks and opportunities. While clearly seeking to maintain control, by offering invited spaces for a conversation that is institutionally driven, moderated and controlled, UNICEF also embraces citizens' need to claim their own voice and the space to articulate it.

UNICEF's communication practice is informed by it being a complex global organization that is experiencing a growing demand for C4D both in the UN system and beyond. UNICEF has in recent years consolidated and further developed its position as the leading UN agency in C4D, thus expanding its communication practice substantially. On the one hand, UNICEF has strengthened its C4D Headquarters Section, offering global leadership and guidance not only to UNICEF worldwide but also beyond to the global C4D community. In addition to the C4D team in New York, seven regional C4D advisers/specialists are now in place working around the world, each responsible for mainstreaming C4D issues into national and regional programming. Finally, the vast majority of staff working with C4D does so at the national level, with C4D officers in 130 country offices across the world.

Highly specific development challenges emerged from the recent humanitarian crises linked to the Zika and Ebola outbreaks, the Nepal earthquake and the Yemen conflict, where UNICEF has had important roles to play. For example, in the Ebola responses in West Africa UNICEF was acknowledged as the UN lead on the social mobilization and community engagement component of the Accra Response Strategy organized by UNMEER (UN Mission for Ebola Emergency Response).

However, these efforts require substantial capacity-building, empowering the organization per se to be able to work competently with communication for development, while facing both the long-term development challenges and the humanitarian crises that call for very different forms of communication practice. To enhance this capacity-building effort led by C4D Headquarters, UNICEF in 2014 signed Long Term Arrangements for Services (LTAS) with twenty-six institutions worldwide, many of them universities and research institutions with expertise across six categories, including C4D research and analysis, C4D planning and strategy development, and C4D curriculum and capacity development. A number of other partnerships were also established to leverage additional funding and in-kind resources. When it comes to assessing the communication for development practice of UNICEF, what can be said is that it is informed strongly by institutional mandates, with all the systemic possibilities and limitations, as well as the programmatic obstacles and opportunities, that this entails.

In conclusion, with regard to the possibilities for agency, voice and empowerment among children and youth across the world, the case offered of U-Report in Uganda and beyond was an example of some of the constraints that children and youth meet. On the one hand, it illustrates the many new opportunities that social media and partnerships with media and civil society offer and that UNICEF capitalize on to push their agendas. On the other hand, it also reveals how difficult it is for large organizations such as UNICEF really to address questions of voice and empowerment. Consequently, while Pradip Thomas has warned us about the commoditization of behaviour change communication, and Mohan Dutta has flagged the role of ideology and values in problem definition, the selection of strategies, the implementation of tactics and the evaluation of results, the UNICEF case has offered a deeper insight into the complexity of communication for social change, and the challenges in ensuring that every voice matters in development. The UNICEF case illustrates that despite the complexities of this global organization, influenced by changing values, power plays and institutional inertia, the organization remains open and seeks to push boundaries and set new standards in communicating for social change in a way that opens up rather than closes down opportunities for citizens to speak up.

8 Towards a New Paradigm and Praxis in Communication and Social Change

Introduction

This book is a call for a new paradigm and praxis in communication for social change. It argues that such communication must be rooted in a more inclusive, people-centred and radically participatory development paradigm. Such a paradigm would cater not only to the dialogic opportunities of new media and developments in communication but also to the need for institutions – governments, CSOs and international development agencies alike – to be in sync with their constituencies. The unfolding argument has been that communication initiatives that are able to communicate social change agendas successfully require a strong embeddedness within, participation by and buy-in from the relevant constituencies. As Tim Markham said at a conference in Copenhagen in October 2015, paraphrasing Charles Taylor: 'If you want to create a new social world, the last thing to do is to be prescriptive and describe how agency should be.'

Based solidly on norms of social justice and human rights, the proposed approach to communication supports and promotes the development of a culture of governance. All this is enhanced by supporting systems of information, communication and knowledge production that are locally rooted, bottom-up in their processes and framed in the glocal reality and political economy of their environments.

Challenging these norms, principles and good intentions in communication and social change are two fundamental problems: the deep crisis of development that the world is currently experiencing and the capacity of citizens not just to aspire but to take action. The crisis of development goes beyond the challenges of climate change, refugee crises or financial crises. From a communication and social change perspective, it manifests itself as a crisis of representation. Furthermore, and contrary to the opportunities the new media developments invite, we are also seeing a critical shrinking of the public space for deliberation, and the exclusion of participation and the experience of ordinary citizens from the general public debate.

As unpacked throughout this book, this crisis of development constitutes a crisis of representation of the ordinary citizen, and the marginalized citizen in particular. It manifests itself as a communicative disconnect and imbalance between the voices, aspirations and hopes of groups of citizens that feel marginalized and unrepresented, on the one side, and the de facto communicative interventions of governments, agencies and civil society, on the other. This disconnect and imbalance begs the question: to what extent are today's representational democracies – and their communicative practices in particular – in sync with their constituencies? Second, and equally important, the crisis of representation is complemented by the major challenge of enhancing the capacities and power of citizens. It is the challenge Arjun Appadurai has termed 'the capacity to aspire' (Appadurai 2004; Stade 2016). This is about the effort to capture not only the unevenly distributed material and measurable assets in people's lives, such as income and education, but also their hopes and visions of the future. To this we must add, as communication scholars and practitioners, the capacity to intervene with communicative practices that influence their lives. This capacity to aspire therefore has a material dimension to it; but equally, and often omitted, it is about the capacity to imagine another future.

Here, I briefly reassess the crises of development and representation as well as the challenge of enhancing the capacity to aspire. I also discuss some of the lines of research and practice that will hopefully strengthen an approach to communication and social change that empowers individuals and collectives to engage and take action for social change. First, I reflect on the crisis of development by briefly revisiting Boaventura de Sousa Santos' call for an epistemology of the South and a 'sociology of emergence'. Second, I discuss the role of communication in such a sociology. The key principles of communication and social change are discussed in an attempt to construct a citizen perspective for communication and social change. Third, I elaborate on the limitations of a representational framework in pursuing the agenda of 'a citizen perspective' for communication and social change. Fourth, I flag some of the risk factors: the exclusion of experience and shrinking public spaces. Finally, the chapter concludes and ends this book by reflecting on the possibilities for and limitations on constructing a space where other social imaginaries can develop and translate into citizen-driven social change processes.

The Crisis of Development

The current crisis of development is fundamentally a crisis of participation and inclusion. The big problem today, reflected in the numerous demonstrations and insurgencies, and even in populist political movements, is the widespread, deep-felt experience of not having any influence on the decisions that affect one's own life. As can be seen from social uprisings, but also in the humanitarian crises surrounding contemporary wars and conflicts, the experience of social injustice and inequality is massive, and the violations of basic human rights and the inability of many to lead a decent life are widespread. An increasing number of citizens across societies are experiencing such challenges, while many more are struggling to maintain their quality of life in times of austerity. These unresolved conflicts and development challenges speak to fundamental shortcomings in the neoliberal, economic-growth-oriented and market-driven model of development that dominates world development today. It is rightly seen as a crisis of development, but it is also a crisis of communication.

Catering to the crisis of development, Boaventura de Sousa Santos has over the years developed an ambitious project to formulate an 'epistemology of the South'. It is a social science project which not only connects well with Alain Touraine's call for a new social thought (Touraine 2009), but goes further in both critiquing the dominant discourse in modern science and suggesting alternative epistemological pathways. Fundamentally, Santos speaks to the need for an epistemological break. He argues for a sociology of emergences:

> The sociology of emergences consists of undertaking a symbolic enlargement of knowledge, practices, and agents in order to identify therein the tendencies of the future (the Not Yet) upon which it is possible to intervene so as to maximize the probability of hope vis-à-vis the probability of frustration. Such symbolic enlargement is actually a form of sociological imagination with a double aim: on the one hand, to know better the conditions of the possibility of hope: on the other, to define principles of action to promote the fulfillment of those conditions. (Santos 2014, 184)

The sociology of emergences explores the possibility of a better future in the present. In this approach, Santos draws substantially on Ernst Bloch's concept of the 'Not Yet'. This is a concept that 'stresses the critique of the mechanical conception of matter . . . and the affirmation of our capacity to think and act productively upon the world' (Santos 2014, 183). In Freirean terms, it explores the hope for a better future through an integrated effort that combines reflection and action. Santos' ideas are rooted in the fundamental claim for global cognitive justice within which he again frames 'a subaltern insurgent cosmopolitanism' (2014, 134). This is a form of cosmopolitanism that refers to the aspirations of oppressed groups to organize their resistance and consolidate coalitions on the same scale as that used by the oppressors to victimize them, that is, the global scale (2014, 135).

In elaborating the epistemological foundations of the subaltern, Santos develops an 'epistemology of seeing', contrasting it with what he calls the dominant 'epistemology of blindness'. This is a blindness to all the absences, needs and injustices of marginalized groups in society. The dominant epistemology of blindness is also what has led to the historical process whereby a particular form of knowledge, a 'knowledge-as-regulation', has come to dominate 'knowledge-as-emancipation'. This dichotomy connects well with the dichotomy often put forward in communication for development and social change debates, that of contrasting a diffusion-oriented communication with that of a participation-oriented communication. Diffusion-oriented communication is based on an epistemology that resonates well with Santos' knowledge-as-regulation, which assumes rational and predictable human behaviour to be a consequence of knowledge acquisition. Participatory communication is based on an epistemology that resonates well with Santos' 'knowledge-as-emancipation'. Santos goes on to develop a critique of the epistemology of absent knowledge – the epistemology of absent agents – and revisits representation, reflecting on its limitations. In these processes, which are all to be found in his 2014 book, Santos' proposal for a knowledge-as-emancipation entails an understanding of the emancipatory as a common-sense project that is 'constructed so as to be appropriated in a privileged way by oppressed, marginalized, or excluded social groups and actually strengthened by their emancipatory practice' (2014, 159). Here we are at the heart of Santos and his book's epistemological basis. It connects very well with the whole project of developing a 'culture of governance' which I unpack and discuss in chapter 5, drawing extensively on Jorge González' notion of 'cibercultur@'.

Connected to his critiques of the epistemology of blindness is Santos' critique of what he calls the 'waste of experience' of the marginalized, in which he argues for the construction of five ecologies against this waste. These are: an ecology of knowledge, an ecology of temporalities, an ecology of recognition, an ecology of trans-scale and an ecology of productivities. They come together in his sociology of emergences and are further substantiated in his meta-concepts of a global cognitive justice and an epistemology of the South (Santos 2014, 182). Central to this approach is an acknowledgement of other forms of knowledge, such as lay, popular, urban, peasant, indigenous, women's and religious. The evaluations of these alternative discourses and practices and their transformative potential constitute a foundational transition towards the construction of a novel, and what Freire might have called a liberating, epistemology of development and social change.

Meanwhile, for communication scholars and practitioners engaged in communication and social change, the crisis of development and its consequences pose an ethical dilemma and call for a normative stand. From an ethical point of view, the crisis of development can hardly be reduced to technical questions about how best to craft communication interventions. Rather, the crisis challenges the fundamental *raison d'être* of communication interventions, their aims and purposes, their content and organization and their expected outcomes. If they are to deal with questions such as social injustice, violations of human rights and the inabilities to lead a decent life or pursue individual or collective aspirations, the key and highly concrete question arises: what communication practices and specific interventions should be carried out to resolve such aspects of the crisis?

Governments, transnational agencies, NGOs, CBOs and social movements are today all faced with the challenge of seeking ways to intervene to reverse the negative spirals of social change, whereby, for example, refugees and forced migrants are offered opportunities to regain hope, and where capacities and capabilities to aspire as individuals and collectives are given a chance to emerge and thrive. This book has spoken to these challenges, offering examples of communication and social change initiatives that deliberately pursue a more inclusive and radically participatory development process.

If we accept this strong normative stand on principles of social justice and human rights, along with Santos' call for an epistemological break with dominant discourses of development, this will create opportunities for another communication which articulates social change processes oriented to a different development to that represented in the dominant neoliberal logic.

A Citizen Perspective on Communication and Social Change

This book's conceptual approach to communication and social change emerges from a critical review of established practice in organizations, combined with a review of social movements and their embodied practice of communication and performance. Through these reviews, a 'new social thought' has been proposed that formulates a critique of the way in which communication for social change has been conceived thus far. It has done this by revisiting key concepts in the field, particularly media, communication, culture, participation and social change, while also introducing new concepts, such as performativity, embodied practices, experience movements, communication movements and cultures of governance. On this basis, this book has formulated an approach to communication and social change and a direction of inquiry based on new types of questions and inquiries that move the emphasis away from the simplicity and superficiality of so much contemporary communication for development and social change research and practice. A core call has been to complexify problem analyses and encourage deeper engagement with the problems at stake. Issues of power dynamics, policy constraints and opportunities for participation have been part and parcel of this call. Recognizing such contexts and complexities challenges researchers and practitioners to be aware of the systemic constraints and the political economy of the field, which otherwise tend far too often to suggest simplistic pathways of intervention vis-à-vis problems that have been too narrowly defined.

In addition to this call to recognize context and complexity, two principles have stood out in the formulation of another communication for another development. First, the emphasis on a 'non-media-centric agenda', a point emphasized in chapter 2 where I distinguish between socio-centric and media-centric approaches, underscoring that social-change-focused communication initiatives would typically have a less exclusive focus on the media sector, that is, on media systems, media content or media uses. Instead, they would be oriented towards understanding communication practices in everyday life and the formation of discursive spaces for radical participation; and they would focus on analyses of the structural determinants influencing both policy and practice. A non-media-centric agenda also complies with and can benefit enormously from the approach to media found, and the insights generated among, many ethnographically oriented media scholars who are exploring media uses as social practice. They tend to align themselves with non-representational communication models. Shaun Moores' comprehensive research into media appropriations is a case in point (Moores 2000; 2012). Non-representational communication models view communication as social practice and the relation between communication and social change as being far less about media representations and much more about social actions.

The second principle for determining what, fundamentally, is the citizen perspective on communication and social change is the emphasis on social imaginaries and the rights, capacities and opportunities of all individuals and collectives to be able both to formulate and articulate these and to see them reflected in communication for social change initiatives.

The epistemology of communication and social change I propose and outline in this book has been anchored in these principles and in enhancing processes of empowerment and collective action. Four components were addressed as the key components of building a framework for communication and social change, a framework that aims to be more inclusive and responsive vis-à-vis its constituencies. First, communication is understood in a holistic and 'ecological' manner, emphasizing a practice approach that focuses on exploring and understanding uses and appropriations, but does this within a broader framework that recognizes and critically navigates within the political economy of the media and other contexts that determine uses and appropriations. Second, media are viewed as deeply embedded in and contributing to the configuration of social and political spaces. Media cannot be dissociated from these contexts. Third, a critical stance towards the ethnocentrism implicit in a lot of social change thinking is crucial, and the vibrant debates on development and social change emanating from post-colonial and post-development debates are critical to the approach advocated here. Santos' proposed epistemologies of the South are a sound basis for such an approach, one that is guided by principles of social justice, equity and the pursuit of positive social change. Social change is here understood as a non-linear, complex and an often contested process open to multi-vocality, diversity and contestation. The complexity embedded in the relation between media use and social change processes is recognized in this approach.

The fourth component underlying this novel communication and social change approach relates to notions of agency and governance. Media uses and appropriations are viewed as active sense-making processes. This, however, is not the same as saying that all sense-making activity is about citizen engagement. With a particular interest in citizen engagement, this book has drawn on González (2014) and others in proposing a notion of bottom-up governance, which is central to a citizen perspective on communication and social change. This entails citizen-driven social change processes that emerge from the development of localized knowledge bases, information systems and communication practice. This volume contains multiple examples of this approach to communication and social change that has demonstrable implications for the way government, international agencies and civil society alike orient and carry out their communicative practice.

The Limits of a Representational Framework of Communication

A core challenge in the practice of communication and social change today is the strong institutional imperative that drives the communication process. Social change agendas here refer to a broad gamut of services and public goods which governments, international agencies and larger NGOs typically communicate about. When analysing the communicative practice of such institutions, many examples highlight the strong emphasis on disseminating centralized information, with limited intention to listen to or understand the constituencies the institutions are communicating with and wish to influence. Public service information, health campaigns, job creation initiatives, public safety arrangements, environmental mitigation efforts and humanitarian communication, along with a wide range of austerity prevention and mitigation initiatives in these and other areas of importance to everyday life, have been communicated mostly as given, defined and agreed agendas, very often with limited opportunities for the constituencies to negotiate the suggested social change agendas.

A severe communication gap exists between numerous institutions communicating social change agendas and the degree of sustained commitment with which constituencies engage around these agendas. The nature of this communication gap is not a technical problem that can be resolved by more precise communication or other refinements, such as different tools of communication. While many institutions in society speak *on behalf of* and *to* citizens, the expressed desire of many citizens is to have their own say in such conversations. Rather than being represented, they want to participate, which is something that social movements offer. Social movements, protests, demonstrations and a variety of other deliberations provide a number of opportunities to be seen, heard and involved. Although many of us live in representative democracies, we are also living in a time of digital media, interactivity and multiple opportunities to crowd-source opinions and engage citizens in large-scale conversations. This begs the fundamental question: what should communication and social change initiatives look like in today's networked society, in which mass self-communication is prevalent and both connective and collective action are features? This sparks a further question: are governmental and non-governmental organizations willing to surrender their agendas when communicating with or on behalf of their constituencies? Finally, how does an organization strategize its way out of such communication disconnects?

The example of UNICEF country offices using social media to crowd-source opinions shows how difficult is it for well-intentioned organizations in times of interactive communication practices to achieve radical participation or anything close to broader citizen engagement. 'Creating' a social movement, which UNICEF aspires to do, is almost a contradiction in terms. This touches on one of the fundamental tensions in this field of research and practice: the tension between citizen-driven process for a better world, often articulated from below through social movements, and the organizations, be they government institutions, international agencies or CSOs, signalling intentions to be participatory and listening, but having difficulties in doing so.

I argue elsewhere for a 'communication at the margins', where the margins signify the grassroots level, but more fundamentally speak to the symbolic and/or physical distance from power (Hemer and Tufte 2016, 18). It underscores the orientation in a communication and social change approach, an orientation towards the most marginalized citizens of the global polity, just as Santos argues with his epistemology of the South. However, the challenge and tension lie in what happens when the margins gain the attention of the centre. If and when 'participatory communication', 'empowerment' and 'social justice' become buzzwords in hegemonic development speak, there is real reason for caution not only due to the devaluation of the concepts, but also because the institutional logic itself tends to be counterproductive and even destructive (Hemer and Tufte 2016, 18). Many examples highlight this tension: from the Indignados movement in Spain partly converging with political parties, to the example of UNICEF that seems to be exactly the systemic straitjacket that impedes the 'creation' of a social movement. As I have said so often in my teaching: 'communication FOR social change' contains a contradiction in terms. The imperative of intentionally creating social change goes against the historical evidence that social change de facto rises from below, a social dynamic that has gained in intensity once more in the past years of social uprisings across the globe. As scholars and practitioners of communication and social change, we must 'be open to the possibility that ultimately the main obstacle to change may be the development industry itself' (Hemer and Tufte 2016, 18).

We have seen in this book the articulation of an important distinction between communicative practices that are open, participatory and horizontal processes, on the one hand, and communicative practices that are more controlled, less inclusive and managed hierarchically, on the other. This distinction serves to clarify the communicative opportunities that the non-representational social movements bring to the field of communication and social change. It contributes the embodied experience, that is, the opportunity for mass participation and social inclusion in communicative processes. It offers communication practices for all as a valid approach and possible action in people's pursuit of social change. This is an approach to communication that most organizations communicating for change have neglected. Others have attempted to take on such approaches, transforming themselves into what Wendy Willems at one point called 'participatory organizations' (Willems 2013).

When organizations and institutions communicate, they tend to emphasize the need for precise texts, correct representation and an emphasis on simple and understandable messages. They seldom offer too much space for negotiation of the message. They typically have clear preferred messages and meanings that they work hard to put across. This limits interactivity and dialogic processes. From a technical point of view, these are relevant discussions. From a normative position, however, with an ethical stand that draws on a non-representational communication model, with all that follows from this position, such considerations are rendered obsolete. Instead, what is needed is a discussion on how to develop communication opportunities and a relevant grammar of communication. I propose a grammar that caters for communication principles that open rather than close dialogues; that generate questions and reflection rather than answers and clarity; and that mobilize and engage rather than satisfy and comfort. Embedded in such principles, communication initiatives and positive social change will be fully integrated social processes.

When Touraine called in 2009 for a new social thought in the social sciences, it was an attempt yet again to reclaim a perspective on social science where non-representational and embodied experience is recognized *along with* the representational and the symbolic. From the perspective of communication and social change it is not necessarily a choice between a representational and a non-representational communication model. Rather, it is about committing to a radically different approach to communication and change. It is an epistemological proposition that can help reposition the field of communication and social change as a field of action research and practice committed to a normative understanding of human rights and social justice. It is thus *not just* about communicating the right thing to the right audience, because the problems communicated about go beyond being problems of information. They are more often complex development problems that require visibility and a lot of dialogue and engagement to be resolved.

A new grammar of communication beyond the valuing of voice, communication and social change is about different discourses and thus different content. It is about the ability to articulate them, and be seen and heard by relevant constituencies, which are often also power holders. This presents practical challenges. This book has revisited the established field of research on and the practice of communication and social change and reviewed the communication experiences of social movements. Together, I have framed these communication challenges as communication *and* social change. As is argued throughout this book, crafting a people-centred, radically participatory approach to communication and social change, embedded in a new social thought, requires consideration of a number of aspects.

My analysis of social movement experiences in chapter 4 identified five innovative communicative features. First, in the processes of mobilization and insurgency characteristic of social movements, mediated communication played a decisive role and showed *new forms and ways of organizing discontent, resistance and political action.* Second, the rapidly emerging online media and communication infrastructures for resistance helped spark strong political momentum, opening *new pathways for practising communication activism.* Third, *the symbolic construction of public space with a dynamic synergy between online and offline practices* provided space for new forms of public deliberation and construction of a civil space of potential and possibility in line with what Roger Silverstone conceptualized in his notion of mediapolis (Silverstone 2007). Fourth, *the role of leadership in social movements took on new dimensions.* The activists claimed they were operating as leaderless movements, but in practice – and embedded in innovative communication practices – they developed subtle new forms of leadership. Finally, the actors in the movements found *new pathways to construct shared meanings and narratives, and to articulate identities* in a social process that was fundamentally a highly embodied and emotional experience movement.

Moreover, my analysis of the contemporary generation of social movements and their communication practices shows that embodied experience is a mode of presence and engagement that goes beyond claims of representation. It signals the important point that to communicate successfully requires a conceptual and analytical openness to understanding the lifeworld of citizens and the emotions and motivations that enhance their engagement and action. The difficult-to-separate fusion of online and offline media and communication practices only emphasizes that the new grammar of change requires an analytical and strategic approach that takes social actors as its point of departure.

Exclusion of Experience and the Shrinking of Public Space

To enhance processes of resilience and empowerment among marginalized groups in a glocal reality requires the articulation of complex social processes. There are few global development challenges that more strikingly illustrate these complexities than the contemporary humanitarian crisis, which contains dynamics of power struggles; complicated policy contexts; opportunities for participation; and unidentified, invisible or blocked capacities for relevant communities to aspire. These are all material elements to consider. These are challenges but also make up the socio-cultural and political-economic web of opportunity in which social change occurs. When social change processes are unfolding in a negative spiral, and voice and action are confounded, it is a tremendous challenge for international organizations, governments and movements, let alone for the affected individuals and groups, to articulate processes of empowerment. However, it is not just because 'communication is difficult', key actors lack technical skills or messages are not crafted well enough. The whole point that this book has built an argument around is that there is a desperate need for 'another communication': a communication that honours and values the point of view of the individual citizen or collectives, and their needs to speak out in order to articulate their aspirations and enhance their abilities to act.

Despite the celebratory promises that infinite and dynamic communication practices would open up with increased access to and use of the Internet and mobile communication platforms, we have the contradictory situation today where civil society increasingly complains about the decreasing public space for communication and action. The space for agency, many NGOs argue, is decreasing rather than increasing (Wagner and Dankova 2016). We also see increases in violations of the human rights of critical journalists, activists, bloggers and others from media and civil society (Wagner and Dankova 2016). A growing political tension surrounds communicative opportunity and action. The logics and dynamics of communication unfold within the political economy and the political reality of the field in ways that seem to reduce the ability not just to represent civil society and its cause-driven initiatives, but to include these actors in formulating common development agendas for the future.

This exclusion of experience and shrinking of public space have a deeper dimension: a weakness not in the ability to communicate but in the will to listen to and understand the constituency concerned. Understanding the participants' point of view, in particular factoring in their experiences and emotions, has emerged as an alarming shortcoming in many strategic communication interventions, and is what social movements seem to have been able to cater for. The civil space of potential and opportunity that Roger Silverstone conceptualized and argued for (2007) is currently threatened and experiencing difficulties in its development.

Furthermore, within the world of organizations communicating for change, we might describe this lack of ability to represent the marginalized, to be inclusive and to listen as a crisis of imagination. Communicative interventions often lack sustainable solutions that involve all relevant groups and stakeholders and their points of view. The social imaginaries of individuals and communities are rarely incorporated.

Constructing a Civil Space of Potential and Possibility

Roger Silverstone's concept of mediapolis is very helpful in situating and understanding communication practices in the context of the globalized world. This framing of a space where we are all constructed as human is interesting to dwell on for a moment. It is such spaces that a participatory and people-centred communication for social change seeks to construct, spaces which open up dialogue, participation and social action. Mediapolis is a civil space of social potential and possibility whose nature Hannah Arendt can also assist us in understanding: 'The polis, properly speaking, is not the city-state in its physical location: it is the organization of the people as it arises out of acting and speaking together, and its true space lies between people living together for this purpose, no matter where they happen to be' (Arendt 1958, 198).

In this context, voice remains a fundamental element of the potentially vibrant, inclusive and empowered body politic. In the sense of both acting and speaking together in the mediapolis, voice signals a way of communicating which is a vital constitutive property, a property we seem to have lost, or never really to have developed sufficiently for it to become a resilient feature of modern-day life. Sharath Srinivasan and Claudia Lopes emphasize this centrality of voice and its dialogic, inclusive and action-oriented virtues:

> we should not treat voices as data points, as dominant neoliberal logics of economic and social ordering do, there to be farmed and harvested and brought into mechanized forms of knowledge production . . . We must foster acts of exchange and listening and new spaces of narrative formation where citizens do not merely give or receive information but are motivated to empathise, understand and form active judgements. (Srinivasan and Lopes 2016, 157)

Silverstone's mediapolis offers us a space for such acts of exchange, listening and narrative formation to unfold.

Pursuing the construction of these spaces opens up opportunities for new social imaginaries to thrive (Appadurai in Stade 2016, 216) and serve as a source for citizen engagement. Charles Taylor helps us formulate what lies at the very core of a citizen perspective on communication and social change:

> By social imaginaries, I mean something much broader and deeper than the intellectual schemes people may entertain when they think about social reality in a disengaged mode. I am thinking, rather, of the ways people imagine their social existence, how they fit together with others, how things go on between them and their fellows, the expectations that are normally

met, and the deeper normative notions and images that underlie these expectations. (Taylor 2004, 23)

Without this emphasis on creating spaces for dialogue where social imaginaries emerge, there will be no opportunity for the radically partici-patory communication processes I have argued for throughout this book. Embryonic and imperfect as this approach may be, it is a necessary starting point for citizen-led processes of communication and social change.

References

Action for Social Change: ADRA Malawi Programme. 2010. http://s243760778. onlinehome.us/adramalawi/our-programs/our-programs/asc.

Airhihenbuwa, C. O., B. Makinwa, B. Frith and Rafael Obregon, eds. 1999. *Communications Framework for HIV/AIDS: A New Direction*. Geneva: UNAIDS.

Anderson, Benedict. 1991. *Imagined Communities: Reflections on the Origin and Spread of Nationalism*. Rev. edn. London; New York: Verso.

Anduiza, Eva, Camilo Cristancho and José M. Sabucedo. 2013. 'Mobilization through Online Social Networks: The Political Protest of the *Indignados* in Spain.' *Information, Communication & Society* 17 (6): 1–15.

Ang, Ien. 1985. *Watching Dallas: Soap Opera and the Melodramatic Imagination*. London; New York: Methuen.

Ang, Ien. 1991. *Desperately Seeking the Audience*. London; New York: Routledge.

Appadurai, Arjun. 2004. 'The Capacity to Aspire: Culture and the Terms of Recognition.' In *Culture and Public Action*, ed. Vijayendra Rao and Michael Walton. Stanford: Stanford University Press.

Arendt, Hannah. 1958. *The Human Condition*. Chicago; London: University of Chicago Press.

Arnstein, Sherry R. 2011. 'A Ladder of Citizen Participation.' In *The Participation Reader*, ed. Andrea Cornwall. London; New York: Zed Books.

Atton, Chris. 2002. *Alternative Media*. London; Thousand Oaks: SAGE.

Barassi, Veronica. 2014. *Activism on the Web: Everyday Struggles against Digital Capitalism*. New York: Routledge.

Barranquero, Alejandro. 2012. 'Redes digitales y movilización colectiva: del 15-M a nuevas practicas de empoderamiento y desarrollo local.' In *Comunicación y desarrollo: practicas comunicativas y empoderamiento local*, ed. Marcelo Martínez Hermida and Francisco Sierra Caballero. Barcelona: Gedisa.

Barranquero, Alejandro. 2014. 'Comunicación, cambio social y ONG en España: pistas para profundizar en la cultura de la cooperación desde los nuevos movimientos comunicacionales: el caso del 15M.' *COMMONS: Revista de Comunicación y Ciudadanía Digital* 3 (1): 6–24. http://reuredc.uca.es/index. php/cayp/article/view/634.

Barranquero Carretero, Alejandro, and Miriam Meda González. 2015. 'Los medios comunitarios y alternativos en el ciclo de protestas ciudadanas desde el 15M.' *Athenea Digital: Revista de Pensamiento e Investigación Social* 15 (1): 139–70.

Bauman, Zygmunt. 1998. *Globalization: The Human Consequences*. Cambridge: Polity.

Bauman, Zygmunt. 2000. *Liquid Modernity*. Cambridge; Malden: Polity.

Beltrán, Luis Ramiro. 2006. 'A Farewell to Aristotle: "Horizontal" Communication.' In *Communication for Social Change Anthology: Historical and Contemporary Readings*, ed. Alfonso-Gumucio Dagron and Thomas Tufte. South Orange: Communication for Social Change Consortium.

Benedicto, Jorge. 2006. 'La construcción de la ciudadania democrática en España (1977–2004): De la institucionalización a las prácticas', https://www.research gate.net/publication/271818643.

Bennett, W. Lance. 2008.'Changing Citizenship in the Digital Age.' In *Civic Life Online: Learning How Digital Media Can Engage Youth*, ed. W. Lance Bennett. Cambridge, MA: MIT Press.

Bennett, W. Lance, and Alexandra Segerberg. 2013. *The Logic of Connective Action: Digital Media and the Personalization of Contentious Politics*. New York: Cambridge University Press.

Bhabha, Homi K. 2004. *The Location of Culture*. London; New York: Routledge.

Boal, Augusto. 2006. 'Theater of the Oppressed.' In *Communication for Social Change Anthology: Historical and Contemporary Readings*, ed. Alfonso Gumucio-Dagron and Thomas Tufte. South Orange: Communication for Social Change Consortium.

Bordenave, Juan Díaz. 2006. 'Participative Communication as a Part of Building the Participative Society.' In *Communication for Social Change Anthology: Historical and Contemporary Readings*, ed. Alfonso Gumucio-Dagron and Thomas Tufte. South Orange: Communication for Social Change Consortium.

Brecht, Bertolt. 2006. 'The Radio as an Apparatus of Communication.' In *Communication for Social Change Anthology: Historical and Contemporary Readings*, ed. Alfonso Gumucio-Dagron and Thomas Tufte. South Orange: Communication for Social Change Consortium.

Brock, Karen, and Jethro Pettit, eds. 2007. *Springs of Participation: Creating and Evolving Methods for Participatory Development*. Rugby: Practical Action.

Cammaerts, Bart. 2012. 'Protest Logics and the Mediation Opportunity Structure.' *European Journal of Communication* 27 (2): 117–34.

Cammaerts, Bart, and César Jiménez-Martínez. 2014. 'The Mediation of the Brazilian V-for-Vinegar Protests: From Vilification to Legitimization and Back?/A mediação dos protestos brasileiros "V-de-Vinagre": da vilificação à legitimação e de volta.' *Liinc em Revista* 10 (1): 44–68.

Cardoso Panel. 2004. *We the Peoples: Civil Society, the United Nations and Global Governance*. https://www.globalpolicy.org/images/pdfs/0611report.pdf.

Castañeda, Ernesto. 2012. 'The *Indignados* of Spain: A Precedent to Occupy Wall Street.' *Social Movement Studies* 11 (3-4): 309–19.

Castells, Manuel. 1997. *The Power of Identity*. Malden: Blackwell.

Castells, Manuel. 2009. *Communication Power*. Oxford; New York: Oxford University Press.

Castells, Manuel. 2010. *End of Millennium*. 2nd edn, with new pref. Oxford; Malden: Blackwell.

Castells, Manuel. 2012. *Networks of Outrage and Hope: Social Movements in the Internet Age*. Cambridge; Malden: Polity.

Certeau, Michel de, Luce Giard and Pierre Mayol. 1998. *The Practice of Everyday Life. Vol. 2: Living and Cooking*. Rev. edn. Minneapolis: University of Minnesota Press.

Chadwick, Andrew. 2006. *Internet Politics: States, Citizens, and New Communication Technologies*. New York: Oxford University Press.

Chadwick, Andrew. 2013. *The Hybrid Media System: Politics and Power*. Oxford; New York: Oxford University Press.

Chambers, Robert. 1981. 'Rapid Rural Appraisal: Rationale and Repertoire.' *Public Administration and Development* 1 (2): 95–106.

Chambers, Robert. 1985. *Managing Rural Development: Ideas and Experience from East Africa*. West Hartford: Kumarian Press.

Chouliaraki, Lilie. 2006. *The Spectatorship of Suffering*. London; Thousand Oaks: SAGE.

Chouliaraki, Lilie. 2012. *Self-Mediation: New Media, Citizenship and Civil Selves*. London: Routledge.

Cooke, Bill, and Uma Kothari, eds. 2001. *Participation: The New Tyranny?* London; New York: Zed Books.

Cornwall, Andrea. 2000. *Beneficiary, Consumer, Citizen: Perspectives on Participation for Poverty Reduction*. http://www.alnap.org/pool/files/beneficiary-consumer-citizens-cornwall.pdf.

Cornwall, Andrea, and Alex Shankland. 2013. 'Cultures of Politics, Spaces of Power: Contextualizing Brazilian Experiences of Participation.' *Journal of Political Power* 6 (2): 309–33.

Costanza-Chock, Sasha. 2012. 'Mic Check! Media Cultures and the Occupy Movement.' *Social Movement Studies* 11 (3-4): 375–85.

Couldry, Nick. 2006. 'Culture and Citizenship: The Missing Link?' *European Journal of Cultural Studies* 9 (3): 321–39.

Couldry, Nick. 2010. *Why Voice Matters: Culture and Politics after Neoliberalism*. Los Angeles; London: SAGE. http://search.ebscohost.com/login.aspx?direct=true&scope=site&db=nlebk&db=nlabk&AN=372428.

Couldry, Nick. 2012. *Media, Society, World: Social Theory and Digital Media Practice*. Cambridge; Malden: Polity.

Couldry, Nick, and Andreas Hepp. 2013. 'Conceptualizing Mediatization: Contexts, Traditions, Arguments: Editorial.' *Communication Theory* 23 (3): 191–202.

Cruikshank, Barbara. 1999. *The Will to Empower: Democratic Citizens and Other Subjects*. Ithaca, NY: Cornell University Press.

Csordas, Thomas J. 1993. 'Somatic Modes of Attention.' *Cultural Anthropology* 8 (2): 135–56.

Custódio, Leonardo. 2016. 'Favela Media Activism: Political Trajectories of Low-Income Brazilian Youth.' PhD thesis, University of Tampere.

Dag Hammarskjöld Foundation. 2014. 'Another Development.' August. http://www.dhf.uu.se/about/another-development.

Dagnino, Evelina. 2011. 'Citizenship: A Perverse Confluence.' In *The Participation Reader*, ed. Andrea Cornwall. London; New York: Zed Books.

Dahlgren, Peter. 2003. 'Reconfiguring Civic Culture in the New Media Milieu.' In *Media and the Restyling of Politics: Consumerism, Celebrity and Cynicism*, ed. John Corner and Dick Pels. London: SAGE. http://sk.sagepub.com/books/media-and-the-restyling-of-politics/n9.xml.

Dahlgren, Peter. 2009. *Media and Political Engagement: Citizens, Communication, and Democracy*. New York: Cambridge University Press.

De Bruijn, Mirjam, Francis Nyamnjoh and Inge Brinkman, eds. 2009. *Mobile Phones: The New Talking Drums of Everyday Africa*. Langaa RPCIG.

Deacon, D., and J. Stanyer. 2014. 'Mediatization: Key Concept or Conceptual Bandwagon?' *Media, Culture & Society* 36 (7): 1032–44.

Della Porta, Donatella, and Mario Diani. 2006. *Social Movements: An Introduction*. 2nd edn. Malden: Blackwell.

Della Porta, Donatella, and Alice Mattoni. 2013. 'Cultures of Participation in Social Movements.' In *The Participatory Cultures Handbook*, ed. Aaron Alan Delwiche and Jennifer Jacobs Henderson. New York: Routledge.

¡Democracia Real Ya! 2014. http://www.democraciarealya.es/page/24.

Denskus, Tobias, and Daniel E. Esser. 2015. 'TED Talks on International Development: Trans-Hegemonic Promise and Ritualistic Constraints.' *Communication Theory* 25 (2): 166–87.

Diaz, Ruben. 2014. 'From the North to the South, from the East to the West: Democracy and Transnational Networks of "*Indignados*": Global Dynamics Seminar.' Roskilde University.

Downing, John. 2001. *Radical Media: Rebellious Communication and Social Movements*. Thousand Oaks: SAGE.

Downing, John, ed. 2011. *Encyclopedia of Social Movement Media*. Thousand Oaks: SAGE.

Downing, John. 2014. 'Social Movement Media in the Process of Constructive Social Change.' In *The Handbook of Development Communication and Social Change*, ed. Karin Gwinn Wilkins, Thomas Tufte and Rafael Obregon. Chichester; Malden: Wiley-Blackwell. http://alltitles.ebrary.com/Doc?id=10830394.

Duncombe, Stephen. 2007. *Dream: Re-Imagining Progressive Politics in an Age of Fantasy*. New York: New Press.

Duncombe, Stephen. 2013. *Creative Activism – Stephen Duncombe – CPH – January 23, 2013*. https://www.youtube.com/watch?v=FXJsWdmlCfA.

Dutta, Mohan J. 2011. *Communicating Social Change: Structure, Culture, and Agency*. New York; London: Routledge.

Enghel, Florencia. 2014. 'Video Letters, Mediation and (Proper) Distance: A Qualitative Study of International Development Communication in Practice.' PhD thesis, Karlstad University. http://urn.kb.se/resolve?urn=urn:nbn:se:kau:d iva-34448.

Enghel, Florencia. 2015. 'Towards a Political Economy of Communication in Development?' *Nordicom Review* 36 (special issue): 11–24.

Enghel, Florencia, and Karin Wilkins, eds. 2012. 'Communication, Media and Development: Problems and Perspectives.' *Nordicom Review* 33 (special issue).

Escobar, Arturo. 1995. *Encountering Development: The Making and Unmaking of the Third World*. Princeton: Princeton University Press.

Escobar, Arturo. 1998. *La invención del Tercer Mundo: construcción y deconstrucción del desarrollo*. Barcelona; Santafé de Bogotá: Norma.

Escobar, Arturo. 2006. 'Imagining a Postdevelopment Era.' In *Communication for Social Change Anthology: Historical and Contemporary Readings*, ed. Alfonso Gumucio-Dagron and Thomas Tufte. South Orange: Communication for Social Change Consortium.

Esser, Frank, and Jesper Strömbäck, eds. 2014. *Mediatization of Politics: Understanding the Transformation of Western Democracies*. Basingstoke; New York: Palgrave Macmillan.

Eyerman, Ron. 1992. 'Modernity and Social Movements.' In *Social Change and Modernity*, ed. Hans Haferkamp and Neil J. Smelser. Berkeley: University of California Press.

Eyken, W. van. 1991. *The Concept and Process of Empowerment*. The Hague: Bernard van Leer Foundation.

Fair, Jo Ellen, and Hemant Shah. 1997. 'Continuities and Discontinuities in Communication and Development Research since 1958.' *Journal of International Communication* 4 (2): 3–23.

Fals-Borda, Orlando. 2006. 'The Application of Participatory Action Research in Latin America.' In *Communication for Social Change Anthology: Historical and Contemporary Readings*, ed. Alfonso Gumucio-Dagron and Thomas Tufte. South Orange: Communication for Social Change Consortium.

Fanon, Frantz, and Constance Farrington. 1968. *The Wretched of the Earth*. New York: Grove Press.

Fanon, Frantz, and Charles Markmann. 1952. *Black Skin, White Masks*. London: Pluto Press.

Fedozzi, Luciano. 2001. *Orçamento participativo: reflexões sobre a experiência de Porto Alegre*. Porto Alegre: Tomo Editorial.

Fenton, Natalie, and Veronica Barassi. 2011. 'Alternative Media and Social Networking Sites: The Politics of Individuation and Political Participation.' *Communication Review* 14 (3): 179–96.

Foster, Susan Leigh. 2003. 'Choreographies of Protest.' *Theatre Journal* 55 (3): 395–412.

Fraser, Colin, and Sonia Restrepo-Estrada. 1998. *Communicating for Development: Human Change for Survival*. London; New York: I.B. Tauris.

Fraser, Nancy. 1997. *Justice Interruptus: Critical Reflections on the 'Postsocialist' Condition*. London: Routledge.

Fraser, Nancy. 2007. 'Transnationalizing the Public Sphere On the Legitimacy and Efficacy of Public Opinion in a Post-Westphalian World'. *Theory, Culture, Society*. 24 (7): 7–30.

Freire, Paulo. 1998. *Extensión o comunicación? La concientización en el medio rural.* México: Siglo XXI.

Freire, Paulo. 2001. *Pedagogy of the Oppressed.* London; New York: Penguin.

Freire, Paulo. 2004. *Pedagogy of Indignation.* Boulder; London: Paradigm.

Fuchs, Christian. 2008. *Internet and Society: Social Theory in the Information Age.* New York: Routledge.

Fuchs, Christian. 2012. 'Behind the News: Social Media, Riots, and Revolutions.' *Capital & Class* 36 (3): 383–91.

Fuchs, Christian. 2014a. 'Review of Manuel Castells' Book "Networks of Outrage and Hope: Social Movements in the Internet Age".' *Media, Culture & Society* 36 (1): 122–4.

Fuchs, Christian. 2014b. *Social Media: A Critical Introduction.* Los Angeles: SAGE.

Galindo Cáceres, Jesús. 2008. *Comunicación, ciencia e historia: fuentes científicas históricas hacia una comunicología posible.* Madrid: McGraw-Hill/Interamericana de España. http://site.ebrary.com/id/10498525.

Galindo Cáceres, Jesús, and José Ignacio González-Acosta. 2013. *#YoSoy132: La Primera Erupción Visible.* Teziutlán: Global Talent University Press

Garcia, D., and G. Lovink. 1997. 'The ABC of Tactical Media.' http://subsol. c3.hu/subsol_2/contributors2/garcia-lovinktext.html.

Gaventa, John. 2011. 'Towards Participatory Local Governance: Six Propositions for Discussion.' In *The Participation Reader*, ed. Andrea Cornwall. London; New York: Zed Books.

Gaventa, John, and Rajesh Tandon, eds. 2010. *Globalizing Citizens: New Dynamics of Inclusion and Exclusion.* London: Zed Books.

Gennep, Arnold van. 1960. *The Rites of Passage.* Repr. Abingdon: Routledge.

Gerace, Frank. 1973. *Comunicación Horizontal.* Lima: Librería Studium.

Gerace, Frank. 2006. 'Participation and Communication: Excerpt from *Comunicación Horizontal*.' In *Communication for Social Change Anthology: Historical and Contemporary Readings*, ed. Alfonso Gumucio-Dagron and Thomas Tufte. South Orange: Communication for Social Change Consortium.

Gerbaudo, Paolo. 2012. *Tweets and the Streets: Social Media and Contemporary Activism.* London: Pluto Press.

Giddens, Anthony. 1986. *The Constitution of Society: Outline of the Theory of Structuration.* Berkeley: University of California Press.

Gitlin, Todd. 1980. *The Whole World Is Watching: Mass Media in the Making & Unmaking of the New Left.* Berkeley: University of California Press.

Gitlin, Todd. 1998. 'Public Sphere or Public Sphericules?' In *Media, Ritual and Identity*, ed. Tamar Liebes, James Curran and Elihu Katz. London: Routledge.

González, Jorge A. 2003. 'Cultura(s) e cibercultur@(s): incursiones no lineales entre complejidad y comunicación.' México: Universidad Iberoamericana.

González, Jorge A. 2012. *Entre cultura(s) e cibercultur@(s): incursões e outras rotas não lineares.* São Paulo: Metodista de São Paulo.

González, Jorge A. 2014. 'Researching and Developing Cybercultur@: Emerging Local Knowledge Communities in Latin America.' In *Reclaiming the Public*

Sphere: Communication, Power and Social Change, ed. Tina Askanius and Liv Stubbe Østergaard. Basingstoke: Palgrave Macmillan. http://www.palgraveconnect.com/doifinder/10.1057/9781137398758.

Grinberg, Máximo Simpson. 1981. 'Comunicación alternativa.' In *Comunicación alternativa y cambio social. 1: América Latina*, ed. Máximo Simpson Grinberg. México: UNAM.

Gumucio-Dagron, Alfonso. 2014. 'Indigenous Communication: From Multiculturalism to Interculturality.' In *The Handbook of Development Communication and Social Change*, ed. Karin Gwinn Wilkins, Thomas Tufte and Rafael Obregon. Chichester; Malden: Wiley-Blackwell.

Gumucio-Dagron, Alfonso, and Thomas Tufte, eds. 2006. *Communication for Social Change Anthology: Historical and Contemporary Readings*. South Orange: Communication for Social Change Consortium.

Gupta, Akhil. 2012. *Red Tape: Bureaucracy, Structural Violence, and Poverty in India*. Durham, NC: Duke University Press.

Hadl, Gabriele, and Arne Hintz. 2009. 'Framing Our Media for Transnational Policy: The World Summit on the Information Society and Beyond.' In *Making Our Media: Global Initiatives Toward a Democratic Public Sphere*, ed. Clemencia Rodriguez, Dorothy Kidd and Laura Stein. Cresskill: Hampton Press.

Hardt, Michael, and Antonio, Negri. 2000. *Empire*. Cambridge, MA: Harvard University Press.

Hardt, Michael, and Antonio, Negri. 2005. *Multitude: War and Democracy in the Age of Empire*. New York: Penguin.

Heller, Ágnes. 1958. *The Human Condition*. Chicago: University of Chicago Press.

Heller, Patrick. 2011. 'Moving the State: The Politics of Democratic Decentralisation in Kerala, South Africa, and Porto Alegre.' *Politics and Society* 29 (1): 131–63.

Hemer, Oscar, and Thomas Tufte. 2016. *Voice & Matter: Communication, Development and the Cultural Return*. Gothenburg: Nordicom.

Hepp, Andreas, and Keith Tribe. 2013. *Cultures of Mediatization*. Cambridge; Malden: Polity. http://www.novanet.eblib.com/EBLWeb/patron/?target=patron&extendedid=P_1180925_0.

Hessel, Stéphane. 2010. *Indignez-vous!* [Montpellier]: Indigène éd.

Hill, Marianne. 2003. 'Development as Empowerment.' *Feminist Economics* 9 (2-3): 117–35.

Hintz, Arne. 2009. *Civil Society Media and Global Governance: Intervening into the World Summit on the Information Society*. Berlin: LIT.

Hjarvard, Stig. 2008. *En verden af medier: medialiseringen af politik, sprog, religion og leg*. Frederiksberg: Samfundslitteratur.

Hjarvard, Stig. 2013. *The Mediatization of Culture and Society*. New York: Routledge.

Holston, James. 2008. *Insurgent Citizenship: Disjunctions of Democracy and Modernity in Brazil*. Princeton; Oxford: Princeton University Press.

Hughes, Neil. 2011. '"Young People Took to the Streets and All of a Sudden All of the Political Parties Got Old": The 15M Movement in Spain.' *Social Movement Studies* 10 (4): 407–13.

Inglehart, Ronald. 1977. *The Silent Revolution: Changing Values and Political Styles among Western Publics*. Princeton: Princeton University Press.

International Development Bank. n.d. http://www.iadb.org/en/inter-american-development-bank,2837.html.

Jacks, Nilda Aparecida, Sérgio Capparelli, Rene Goellner, Thomas Tufte, Yhevelin Guerin and Luciana Dorneles, eds. 2006. *TV, família e identidade: Porto Alegre 'fim de século.'* Porto Alegre: EDIPUCRS.

Jacks, Nilda Aparecida, and Thomas Tufte. 1998. *Televisão, identidade e cotidiano: parte de um projeto integrado*. Vozes: Petropolis.

Jansson, André, and Miyase Christensen, eds. 2014. *Media, Surveillance and Identity: Social Perspective*. Digital Formations, volume 84. New York: Peter Lang.

Jensen, Klaus Bruhn. 1995. *The Social Semiotics of Mass Communication*. London; Thousand Oaks: SAGE.

Johnston, H. 2011. *States and Social Movements*. Cambridge: Polity.

Johnston, Hank, and Bert Klandermans, eds. 1995. *Social Movements and Culture*. Minneapolis: University of Minnesota Press.

Jordan, Lisa, and Peter van Tuijl, eds. 2006. *NGO Accountability: Politics, Principles and Innovations*. London; Sterling, VA: Earthscan.

Jørgensen, Rikke Frank. 2013. *Framing the Net: The Internet and Human Rights*. Northampton, MA: Edward Elgar.

Junge, Benjamin. 2012. 'NGOs as Shadow Pseudopublics: Grassroots Community Leaders' Perceptions of Change and Continuity in Porto Alegre, Brazil.' *American Ethnologist* 39 (2): 407–24.

Juris, Jeffrey S. 2008. *Networking Futures: The Movements against Corporate Globalization*. Durham, NC: Duke University Press.

Juris, Jeffrey S. 2012. 'Reflections on #Occupy Everywhere: Social Media, Public Space, and Emerging Logics of Aggregation.' *American Ethnologist* 39 (2): 259–79.

Kavada, Anastasia. 2011. 'Digital Communication Technologies and Collective Action: A Conceptual Framework.' Presented at the 2011 IAMCR conference, Istanbul.

Kavada, Anastasia. 2012. 'Engagement, Bonding, and Identity across Multiple Platforms: Avaaz on Facebook, YouTube, and MySpace.' *MedieKultur: Journal of Media and Communication Research* 28 (52): 28–48.

Kavada, Anastasia. 2014. 'Transnational Civil Society and Social Movements.' In *The Handbook of Development Communication and Social Change*, ed. Karin Gwinn Wilkins, Thomas Tufte and Rafael Obregon. Chichester; Malden: Wiley-Blackwell. http://alltitles.ebrary.com/Doc?id=10830394.

Klandermans, Bert. 1994. 'Transient Identities? Membership Patterns in the Dutch Peace Movement.' In *New Social Movements: From Ideology to Identity*, ed. Enrique Laraña, Hank Johnston and Joseph R. Gusfield. Philadelphia: Temple University Press.

Kleine, Dorothea. 2013. *Technologies of Choice? ICTs, Development, and the Capabilities Approach.* Cambridge, MA: MIT Press.

Koggel, Christine. 2003. 'Globalization and Women's Paid Work: Expanding Freedom?' *Feminist Economics* 9 (2-3): 163–84.

Laclau, Ernesto, and Chantal Mouffe. 1985. *Hegemony and Socialist Strategy: Towards a Radical Democratic Politics.* London: Verso.

Laraña, Enrique, and Rubén Díez. 2012. 'Las raíces del movimiento 15-M: orden social e indignación moral.' *Revista Española del Tercer Sector* 20: 105–44.

Larsen, Bent Steeg, and Thomas Tufte. 2003. 'Rituals in the Modern World: Applying the Concept of Ritual in Media Ethnography.' In *Global Media Studies: Ethnographic Perspectives,* ed. Patrick Murphy and Marwan M. Kraidy. New York: Routledge.

Leistert, Oliver. 2013. *From Protest to Surveillance: The Political Rationality of Mobile Media: Modalities of Neoliberalism.* Frankfurt am Main; New York: Peter Lang.

Lennie, June, and Jo Tacchi. 2013. *Evaluating Communication for Development.* London; Routledge.

Lievrouw, Leah A. 2011. *Alternative and Activist New Media.* Cambridge; Malden: Polity.

Lull, James, ed. 1988. *World Families Watch Television.* Newbury Park: SAGE.

Lundby, Knut, ed. 2009. *Mediatization: Concept, Changes, Consequences.* New York: Peter Lang.

Madianou, Mirca. 2012. *Migration and New Media: Transnational Families and Polymedia.* Abingdon; New York: Routledge.

Mamdani, Mahmood. 1996. *Citizen and Subject: Contemporary Africa and the Legacy of Late Colonialism.* London: James Currey.

Manyozo, Linje. 2004. 'Locating the Praxis of Development Radio Broadcasting within Development Communication.' *Journal of Global Communication Research Association,* December.

Manyozo, Linje. 2006. 'Manifesto for Development Communication: Nora Quebral and the Los Baños School of Development Communication.' *Asian Journal of Communication* 16 (1): 79–99.

Manyozo, Linje. 2012. *Media, Communication and Development: Three Approaches.* New Delhi; Thousand Oaks; London: SAGE.

Marí Sáez, Víctor Manuel. 2011. *Comunicar para transformar, transformar para comunicar: tecnologías de la información, organizaciones sociales y comunicación desde una perspectiva de cambio social.* Madrid: Editorial Popular.

Martín-Barbero, Jesús. 1987. *De los medios a las mediaciones: comunicación, cultura y hegemonía.* Santafé de Bogotá: Convenio Andrés Bello.

Martín-Barbero, Jesús. 1993. *Communication, Culture and Hegemony: From the Media to Mediations.* London; Newbury Park: SAGE.

Martín-Barbero, Jesús. 2010. Unpublished interview by Thomas Tufte.

Mattoni, Alice, and Emiliano Treré. 2014. 'Media Practices, Mediation Processes, and Mediatization in the Study of Social Movements.' *Communication Theory* 24 (3): 252–71.

Mbembe, Achille. 2001. *On the Postcolony*. Berkeley: University of California Press.

McDonald, Kevin. 2006. *Global Movements: Action and Culture*. Malden; Oxford: Blackwell.

McPhail, Thomas L., ed. 2009. *Development Communication: Reframing the Role of the Media*. Chichester; Malden: Blackwell.

Mefalopulos, Paolo. 2008. *Development Communication Sourcebook: Broadening the Boundaries of Communication*. Washington, DC: World Bank. http://siteresources.worldbank.org/EXTDEVCOMMENG/Resources/DevelopmentCommSourcebook.pdf.

Melkote, Srinivas R., ed. 2012. *Development Communication in Directed Social Change: A Reappraisal of Theory and Practice*. Singapore: AMIC and WKWSCI-NTU.

Melkote, Srinivas R., and H. Leslie Steeves. 2015. *Communication for Development: Theory and Practice for Empowerment and Social Justice*. 3rd edn. New Delhi; Thousand Oaks: SAGE.

Melucci, Alberto. 1985. 'The Symbolic Challenge of Contemporary Movements.' *Social Research* 52: 789–816.

Melucci, Alberto. 1989. *Nomads of the Present: Social Movements and Individual Needs in Contemporary Society*, ed. John Keane and Paul Mier. Philadelphia: Temple University Press.

Melucci, Alberto. 1994. 'A Strange Kind of Newness: What's "New" in New Social Movements?' In *New Social Movements: From Ideology to Identity*, ed. Enrique Laraña, Hank Johnston and Joseph R. Gusfield. Philadelphia: Temple University Press.

Melucci, Alberto. 1996. *Challenging Codes: Collective Action in the Information Age*. Cambridge; New York: Cambridge University Press.

Milan, Stefania. 2013. *Social Movements and Their Technologies: Wiring Social Change*. Basingstoke; New York: Palgrave Macmillan.

Mohan, Giles, and Kristian Stokke. 2000. 'Participatory Development and Empowerment: The Dangers of Localism.' *Third World Quarterly* 21 (2): 247–68.

Mollerup, Nina Grønlykke. 2016. 'Media and Place in Revolutionary Egypt. An Anthropological Exploration of Information Activism and Journalism.' PhD thesis, Roskilde University.

Moores, Shaun. 1996. *Satellite Television and Everyday Life: Articulating Technology*. Luton: Libbey.

Moores, Shaun. 2000. *Media and Everyday Life in Modern Society*. Edinburgh: Edinburgh University Press.

Moores, Shaun. 2012. *Media, Place and Mobility*. London: Palgrave.

Morley, David. 1986. *Family Television: Cultural Power and Domestic Leisure*. London: Comedia.

Morozov, Evgeny. 2011. *The Net Delusion: How Not to Liberate The World*. London: Allen Lane.

Mosco, Vincent. 2009. *The Political Economy of Communication*. London: SAGE.

Moser, C. 1991. *Gender Planning and Development*. London: Routledge.

Mouffe, Chantal. 2000. *The Democratic Paradox*. London: Verso.

Narayan, Deepa, Robert A. Chambers, Meera K. Shah and Patti Petesch. 2000. *Voices of the Poor: Crying Out for Change*. New York: Oxford University Press for the World Bank.

Negt, Oskar, and Alexander Kluge. 1972. *Public Sphere and Experience: Toward an Analysis of the Bourgeois and Proletarian Public Sphere*. Minneapolis: University of Minnesota Press.

Nordenstreng, Kaarle, and Tapio Varis. 1974. *Television Traffic: A One-Way Street? A Survey and Analysis of the International Flow of Television Programme Material*. Paris: UNESCO.

Obregon, Rafael, and Mario Mosquera. 2005. 'Participatory and Cultural Challenges for Research and Practice in Health Communication.' In *Media and Glocal Change: Rethinking Communication for Development*, ed. Oscar Hemer and Thomas Tufte. Buenos Aires: CLACSO and Nordicom.

Obregon, Rafael, and Thomas Tufte. 2014. 'Rethinking Entertainment-Education for Development and Social Change.' In *The Handbook of Development Communication and Social Change*, ed. Karin Gwinn Wilkins, Thomas Tufte and Rafael Obregon. Chichester; Malden: Wiley-Blackwell. http://alltitles.ebrary.com/Doc?id=10830394.

Olesen, Thomas. 2005. *International Zapatismo: The Construction of Solidarity in the Age of Globalization*. London; New York: Zed Books.

Ordóñez, V. 2015. 'Fighting Evictions: A Reflection on the New Strategies of PAH.' Roskilde University, March.

Peruzzo, Cicilia Krohling. 1996. 'Participation in Community Communication.' In *Participatory Communication for Social Change*, ed. Jan Servaes, Thomas Jacobson and Shirley A. White. New Delhi: SAGE.

Peruzzo, Cicilia Krohling. 2014. 'Communication in Social Movements: A New Perspective on Human Rights.' In *Reclaiming the Public Sphere: Communication, Power and Social Change.*, ed. Tina Askanius and Liv Stubbe Østergaard. Basingstoke: Palgrave Macmillan.

Pew Research Center. 2015. 'Cell Phones in Africa: Communication Lifeline.' April. http://www.pewglobal.org/2015/04/15/cell-phones-in-africa-communication-lifeline.

Pieterse, Jan Nederveen. 2010. *Development Theory*. 2nd edn. Thousand Oaks: SAGE.

Piketty, Thomas. 2014. *Capital in the Twenty-First Century*. Cambridge, MA: Belknap Press of Harvard University Press.

Postill, John. 2014a. 'Democracy in an Age of Viral Reality: A Media Epidemiography of Spain's *Indignados* Movement.' *Ethnography* 15 (1): 51–69.

Postill, John. 2014b. 'Field Theory, Media Change and the New Citizen Movements: Spain's "Real Democracy Turn", 2011–2014.' RMIT University. https://www.academia.edu/11286950/Field_theory_media_change_and_the_new_citizen_movements_Spain_s_real_democracy_turn_2011–2014 .

Quarry, Wendy, and Ricardo Ramírez. 2009. *Communication for Another Development: Listening before Telling*. London; New York: Zed Books.

Reich, Ebbe Kløvedal. 2002. *Frederik: en folkebog om N.F.S. Grundtvigs tid og liv.* [Copenhagen]: Gyldendal.

Renó, Denis, Marcelo Martínez Hermida and Carolina Campalans. 2015. *Medios y opinión pública.* Bogotá: Editorial Universidad del Rosario.

Ribot, J. C. 2011. 'Participation without Representation: Chiefs, Councils and Forestry Law in the West African Sahel.' In *The Participation Reader*, ed. Andrea Cornwall. London; New York: Zed Books.

Rodriguez, Clemencia. 2001. *Fissures in the Mediascape. An International Study of Citizens' Media.* Cresskill: Hampton Press.

Rodriguez, Clemencia, and Ana María Miralles. 2014. 'Citizens' Journalism: Shifting Public Spheres from Elites to Citizens.' In *The Handbook of Development Communication and Social Change*, ed. Karin Gwinn Wilkins, Thomas Tufte and Rafael Obregon. Chichester; Malden: Wiley-Blackwell.

Rogers, Everett M. 1995. *Diffusion of Innovations.* 4th edn. New York: Free Press.

Rosanvallon, Pierre. 2008. *Politics in an Age of Distrust.* Cambridge: Cambridge University Press.

Santos, Boaventura de Sousa. 1998. 'Participatory Budgeting in Porto Alegre: Toward a Redistributive Democracy.' *Politics and Society* 26 (4): 461–510.

Santos, Boaventura de Sousa. 2014. *Epistemologies of the South: Justice against Epistemicide.* Abingdon: Routledge.

Sanz Cortell, Mariona. 2015. 'From Victims to Activists: The Role of Communication for the Empowerment and Impact of the PAH Anti-Evictions Movement in Spain.' Malmö: Communication for Development, Malmö University. https://dspace.mah.se/handle/2043/19452.

Saxena, N. C. 2011. 'What Is Meant by People's Participation?' In *The Participation Reader*, ed. Andrea Cornwall. London; New York: Zed Books.

Scholte, Jan Aart. 2001. 'Global Civil Society.' In *The Political Economy of Globalization*, ed. Ngaire Woods. Repr. Basingstoke: Palgrave.

Scott, Martin. 2014. *Media and Development.* New York; London: Zed Books. http://search.ebscohost.com/login.aspx?direct=true&scope=site&db=nlebk&db=nlabk&AN=771970.

Segerberg, Alexandra, and W. Lance Bennett. 2011. 'Social Media and the Organization of Collective Action: Using Twitter to Explore the Ecologies of Two Climate Change Protests.' *Communication Review* 14 (3): 197–215.

Sen, Amartya. 1999. *Development as Freedom.* New York: Oxford University Press.

Shildrick, Margrit. 2002. *Embodying the Monster: Encounters with the Vulnerable Self.* London; Thousand Oaks: SAGE.

Shirky, Clay. 2011. 'The Political Power of Social Media: Technology, the Public Sphere, and Political Change.' *Foreign Affairs*, January/February.

Silva, José de Souza. 2011. *Hacia el 'dia después del desarrollo.'* Asunción: Editorial Arandurã.

Silverstone, Roger. 1994. *Television and Everyday Life.* London; New York: Routledge.

Silverstone, Roger. 2007. *Media and Morality: On the Rise of the Mediapolis.* Cambridge; Malden: Polity.

Silverstone, Roger, and Eric Hirsch, eds. 1992. *Consuming Technologies: Media and Information in Domestic Spaces.* London; New York: Routledge.

Sparks, Colin. 2007. *Globalization, Development and the Mass Media.* Los Angeles; London: SAGE.

Spitulnik, Debra. 1993. 'Anthropology and Mass Media.' *Annual Review of Anthropology* 22: 293–315.

Spitulnik, Debra. 2011. 'Media Machines and Fluid Audiences: Rethinking Reception through Zambian Radio Culture.' In *Media Worlds: Anthropology on New Terrain*, ed. Faye D. Ginsburg, Lila Abu-Lughod and Brian Larkin. Berkeley: University of California Press.

Srinivasan, Sharath, and Claudia Abreu Lopes. 2016. 'Africa's Voices Versus Big Data? The Value of Citizen Engagement through Interactive Radio.' In *Voice & Matter: Communication, Development and the Cultural Return*, ed. Oscar Hemer and Thomas Tufte. Gothenburg: Nordicom.

Stade, Ronald. 2016. 'On The Capacity to Aspire. Conversation with Arjun Appadurai.' In *Voice & Matter: Communication, Development and the Cultural Return*, ed Oscar Hemer and Thomas Tufte. Gothenburg: Nordicom.

Stark, Birgit, and Peter Lunt. 2012. 'An Introduction to Public Voice and Mediated Participation.' *Communications: The Eurpean Journal of Communication Research* 37 (3): 225–31.

Stenersen, Johanna. 2014. 'Citizens in the Making: Critical Perspectives on Civic Identity and Culture.' PhD thesis, Örebro University.

Stiefel, Matthias, and Marshall Wolfe. 2011. 'The Many Faces of Participation.' In *The Participation Reader*, ed. Andrea Cornwall. London; New York: Zed Books.

Tacchi, Jo. 2016. 'When and How Does Voice Matter? And How Do We Know?' In *Voice & Matter: Communication, Development and the Cultural Return*, ed. Oscar Hemer and Thomas Tufte. Gothenburg: Nordicom.

Taylor, Charles. 2004. *Modern Social Imaginaries.* Durham, NC: Duke University Press.

Thomas, Pradip Ninan. 2014. 'Development Communication and Social Change in Historical Context.' In *The Handbook of Development Communication and Social Change*, ed. Karin Gwinn Wilkins, Thomas Tufte and Rafael Obregon. Chichester; Malden: Wiley-Blackwell. http://alltitles.ebrary.com/Doc?id=10830394.

Thomas, Pradip Ninan. 2015. 'Communication for Social Change: Making Theory Count.' *Nordicom Review* 36: 71–78.

Thompson, Lisa, and Chris Tapscott, eds. 2010. *Citizenship and Social Movements: Perspectives from the Global South.* London; New York: Zed Books.

Tilly, Charles. 2008. *Contentious Performances.* New York: Cambridge University Press.

Touraine, Alain. 2007. *A New Paradigm for Understanding Today's World.* Cambridge: Polity.

Touraine, Alain. 2009. *Thinking Differently*. Cambridge; Malden: Polity.

Touraine, Alain, Alan Duff and Richard Sennett. 1981. *The Voice and the Eye: An Analysis of Social Movements*. Cambridge; Paris: Cambridge University Press and Maison des Sciences de l'Homme.

Treré, Emiliano. 2011. 'Studying Media Practices in Social Movements.' In *CIRN Prato Community Informatics Conference 2011: Refereed Stream*, 1–14. http:// ccnr.infotech.monash.edu/assets/docs/prato2011papers/trere.pdf.

Tufte, Thomas. 2000. *Living with the Rubbish Queen: Telenovelas, Culture and Modernity in Brazil*. Luton: University of Luton Press.

Tufte, Thomas. 2004. 'Eduentretenimiento en la comunicación para el VIH/ SIDA: más allá del mercadeo, hacia el empoderamiento.' *Investigación & Desarrollo* 12 (1).

Tufte, Thomas. 2006. 'Your Future Gets Stuck! Challenges for HIV/AIDS Communication.' *Media Development* 3: 25–9.

Tufte, Thomas. 2011. 'Mediápolis, Human (In)Security and Citizenship Communication and Global Development Challenges in the Digital Era.' In *Online Territories: Globalization, Mediated Practice and Social Space*, ed. M. Christensen, A. Jansson and C. Christensen. New York: Peter Lang.

Tufte, Thomas. 2012. 'Facing Violence and Conflict with Communication: Possibilities and Limitations of Storytelling and Entertainment-Education.' In *Development Communication in Directed Social Change: A Reappraisal of Theory and Practice*, ed. Srinivas R. Melkote, AMIC and Wee Kim Wee School of Communication and Information. Singapore: AMIC and WKWSCI-NTU.

Tufte, Thomas. 2013. 'Towards a Renaissance in Communication for Social Change: Redefining the Discipline and Practice in the Post "Arab Spring" Era.' In *Speaking up and Talking Back? Media Empowerment and Civic Engagement among East and Southern African Youth*, ed. Thomas Tufte, Norbert Wildermuth, Anne Sofie Hansen-Skovmoes and Winnie Mitullah. Gothenburg: Nordicom.

Tufte, Thomas. 2014a. 'Civil Society Sphericules: Emerging Communication Platforms for Civic Engagement in Tanzania.' *Ethnography* 15 (1): 32–50.

Tufte, Thomas. 2014b. 'Emerging Issues in Activism and Social Change Communication.' In *The Handbook of Development Communication and Social Change*, ed. Karin Gwinn Wilkins, Thomas Tufte and Rafael Obregon. Chichester; Malden: Wiley-Blackwell. http://alltitles.ebrary.com/Doc?id=10830394.

Tufte, Thomas. 2015. *Comunicación para el cambio social: La participación y el empoderamiento como base para el desarrollo mundial*. Barcelona: Icaria.

Tufte, Thomas, and Florencia Enghel, eds. 2009. *Youth Engaging with the World: Media, Communication and Social Change*. Gothenburg: Nordicom.

Tufte, Thomas, and Paolo Mefalopulos. 2009. *Participatory Communication: A Practical Guide*. Washington, DC: World Bank.

Turner, Eric. 2013. 'New Movements, Digital Revolution, and Social Movement Theory.' *Peace Review* 25 (3): 376–83.

Turner, Ralph H., and Lewis M. Killian. 1957. *Collective Behavior*. 2nd edn. Englewood Cliffs: Prentice Hall.

Turner, Victor W. 1995. *The Ritual Process: Structure and Anti-Structure.* New York: Aldine de Gruyter.

UNICEF. 2014. *Communicate to Advocate for Every Child: UNICEF's Global Communication and Public Advocacy Strategy, 2014–2017.* http://amecinter nationalsummitstockholm.org/wp-content/uploads/2015/06/UNICEF-Global-Communication-and-Public-Advocacy-Strategy1.pdf.

UNICEF SLDP Cohort 4, Team B. 2014. 'Towards a Child Spring: How Can UNICEF Adjust Its Programming to Empower Local Communities by Learning from Social Movements?' https://prezi.com/xxfmqg39x--x/sldp-cohort-4-team-b.

Ura, Karma, Sonam Kinga, and Centre for Bhutan Studies, eds. 2004. *The Spider and the Piglet: Proceedings of the First International Seminar on Bhutan Studies.* Thimphu: Centre for Bhutan Studies.

U-Report Uganda: Voice Matters. 2016. http://www.ureport.ug/about.

Vidali, D. S. 2014. 'The Ethnography of Process: Excavating and Re-Generating Civic Engagement and Political Subjectivity.' *Ethnography* 15 (1): 12–31.

Wagner, Rebecca, and Julia Dankova. 2016. 'The CSO's Shrinking and Closing Space Tendency: How EU Institutions Can Support CSOs Worldwide.' 7 April. https://eu.boell.org/en/2016/04/07/csos-shrinking-and-closing-space-tendency-how-eu-institutions-can-support-csos-worldwide.

Waisbord, Silvio R. 2014. 'The Strategic Politics of Participatory Communication.' In *The Handbook of Development Communication and Social Change*, ed. Karin Gwinn Wilkins, Thomas Tufte and Rafael Obregon. Chichester; Malden: Wiley-Blackwell.

Watkins, Jerry, Jo Tacchi and UNESCO. 2008. *Participatory Content Creation for Development: Principles and Practices.* New Delhi: UNESCO.

White, S. 2011. 'Depoliticizing Development: The Uses and Abuses of Participation.' In *The Participation Reader*, ed. Andrea Cornwall. London; New York: Zed Books.

Wildermuth, Norbert. 2013. 'Information and Communication Technology-Facilitated E-Citizenship, E-Democracy and Digital Empowerment in Kenya: The Opportunities and Constraints of Community-Based Initiatives.' In *Speaking up and Talking Back? Media Empowerment and Civic Engagement among East and Southern African Youth*, ed. Thomas Tufte, Norbert Wildermuth, Anne Sofie Hansen-Skovmoes and Winnie Mitullah. Gothenburg: Nordicom.

Wildermuth, Norbert. 2014. 'Communication for Transparency and Social Accountability.' In *The Handbook of Development Communication and Social Change*, ed. Karin Gwinn Wilkins, Thomas Tufte and Rafael Obregon. Chichester; Malden: Wiley-Blackwell. http://alltitles.ebrary.com/Doc?id=10830394.

Wilkins, Karin Gwinn. 2014. 'Advocacy Communication.' In *The Handbook of Development Communication and Social Change*, ed. Karin Gwinn Wilkins, Thomas Tufte and Rafael Obregon. Chichester; Malden: Wiley-Blackwell. http://alltitles.ebrary.com/Doc?id=10830394.

Willems, W. 2013. 'Participation – In What? Radio, Convergence and the

Corporate Logic of Audience Input through New Media in Zambia.' *Telematic and Informatics* 30 (3): 223–31.

World Bank. 1997. *World Development Report 1997: The State in a Changing World.* Oxford: Oxford University Press.

World Bank Institute. 2005. *Social Accountability in the Public Sector: A Conceptual Discussion.* Washington, DC: International Bank for Reconstruction and Development/ World Bank. http://siteresources.worldbank.org/WBI/Resources/ Social_Accountability_in_the_Public_Sector_with_cover.pdf.

Index